Books by Herbert Feis

EUROPE, THE WORLD'S BANKER: 1870–1914

SEEN FROM E.A.

THE SPANISH STORY

THE ROAD TO PEARL HARBOR

THE DIPLOMACY OF THE DOLLAR

THE CHINA TANGLE

CHURCHILL — ROOSEVELT — STALIN

BETWEEN WAR AND PEACE — THE POTSDAM
CONFERENCE

JAPAN SUBDUED: THE ATOMIC BOMB AND THE
END OF THE PACIFIC WAR

FOREIGN AID AND FOREIGN POLICY

1933: CHARACTERS IN CRISIS

1933:
CHARACTERS IN CRISIS

1933:

CHARACTERS IN CRISIS

by Herbert Feis

Little, Brown and Company · Boston · Toronto

FIRST EDITION

cam

Published simultaneously in Canada
by Little, Brown & Company (Canada) Limited

PRINTED IN THE UNITED STATES OF AMERICA

To the memory of my old friend Felix Frankfurter,
whose death leaves a void which I and so many
others will never be able to fill

Author's Note

MANY of the "characters" who appear in this narrative helped me to write it. It is my agreeable obligation to thank them and others for their assistance. I do so in the sobering knowledge that those of them who read it will find inaccuracies of fact, and faults in perception and interpretation. But I trust that none are inexcusable.

The Honorable McGeorge Bundy authorized me to consult and quote the diary kept by Henry L. Stimson, Secretary of State under President Herbert Hoover. Justice Felix Frankfurter agreed that I might freely learn from such of his correspondence as bore on the matters of which I have written; my search for them was aided by Mrs. Elsie Douglas, his devoted and able secretary, whom I could not annoy by my persistence. Mr. Raymond Moley generously allowed me to quote from his informative book *After Seven Years,* discussed some of its main episodes with me, and gave me a copy of a memo that he and Herbert Swope made of their dramatic trip to London. The Honorable Henry Morgenthau, Jr., former Secretary of the Treasury, kindly granted me permission to read and draw upon the diary which he kept during this period; and Professor John Morton Blum of Yale University and the staff of the Franklin D. Roosevelt Library at Hyde Park made it convenient for me to do so. Mr. James P. Warburg was kind enough to give me permission to read and quote from the recording he made for the Oral

History Project carried on at Columbia University, a lively and candid account, as would be expected of him; and I have to thank the staff of the Special Collections Division of the Library of Columbia University for making available this Warburg recording and also the informative papers of George L. Harrison, who was at the time president of the Federal Reserve Bank of New York. Among the journals and papers of former colleagues which I was able to use were those of William Phillips, former Under-Secretary of State; of Pierrepont Moffat, former head of the European Division of the State Department, through the kindness of his widow, Mrs. Albert Levitt; of Mr. Walter Prendergast, who gave me a copy of the entertaining memo he wrote about his flight from London to Ireland to meet Raymond Moley; and of Robert Kelley, former head of the Eastern European Division of the State Department, whose memos about the negotiations preceding the recognition of the Soviet government are now in the custody of the National Archives. Mr. Bernard M. Baruch gave me permission to quote from his letters and indicated his willingness to have me extend my search if time had permitted.

The staff of the Library of Congress expedited my effort to scan the papers of former Secretary of State Cordell Hull and former Ambassador Norman H. Davis — the most important of which, however, had already been published; and of Ogden Mills, former Secretary of the Treasury. Similarly Professor Brooks Kelley, Archivist of Yale University, and other members of the staff of that library facilitated my consultation of the Stimson diary and the papers of Colonel Edward M. House; as did the staff of the Houghton Library of Harvard University and the Firestone Library of Princeton University. Mr. Gordon Wasson, Librarian of the Council on Foreign Relations, with patient good nature located the books I wanted to read.

I am grateful to Joseph E. Johnson, president of the Carnegie Endowment for International Peace, for his kindness in assigning me a spacious room in the headquarters of the Endowment in which to do my writing, and to the staff of the Endowment, especially those in its library.

Mrs. John F. Rowe, with unfailing good humor and reliability, transformed my scribbles into an acceptable typed manuscript, and my wife, Ruth Stanley-Brown Feis, despite many years of trying experience, again acted as reader, critic and index maker.

To one and all who helped me, as well as to those who may read this book, I wish to say that I am sincerely sorry if my thoughts and memory so often — but surely not always — have produced prickles rather than pineapples. Let them blame the romp of historical circumstance, not me.

H.F.

Contents

PART I

From Hoover to Roosevelt

CHAPTER 1

Introduction

In 1933 the storm lowering over the nations turned into a tempest. The deranged currents of history cut a channel and swirled toward the bloody marshes of the Second World War.

The United States, in the depths of a confounding depression and in distress, tried hard to right itself and find a steadier course. The American government, amazed at the calamity which had befallen the country, and believing foreign nations to be self-centered, strove to save itself. When it did, it would gladly come to the assistance of other countries and be more able to do so.

Of this storm and the efforts made by the American government, and the strains within it, I, at the time Economic Adviser for the State Department, was a witness, a participant, and a chronicler of what I heard and watched — an industrious gull, as it were. When I started this narrative I had intended only to tell of my own experiences and observations. But as I went along, these seemed subordinate and marginal. Professional training impelled me to try to secure the testimony of important figures — from their books, from their unpublished notes and correspondence, and from the memories of those still alive, as fading and selective as my own.

Yet I know this narrative does not cover the whole historical horizon. It is rather a telescopic view of the tempest as it blew upon and through Washington during a short period in which nations and men were awash.

The sun shines brightly in the temporal sky while I am writing this, but there on the horizon is that mushroom cloud, more ominous than any visible in 1933. For nations and men are today beset and baffled by torrents in a changed universe of time and space, which they have not learned to master. By which I mean that they have not learned to master themselves and their societies. The travails and triumphs ahead are hidden around the bend of history.

CHAPTER 2

The Dégringolade

WELL I remember standing with Pierrepont Moffat on the front steps of Woodley, Secretary of State Henry L. Stimson's home, in Washington, in the early darkness of an evening late in 1931. We had gone there to discuss with him the report just received that the Kredit Anstalt, the great Austrian bank, had collapsed. As he was seeing us off, Moffat remarked, "What a debacle!" (*Dégringolade* was the word he used.) The Secretary, puzzled and grim, nodded his head in appreciation of the meaning of this event. But, as will appear, the emergency energized him even while it depressed him.

Most members of the administration in office grasped the seriousness of the depression and the distress it was causing, belatedly. Time after time President Herbert Hoover himself and Secretary of the Treasury Andrew Mellon strove to reassure the American people and stimulate American business leaders by bullish public statements. They thought that if only the fears of those who directed finance, industry and trade could be dispelled our troubles would be transient and prosperity would return. But even though these controllers echoed official incantations, they failed to change the gradient of our declining economy.

To most of the comfortably employed civil servants in the District of Columbia, the extent of the distress and its dangerous character were for the first time made vivid by the invasion of the thousands of veterans who camped along Pennsylvania Avenue. There, bedraggled, many homeless and hungry, they pitched tents and built shacks out of discarded lumber and rusty corrugated iron. When they dispersed, most public officials relapsed into the belief that our economic system would soon regain its health and vitality.

The reread carbons of my memos to Secretary Stimson during the onset of the depression justify, I think, the opinion that my belief that the situation was going to turn for the better waned earlier and more sharply than that of most of my colleagues. This was due to my training and to my exposure to the news from Europe rather than to superior prescience. My study of the Keynesian analysis of the operation of contemporary capitalist societies had let me accept Keynes's conclusion that stagnation and depression could last long, since there were propensities which thwarted the tendency to recover. This meant that I remained reserved about the lilting reassurances that were diffused. Indeed, they accentuated my pessimism, which so frequently tinged my memos and remarks that Secretary Stimson took to calling me Jeremiah in our small circle. As when upon his return from Geneva in May 1932, where he had witnessed the fadeaway of plans for collective action to restrain Japan, he had read a memo I had written on "Economic Events in the State Department Sphere of Interest During the Secretary's Absence," he called it a jeremiad, and added that he would not send me to Geneva lest I commit suicide. But he had then gone on to add that without sharing my bathos he knew that national and international affairs were at an acute pass. His kindness toward me, no matter how disturbing my forecasts or comments were to him, was constant; and his tolerance allowed me to indulge my pessimism without anxiety about my position.

President Hoover was not an insensitive nor inhumane man; quite the contrary. But he could not grasp or would not face the grim realities which called for deviations from principles and practices that he deemed essential to American greatness and freedom.

The policies and proposals which he expounded so earnestly might have served to end the depression, let us say, in the 1870's or 1880's, but not the one by which the United States was then beset.

He could not believe that the American economy would not rebound if loans were offered to industries, railways, banks, merchants, farm mortgage associations and like enterprises — thereby replenishing their capital and restoring their credit — while their nerve was being revived by hopeful prognostications. Credit and confidence were the talismans of recovery. If their magic failed it could only be, he thought, because of baneful events or malign influences at home and abroad.

Any remaining trickle of confidence that the Hoover administration would develop a program of enough vitality to correct the situation seeped away on August 11, 1932. On that night in Constitution Hall in Washington I listened to Hoover deliver his speech accepting the Republican presidential nomination, numbered point trooping after numbered point until attention was numbed. That speech, over which he had labored so hard, was limp and drab. The combination of policies propounded would, I was almost sure, condemn our economy to a longer stay in the trough of depression. His judgment was riveted to the belief that its duration was due to the political troubles abroad and the economic and fiscal disorder in other countries. Yet he claimed that to protect itself against these external disturbances the United States must maintain its high tariff structure. The governments of Western Europe, it may be interjected, were in turn attributing their troubles to the depression in the United States and our insistence on collecting the debts they owed. The President also assured prospective voters that he was opposed to cancellation of the debts owed by our former associates in the First World War to the American government; but he added that he was sure that the American people would consider proposals for foregoing particular annual payments if compensated by expanded purchases of American products. We would insist on a balanced budget, since "The first necessity of this nation, the wealth and income of whose citizens have been reduced, is to reduce expenses of government — national, state, and local."

This address that night seemed to me to portend, should Hoover be re-elected, a long continuation of the depression after a collapse of our banking system. But all I found to do next morning was to write another memo for the Secretary of State and invite the wrath of the likable but choleric Secretary of the Treasury, Ogden Mills, who had succeeded the secretive and acquisitive Andrew Mellon. While Mills, like the President, was cheered by incoming messages of praise for the speech, I found him irritated over what he termed "the bear raid of the Democrats." These onslaughts on values, both believed, were timed by their opponents to occur on the day after the speech. Names of short sellers were being listed.

The vocal members of the Hoover administration defended it against every kind of charge made by critics — some of which were valid, some dubious, some unfair, some cruelly mocking. They would not accept any blame for the plight of the country and they indignantly denied that their policies had been faulty. They averred that recovery in the United States had been well under way in the summer.

For the recession that was ensuing they blamed, as the campaign barged along, not themselves but Democratic nominee Franklin Delano Roosevelt and the group about him. These aspirants for power, the defenders of their own record declared, were recklessly scaring the American people out of their wits and sapping their free-flowing energy. President Hoover did not tire of telling his confidants and members of the press that he was sure recovery would have been far along if the business and banking community had not been frightened by the agitation for inflation and wild schemes for changing our monetary system.

Roosevelt's acceptance speech had not impressed me either. Though incisive and almost coherent, it was primarily critical rather than positive. His statements about some primary issues seemed to me so ambiguous that voters could read any meaning they wanted into them. He could and he did discuss the actions of foreign countries without Hoover's note of complaint and irritability. But what he said then and in subsequent campaign speeches about foreign political and economic affairs slithered; there was no firm promise for change for the better. I found myself set up, for example, by the section in his speech of June 20 which averred, "Trade barriers ought to be lowered, not by rule of thumb but with due regard to safety and justice; lowered, nevertheless, as quickly and definitely as possible," only to be let down again when, by the end of September, the candidate promised to maintain a tariff at least high enough to prevent competitive imports and ruled out all reductions of tariffs on farm products. As for the intergovernmental debts, he lurched about in much the same way as Hoover. He did propose at one time, as had Hoover, that debts might be reduced or forgiven if debtors bought more American products. But in face of objections he allowed the proposal to fade out.

In sum, the course of the campaign brought me no comforting assurance that our foreign policies would be revamped. After a while I ceased to read the headlines for signs of clear and candid thought.

As Election Day neared, I passed on my impressions in a letter to a friend, writing: "Much of everybody's thoughts has been on politics. I think that the passage of the days and the course of events are each day making clearer that the administration has made important mistakes and has failed badly. No member of it seems to be able to find a new inner truth about the administration's theories or record, and impress the country with it. The people have ceased reading their statements and walked out on their speeches, while they seem to be lifting eager faces to Franklin Roosevelt, having the impression that he is talking intimately to them. I am glad of his enthusiasm and buoyancy but I cannot escape the sense that he really does not understand the full meaning of his own recitations. I await confirmation that he realizes where the work is, what is going on, and what should be done."

On Election Day, Hoover's policies and attitudes were conclusively judged at fault by the American people. Roosevelt won by an impressive majority. Those who elected him to office took fresh heart for the future, hopeful that the change would be for the better. But Hoover and his men were responsible for the government until

March 4. During that interval the weal or woe of the nation would depend on those to whom the people had refused another term of office.

Hoover and Mills, worried about the deficit in our national public finances, continued to resist any and all proposals that would have required greatly enlarged public expenditures. They did so although the stock of money (currency and bank deposits) was one-third smaller than at the peak. Substantial (but much less than enough) federal aid was being given to local communities. These were being compelled to provide relief for more and more needy people while their tax revenues were falling. Doubts were mounting whether many municipalities and states would be able to continue to pay interest on their bonds, or even the salaries of teachers, policemen, firemen, trash and garbage collectors and others who performed essential services, of even the tax gatherers themselves.

Between 1929 and 1933 the net national product in current prices fell by more than one-half; in constant prices by one-third.

Between November 1932 and March 1933 the American people fell on much harder times than they had ever experienced before. About fifteen million men and women who wanted jobs could not find them. Many others were working shorter hours for lower wage rates. At least three million people were receiving relief, barely enough to keep themselves alive. The prices of farm products such as wheat, cotton and corn were ruinously low. In Kansas, as I recall from an article written by a former colleague, they had fallen so much that a wagonload of corn would not pay for the shoeing of a pair of horses; a truckload of hogs would hardly pay for a set of new tires. Hundreds of thousands of hard-working farmers and rural shopkeepers were facing bankruptcy or expulsion from their homes and stores because they could not meet mortgages and other debts. The money value of American exports was the lowest in thirty years.

This was poverty amid plenty. Much wheat remained unharvested or was allowed to decay in heaps because it did not pay to bring it to market. Cotton was left to shrivel because its price was not enough to pay the cost of picking it. Sheep were allowed to die because their owners could not get enough for them to repay the cost of transport. Woolen mills stood idle while men without overcoats shivered in the snow and brooded in bread lines. Sky signs burned bright over Times Square in New York City, advertising comforts and luxuries that fewer and fewer Americans were able to buy.

Even many of the affluent members of American society were being impoverished. The total value of the common stocks listed on the New York Stock Exchange had fallen from about ninety billion dollars at its height to about fifteen billion. The price of the common stocks of United States Steel and General Motors had fallen to about 8 per cent of the peak prices at which they had been bought and sold in 1929. Millions of people who had considered themselves comfortable and protected had lost or were in danger of losing their life's savings as banks became insolvent or closed their doors — over four thousand of them before the end of 1932.

Many American banks were calling the loans they had made to businessmen and farmers, or trying to reduce them. Those who had mortgages on real estate, rural and urban, were pressed to foreclose when payments fell in arrears. This caused other defaults and bankruptcies. Even the great city banks were coming within the circle of peril. Some had loaned sums greater than the whole of their capital to governments and financial institutions of Central Europe — to secure somewhat higher interest on what they intended to be liquid short-term credits that could be turned into cash on short notice. The National City Bank of New York, for example, had invested more than fifty million dollars of its own funds in Germany alone. But the financial situation of the foreign debtors was growing worse and worse, and the chances of collection on demand poorer and poorer.

The Federal Reserve System was proving unwilling or incapable of countering the monetary and banking collapse — partly because of the way it was constituted, partly because of its policies.

During January and February 1933 the flight of American capital out of the United States quickened. Domestic hoarding and exports of gold soared. Banks became still more urgent in their demands for repayment of the loans they had made to domestic industry. Those in the great financial centers which had deposited in or loaned their liquid funds on short term to banks in the interior were withdrawing their balances. In Michigan, where the banks were deeply involved with the automobile industry, the vulnerable situation cracked on February 14. The Governor declared a banking holiday for the state to protect the assets of the banks and preserve them for equitable distribution among the depositors. A few days later the Governor of Maryland was compelled to take similar action — to close the banks in which many government workers had their savings. No one was sure what the next day would bring. The queues before the windows of the tellers lengthened. Almost all Americans who could tried to get cash in hand to carry them over until rescue measures could be taken.

The contrast between the secure and easy past and the anxious end is marked in my memory by a farewell dinner which the Spanish ambassador gave for Secretary of the Treasury Mills on February 27. The magnificent floral displays in the embassy and scattered over the dining table had been flown up from the South. The Dover sole had been shipped down from New York. The wines had been procured from the best vineyards of Spain and France.

But scarcely had Mills taken his seat at the table when he was called to the telephone. On his return he told a few of us of the latest bank closings. Hardly had he begun to taste the fish on his plate when he was summoned to the telephone again. He learned that during the day withdrawals of gold by depositors of the banks that still remained open had speeded up.

The glimmer of the jewels worn by the ladies led some of the more fearful members of the company to recall how former Russian aristocrats had been forced to sell their heirlooms to support themselves in the distant countries to which they had fled.

My view of the plight of the country at this time recurs to me as

I reread a letter written to a friend: "It has been traditional to engrave on the bonds and stock certificates of American enterprises, and even on some kinds of money currency, pictures of fertile prairies, powerful machines, speeding locomotives and busy factories. These were representations of the faith of Americans about the future of their country and their satisfaction in the efforts to develop its wealth. But in the winter of 1932–1933 the engravers, if they were true reporters and courageous artists, would have had to substitute pictures of lines of men before factory gates or in relief lines under dark skies, and of distraught farmers in fear of losing their houses and lands and burning their wheat and dumping their milk into the gutters rather than accept the miserable prices which they could get."

This was an ironical attempt to lighten the mood in which I found myself as the interim between the election and inauguration neared its end. I had lost faith in the chance that the departing group could, or would, do what was essential to salvage the situation. I was uncertain about the ability of the incoming group to do so.

My first talks with the assorted members of the Brain Trust, the publicized set of Roosevelt's assistants and ghost writers, left me puzzled. Their knowledge of foreign affairs seemed to be slighter than their intellectual assurance. Moreover, there were signs of schism within the Democratic Party in this field. Some of its leading figures were ardent believers in the necessity for cooperation in both economic and political spheres with the rest of the world. Others were equally ardent advocates of the view that the American government should remain free to take any and all measures that might help economic recovery regardless of their effect on other nations. Another group was just as devoted to the traditions of high tariff protection and political isolation as the Republicans. Roosevelt seemed to be teetering beween these divergent groups of supporters.

But as I shall tell when recalling the effort to effect liaison between those in office and those that would soon succeed them, my personal anxieties were soothed by indications that some members of the new group wanted me to work with them and that I was likely to continue to receive my monthly salary check. Despite uncertainty as to what the new administration would do, I awaited with barely suppressed eagerness the day they would take over authority.

CHAPTER 3

The Need for Liaison

THOUGH their prestige was gone, their influence shrunken, and their power to lead Congress shaken, Hoover and his aides had to carry on for the four dreaded months after defeat. The need for liaison with the victors was imperative.

Among the many questions confronting Hoover during this interval, three were within my own field of observation and activity. They were connected with each other. The first was how to answer the requests of foreign governments for relief from their debt obligations to the American government. The next was how to proceed to prepare for the international Monetary and Economic Conference in which the American government had promised to participate. The third was what, if anything, should be done about the disturbing crisis in the Far East. These were the original reasons why the cooperation of those who would take over power in March was sought.

The story of the efforts to effect and maintain the desired liaison will have more meaning if I briefly recall the previous history of those several questions which engaged attention.

The debts were sludge left after the fires of the First World War had died down. Long after grass and wildflowers covered over the dank and rat-ridden trenches of Flanders, and time had assuaged the grief of the widows and mothers of those who had lost their lives, the loans made to our former European allies continued to corrode their relations with us.

To the borrowing governments these debts had been incurred for a cause which they thought to be almost as much ours as theirs. They had been spent to finance their war effort and replenish the supplies of food, raw materials and industrial materials used up during the struggle. Many of their people even thought the United States ought to be more generous because they had fought the enemy for three years before we entered the war and had thus spared us loss and suffering.

But the viewpoint of most Americans was quite different. They believed that without being compelled to do so in our own interest, we had saved the debtors from disastrous defeat and preserved their countries. Was it not only just that in gratitude they should repay their debts to us? Moreover, how could the American government — while resisting the demands of our own war veterans and still paying interest on the bonds it sold to provide help for our foreign allies — ease their lot? And, many Americans thought in all fairness, *why* should we do so?

Animated by these views and sentiments, Congress had, during the 1920's, deplored any impulse to forgo payment and relieve the debtors. With the approval of two Presidents, Warren G. Harding and Calvin Coolidge, it had passed a law prohibiting new loans — even private loans — to debtor countries until they agreed to settle the old bills.

They did so; some in order to keep their word and preserve their credit, others under duress. The terms of the debt agreements differed, principal and interest in each being presumably adjusted to capacity to pay. We drove hard bargains but ones that would have been bearable had the depression not occurred. Woodrow Wilson had renounced almost all American claims for reparations from Germany in favor of our debtors, so the sums they were extracting from Germany made it easier for them to transfer funds to us.

In 1931, when disaster struck, they had asked to be let off. Since the monetary and banking crisis in Europe was becoming dangerously serious, President Hoover managed to secure congressional approval of a one-year moratorium on the debt payments due, linked with a suspension of reparations payments from Germany. But in the autumn of 1932, when the end of that reprieve was in sight, their situation was worse, not better. So was that of the United States. Thus Hoover and the officials under him, aware of the temper of Congress, had not asked it to extend the moratorium.

The debtors then took matters into their own hands. The British government in May omitted from its budget for the fiscal year 1932–1933 all provision for both payments to the United States and receipts of reparations from Germany. The Chancellor of the Exchequer explained that this was done because ordinarily these two items were self-balancing, and also because their amounts were so uncertain in the light of future events. The German government similarly omitted all provision for payments of reparations except some due under particular loans. Chancellor Heinrich Bruening said this was not intended as repudiation.

By then the surplus of German exports over imports was only about one-third the sum required to maintain reparations payments and service Germany's other debts to foreigners. The recipients of reparations arranged to meet with German representatives once again at Lausanne on June 16, 1932.

On Stimson's return from Europe on May 11, in the brief review of the situation which I submitted to him I observed that "Government defaults are becoming all-inclusive, and financial difficulties are again creeping up from Austria-Hungary to Germany. It may or may not provide exchange even to meet its debts to private creditors until it knows what the outcome of the Lausanne Conference, scheduled to meet June 16, may be. If that conference fails, I anticipate a worse crisis than that of June 1931, striking first Germany and England and then the United States. No steady and substantial improvement in American economic conditions can be achieved until the doubtful elements in the international field are settled. . . .

"It is possible that during the Lausanne Conference the American government may be approached for some expression of its intention as regards the debt to it.

"In the absence of any indication from us as to what program of debt revision the Executive may be willing to sponsor, it is possible that various debtor governments may simply inform us that they do not intend to pay."

However, President Hoover and the State Department were afraid to give any ground for accusation that they were agreeing to renounce debts due the American government in order to lessen the strain over reparations. When rumors were heard that the American representatives, Norman Davis and Hugh Gibson, who were in Geneva discussing disarmament, had also talked about the debts, the State Department, prompted by the President, informed the press on May 21 that "There is no truth whatever in the statements from Lausanne that the American government or its representatives have had any negotiations or made any suggestions as to debt questions at Lausanne."

In June, as our national crisis took a definite turn for the worse, I tried again to overcome inertia by fear. Talking even more like Jeremiah than usual, I predicted "universal bankruptcy" if some bold initiatives were not quickly taken. But my colleagues were of the opinion that any remarks that the American government might make at this time about the Lausanne Conference would be neither useful nor advisable. Even a conditional indication of the chance of a debt reduction, they argued, would be taken up and twisted by the Democratic contenders, and compel President Hoover to stand stubbornly for full collection. The officials in office felt they had to continue to repeat publicly that they were opposed to cancellation, as they privately complained that the Democrats were trying to place "the cancellation tag" on them.

Despite American abstention, the conferees at Lausanne reached an agreement in July. The British authorities had made up their

minds firmly that it was essential to end all political payments —
both reparations and intergovernmental debts — not only to revive
European economic prosperity but also to preserve European political order. This conclusion prevailed over French anxiety at the
loss of reparations receipts from Germany.

The Lausanne accord stipulated that except for a relatively
small token amount, German reparations were to cease. This action ended almost fifteen dreadful years of bickering between Germany and its former enemies over these obligations. It is most regrettable that the allies did not respond to the pleas for relief made
while democratic regimes were still in power in Germany, but
bowed before fear of disaster and warnings of the government
headed by that notorious schemer Franz von Papen. For the agreement had wider and deeper meaning than the mere cancellation of
reparations. In effect it meant also repudiation of that article in the
Versailles Treaty, known as the War Guilt Article, in which "The
Allied and Associated Governments affirm and the German Government accepts the responsibility of Germany and her Allies for
causing all the loss and damage to which the Allied and Associated
Governments and their nationals have been subjected as a conse-
quence of the war imposed upon them by the aggression of Germany and her Allies."

When news of this accord reached at Lausanne was received on
July 8, I, along with several of my colleagues, advised that the
American government should show a friendly interest in what had
been done. Secretary Stimson readily agreed and telephoned the
President. But Hoover said, "I'll wait and see. If they have tried to
tie in the debts to the United States I shall at once issue a statement
of dissent. If not tied in, I'll merely keep silent."

His hesitation to hail the Lausanne accord turned out to be warranted. Several days later it was learned that the agreement between Germany and the recipients of reparations was supplemented by another between the representatives of Great Britain,
France, Belgium and Italy. This was called the Gentlemen's Agreement.[1] It stipulated that the accord on reparations was not to
come into final effect until ratified; and that "so far as the creditor

governments on whose behalf this *procès verbal* is initiated are concerned, ratification will not be effected until a satisfactory settlement has been reached between them and their own creditors." Neville Chamberlain, the Chancellor of the Exchequer, with whom the American government was going to have to deal not only in regard to the debts but also about international monetary matters, had signed for the British government. We will meet him again at London during the Monetary and Economic Conference.

A buzzing bevy of Senators — including Hiram Johnson of California, Arthur Vandenberg of Michigan and Key Pittman of Nevada, chairman of the Foreign Relations Committee — expressed their views with emphasis that justified the headlines that the *New York Times* attached to a list of their statements: CONGRESS UNMOVED ON STAND ON DEBTS; LEADERS HAIL ECONOMIC PROMISE OF LAUSANNE AGREEMENT BUT ARE FIRM ON PAYMENT.

Thus, this troublemaking question had simmered along while the 1932 election campaign went on to its tired end. Even before then, the British and French governments had informed us that they believed the existing debt accords should be reviewed as soon as possible. Since the time remaining was so short, they had asked for suspension of that next payment due on December 15. What answer was to be made to them?

Stimson and Mills were afraid, however, that a refusal to afford the debtors a chance to discuss the possibility of adjusting their obligations to current circumstances could cause so bitter a quarrel as to debar cooperation in all else.

But even in the unlikely event that a new agreement could be reached before December 15, what chance had Hoover, a defeated President, to persuade Congress to approve it? Was the only other course open to us to send out the usual semiannual dunning notices and passively await payment or default? Our reports indicated it would probably be unsanctioned default rather than payment. The officials of the Federal Reserve System in particular were worried about the impact of default on the nearly shattered financial community.

Could anything be said to the debtors that might avert it unless the President-Elect associated himself with the policy pursued? To find out was one of the first reasons for trying to get him to cooperate.

Related to that dilemma, and deemed hardly less pressing, was the need to know whether the incoming administration wanted to participate in the Monetary and Economic Conference which had been arranged. If it did, how did it wish the preparatory work, already begun, to be carried on, and by whom?

The events which had engendered the proposal that the conference be convoked had also centered on Germany, just before the conference at Lausanne. As observed, a crisis akin to that of the early 1920's had loomed. The German government had an enormous deficit and its principal sources for taxation were exhausted. Unemployment was very large; over 44 per cent of the members of trade unions were out of work. National Socialism and Communism were gaining converts every day and fighting each other in beer halls and gutters.

While Secretary Stimson was quizzing me about my disconsolate report on the situation — this was at Woodley on May 11, 1932 — the British ambassador was calling on Under-Secretary of State William R. Castle, Jr. Sir Ronald Lindsay said that the British government was alarmed by the further fall in the prices of commodities measured in gold. He inquired whether the American government would join in a world economic conference. Castle replied that the American government would give the question careful consideration when advised of the agenda the British government had in mind. When Lindsay advanced the idea that this conference might be convened in June as a sequel to the Lausanne Conference on reparations, Castle said that this would be inadvisable. During that month, he explained, the Democratic political convention would be going on, and the Democratic leaders would almost surely try to turn any Republican initiatives to their partisan advantage.

Thinking that the halt in American recovery was largely due to the ailments of Europe, Hoover was attracted to the British proposal. He was impressed by its psychological potential rather than by belief that it could have quick substantial results. Moreover, it offered a way of pleasing the Senators who were plaguing him to call a conference on silver. He told Stimson that he was inclined to go along with the British proposal — but only on our terms: (1) that the conference would not discuss the debts due the American government; (2) that it would not discuss specific tariff rates; and (3) that it would do something for silver.

When the Secretary of State told me of them I grimaced. The memo outlining what I thought might be achieved in such a conference, which I wrote at Stimson's direction, he found disconcerting. Its first paragraph read: "Considering (a) the deranged economic conditions and the damaged debtor-credit relationship between countries that now prevail, and the conditions imposed by the President, and (b) existing tariff and fiscal policies of the United States, it seems to me that the proposed conference could achieve nothing important *except possibly in one direction*. . . . Under present conditions where every existing claim on wealth (that is, all debts and promises to pay) is in distinct danger of further loss of value and possibly of complete depreciation, it may be that the world is ready to entertain types of monetary measures that a few years ago it would have regarded almost with abhorrence. . . . The line of attack that seems to have won the widest interest would involve in some way a devaluation of gold — that is, a reduction of the number of grains of gold metal corresponding to the dollar and other units of currency. These measures might give increased place to silver in the monetary sphere. . . . [They] would seem to belong to what may be called the world of H. G. Wells. But if the period in which we are now has become sufficiently Wellsian (and there is reason for believing that it may be), the Wellsian measures may be in order. Another reason for considering them is the likelihood that if no action is taken by international agreement in the monetary sphere, there is an excellent chance that each country will head in its own way along the path of inflation and devaluation anyhow."

The Secretary chided me for this negative analysis and disturbing forecast. He told me that he thought I had taken the President's limitations too seriously and handled my assignment as though it were an academic disquisition rather than an official necessity. The President, he remarked, was very hard pressed and "grasping at any straw and wanted some positive suggestions." None could be found, I ventured to reply, which fitted his conceptions. A few days later I learned that I had company in my negativism. George Harrison, head of the Federal Reserve Bank of New York, asked Montagu Norman, governor of the Bank of England, whether he thought anything would come out of the proposed conference, and Norman replied, "Not a thing."

The Secretary soon thereafter had gone down to his camp at Rapidan, Virginia. He had not been able to persuade Hoover to relax the restrictions which he wanted to impose on the conference should it be held. Still Stimson's positive spirit sprang forth. He telephoned British Prime Minister Ramsay MacDonald on May 25. The President, he said, had two purposes in mind. One was to seek joint actions which might raise commodity prices. But the measures to this end which Stimson enumerated were the same ones that had proven inadequate in the United States — the easing of credit and the lowering of interest rates (and possibly some program of synchronized public expenditure). The other purpose was to encourage private economic groups throughout the world by evidence that governments were striving to find common means of meeting what were largely shared difficulties.

Perhaps also, Stimson had added, order could be brought into international currency relationships, thereby making merchants more confident and checking the tendency to adopt more and more stringent measures of trade control. But neither he nor MacDonald in this talk took note of the question which was later to stalk through the conference — *how and on what terms* was order to be restored in this turbulent field?

In suggesting to MacDonald that the conference be summoned by the British government and held in London, Stimson gave one reason which indicated that the American government expected other countries to do what was necessary rather than the United States. He told the Prime Minister that Hoover thought that since

Great Britain had departed from the gold standard, it could convoke the conference without raising undesirable and premature
fears; while if the American government were to call it, a new set
of speculations about American monetary policy might be born
which would further disturb our gold and monetary situation.

Lastly, Stimson suggested that the conference should bring together important officials, probably heads of state, and that there
would have to be suitable preliminary discussions and expert preparation.

Andrew Mellon, at that time American ambassador to England,
had been informed of these views and ideas and asked to discuss
them with the Prime Minister or such members of the British cabinet as the Prime Minister might designate. After talking with the
Secretary of State for Foreign Affairs, Sir John Simon, he had sent
back word that the British authorities were willing to accept our
conditions.

Up to then the project had been a well-kept secret. But while
Stimson and Mills were in conference at the White House on the
afternoon of May 31, Castle brought over accounts which had
leaked in London about the Mellon-Simon conversations. Hurriedly, the press was told that the American government thought
that the proposed international conference might be of real value in
the present depression, and of our conditions for the meeting.

I remember well this night of May 31. After dinner I went over
to the Treasury to talk with Secretary of the Treasury Ogden Mills
and Under-Secretary Arthur Ballantine, both pallid and near exhaustion. While I was trying to enlist their interest in the conference, news came which they mistakenly regarded as genuine relief
for the country as well as themselves. The Senate had passed the
Revenue Bill, which, they thought would, in conjunction with the
Economy Bill, assure a balanced budget during the next fiscal year.
They were deeply convinced that this was essential in order to avert
a panic due to fear of deficit financing and inflation. They had
chuckled over the surmise that the Senate had been induced to pass
this bill because they had "scared the pee" out of some of the leading members at a recent meeting at the White House. Even then

Mills's mind had harbored partisan thought, as indicated by his remark that "if they [the Senate] had not acted today and calamity had come, the country would have put the blame on the Democratic Senators."

In July the governments of the chief European countries agreed that the Council of the League of Nations should be asked to appoint an organizing committee for the conference. After a tardy presentation by Stimson, the President decided to accept membership on that committee.

It had also been agreed that preparatory work should be done by a commission of experts to be designated by the British, French, German, Japanese, Italian and American governments. This would meet in late September or early October in Geneva. Hoover and Stimson at this time contemplated that the conference itself might be convoked not later than December 1932, with the Republicans still in charge of our national affairs.

Who were to be the American representatives on the organizing committee and the two American representatives on the expert committee? There was a tussle over their selection. Mills wanted to make sure that the views of those named jibed with his own. For the organizing committee he did his utmost to persuade Hoover to appoint Mellon. But several members of the State Department, including myself, had pleaded with the Secretary of State to oppose this nomination. We argued that in the eyes of most of Europe, Mr. Mellon represented past practices that had fallen into disrepute. We predicted that if he were selected liberals in the United States and Europe would be alienated, and by their criticism lessen the chance that the conference would achieve anything. Moreover, we were even bold enough to say that we thought Mellon poorly informed about recent events, both in the United States and in foreign countries.

Mr. Stimson was hard to convince, at least to the point of having a set-to with Mills (and maybe with the President). He thought that Mellon would bring both prestige and experience to the task, and he denied that age had dimmed Mellon's capabilities. We sustained our point of view by saying that even if what Stimson said were so, Mellon's intellect and views of human affairs were not what most people in the world wanted today; he was canny and rigid, when what was needed was imaginativeness and flexibility.

Whether or not Mellon was asked to serve, I do not know. If he was asked and refused, I do not know the reason. At any rate Norman Davis was given the assignment — to the dismay not only of some of the more partisan Republicans but also of some members of Franklin Roosevelt's inner circle, particularly Raymond Moley, and of isolationists in Congress.

For the other commission — the Preparatory Commission — two experts were wanted, one qualified to deal with financial questions, the other with economic questions. Mills favored Professor John H. Williams of Harvard University, since he believed Williams to be a firm advocate of what he regarded as sound monetary policy, including the conviction that the return of countries off the gold standard — particularly Great Britain — to that hallowed system was essential. To those of us in the State Department whom Stimson consulted, Williams was also an acceptable selection. He was professionally qualified. We thought him independent-minded, so that he would not be subservient to the Hoover-Mellon-Mills view of monetary and fiscal policies should circumstances make them appear wrong. (In time, if I may interject, I came to regret this choice. He was one of the persons who set the scene for the smash-up of the conference.)

A squall blew up over the selection of the American member of the Preparatory Commission who was to concern himself with economic questions. Hoover had his own candidate. He said he wanted a protagonist, someone on whom he could rely to present his views and maintain the integrity of the policies he was propounding. He proposed Julius Klein, the Assistant Secretary of Commerce. Klein was a serious but undistinguished student of commercial activities, chained to the past performance of his present superiors. Harvey Bundy, Assistant Secretary of State, and I, while talking with Williams about the program for the meeting of experts, found him in agreement that if Klein were selected the conference would be doomed to futility. Opinion in academic and journalistic circles would range itself against the effort.

The question seemed to us so grave that we ventured to put our doubts before Secretary of Commerce Roy D. Chapin. After a candid talk he said that he understood our point of view, and he asked the President not to announce the appointment pending further discussion. Out at Woodley, in the late afternoon, we explained our thoughts to the Secretary of State. Stimson had so many more urgent matters before him that he was very reluctant to enter into a contest which he thought might be extremely embarrassing because of Klein's past connections with the President. However, he listened to our full story, and when he and Chapin went to see the President early the next morning, Hoover said good-naturedly, "Well, if both of you feel this way about it, I'll change my mind, especially since I don't think the work of the experts will have consequential results anyhow."

Hoover then assented to the selection of Edmund Day, director for the social sciences of the Rockefeller Foundation, who was asked to come to Washington. On the next day, when Bundy and I met with the Secretary to try to tell him what we thought was the most impressive way of dealing with Day, he almost threw us out of his office. He had taken up our cause because we seemed to feel so strongly about it, but he thought it trivial compared to the political situations such as those confronting him in the Far East and Europe. Events were to show that we had not only made a tempest in a teapot but we had done so without improving the quality of the tea.

The experts had to be in Geneva late in October. In the interval, the statements of American high officials did not make their assignment any brighter.

The steamship *Exeter,* with Williams, Day and myself among those on board, left New York on October 18. The voyage was unremarkable. I remember it chiefly because of my sense that Williams's mind had already fixed on the conclusion that the first and essential thing to be done was to bring about stabilization of the pound sterling.

Most members of the Preparatory Commission of Experts were permanent officials who were preoccupied with their national troubles. Many represented governments which were floundering as was ours. The group agreed on the indemnification of three principal and conjunctive lines of action, but there was much difference of opinion about their relative importance and precedence. The majority was of the opinion that Great Britain and Japan should quickly return to the gold standard at firm rates. But the representatives of these countries argued that neither their domestic situation nor the international outlook was clear enough to set a definite date for doing so; that decision must await improvement in their debt situation, expansion of trade and a rise of prices.

When President Hoover read the first report of the American experts, he was noncommittal. Stimson had thought that with good will all around and a firm determination to cooperate to end the depression, agreement could be reached. Mills, though pleased with the way in which Williams had so firmly advocated the primacy of stabilization, distrusted what the conference might produce. He feared that the foreign countries might align themselves against American tariff policy and resolve on measures that would make it more difficult for the United States to maintain the gold value of the dollar.

The Preparatory Commission of Experts was scheduled to meet again in January 1933 to produce a more conclusive analysis and further recommendations. At that time the sense still prevailing was, as I informed a friend, "that the conference itself must not be permitted to meet until the lines of agreement are definitely outlined and a fair measure of consent assured. The final conference should be little more than a play for which the lines have already been written."

By this time, elections had taken place and their outcome had cast uncertainty on everything planned. Did Roosevelt want the American government to participate in this conference? If so, would he be willing to have Day and Williams represent us on the

Preparatory Commission? Did he want them to return to Geneva? Would he instruct his staff to join them and officials still in office in formulating instructions that other governments could rely on? To find out, it was essential to consult him. That was another imperative reason for trying to concert a liaison.

There was also an intense wish to know whether the President-Elect would endorse Stimson's course of resolute resistance to Japanese aggression in China. Japanese armies were overrunning Manchuria and large areas of North China, killing and pillaging as they went along. Their thrust was destroying the whole treaty and peace structure for the Pacific which the American government had so earnestly striven to erect. It was menacing our own future security in the area.

The Japanese authorities had not been deterred by our disapproval. Early in 1931 the American government had made known that it would not recognize any treaty or agreement which impaired our treaty rights, including those which related to the sovereignty, the independence, or the territorial and administrative integrity of the Republic of China, nor any situation brought about by means contrary to the covenant of the pact renouncing war, commonly known as the Kellogg-Briand Pact, which had been signed in Paris in 1928.

Nevertheless, Japan had proceeded to consummate the plan to create a puppet state of Manchukuo by which to control Manchuria. Stimson's ire had been aroused by Japanese disregard of his friendly warnings. On the evening of Washington's birthday, 1932, he dictated a letter to Senator William E. Borah of Idaho, chairman of the Senate Foreign Relations Committee, publicly confirming a policy of non-recognition of the new state; he was not sure what Borah's response would be until the next day, when the Senator told him he was much pleased.

Some members of Congress — Senator Hiram Johnson of California among them — and some newspapers stressed one section of the letter that could be construed as an implication that if Japan insisted on territorial acquisitions contrary to treaties, the United

States would feel itself free to seek revision of the pact which provided for limitation of naval armaments. This caused both the President and Senator Borah to be uneasy; they feared the letter would be used by advocates of a larger navy to get Congress to authorize further construction.

Foreign governments had thus far refrained from commenting on the crisis. A special session of the Assembly of the League of Nations, called to consider the Far Eastern situation, was due to meet on March 4. The American government refused to send a representative to attend the sessions, but waited for the members of the League to make the next move. On March 11 (we are still in the year 1932), it declared that it was incumbent upon members of the League not to recognize any situation, treaty or arrangements brought about by means "contrary" to the covenant of the Pact of Paris.

Borah's endorsement of his stand gave Stimson satisfaction. But that waned as passing events revealed the ineffectiveness of the verbal and legal reprimand to Japan. Lacking support of the President and American public opinion for any independent initiative, Stimson had waited with suppressed impatience the report of a special League of Nations commission of inquiry — known by the name of the chairman, the Earl of Lytton, as the Lytton Commission — to investigate and advise upon all aspects of the dispute.

The somberness of Stimson's views of the situation may be recalled by extracts from a memorandum in which I jotted down what he said to his staff in the State Department: "The course of recent events in Japan was ominous. He [Stimson] had correctly diagnosed the first crisis as the assertion of military feudal elements in Japan over the civilian elements. They seemed to be getting more and more out of control. Up to recently all had hoped that Japan would prove itself a stabilizing influence in the Far East, proceeding by parliamentary means and supporting Western tendencies towards the maintenance of permanent peace, based on treaties and rules for peaceful settlement of disputes.

"But there had come about the brute assertion of force and the elevation of military groups in a country of sixty-five million people, with an army larger than ours and a navy as great. It was a grave issue. The one phrase that expressed our central purpose during the last war was 'To make the world safe for democracy.' This was not merely the rhetoric of a wartime President. It was one of the abiding principles of American life that military must be subordinate to civil authority and always under its command. A king's head had been cut off to establish that principle. He was praying that the new Prime Minister, Makoto Saito, would move to restore civilian control, for the military were out of hand."

The prayer was not answered. The Japanese did not retreat from the positions acquired from China, and their army and navy became still more bold in their demands for support and expansion. The Secretary's indignation was complemented by a sense of frustration at the failure of his attempts to cause Japan to desist. Moreover, he was troubled because Japanese actions were making it hard — perhaps impossible — to put forth proposals for disarmament he and the President had at heart.

In September 1932 the Japanese government formally recognized Manchukuo and concluded an alliance with it. This was construed as a way of confronting the League of Nations and the American government with an accomplished fact before they considered the report of the Lytton Commission, which was published on October 2. That condemned Japanese military action, declaring in substance that the state of Manchukuo was neither genuine nor independent, and that it would be incompatible with existing international obligations and prejudicial to the prospects of peace. Stimson hailed this report with enthusiasm, stating publicly that the American government firmly endorsed its conclusions.

But could its judgments be made effective? Would the incoming administration stand by them? Would it join in securing the assent of the American people if the Secretary of State associated the American government with the Assembly of the League if it approved the Lytton report and adopted its recommendation that members should refuse to recognize Manchukuo and continue to challenge Japanese control of it? If not upheld by us, the Assembly might falter. Even if the Assembly were upheld, the chance that

Japan might be brought to pause and retreat would be small if there were not a common front between the League and the United States. In sum, Stimson concluded that how far he might venture in his efforts to preserve the treaty structure in the Far East, how firmly he might repel the Japanese contentions, was dependent on whether or not the President-Elect would stand with and behind him.

The converging needs to make decisions about these three situations — debts, the arrangements for the Monetary and Economic Conference, and the Far East — made it imperative for the Hoover administration to seek to enter into and maintain a liaison with Roosevelt before he took office on March 4. The tale of the uneasy and unfruitful contacts that were made, retains, I believe, lively historical interest.

CHAPTER 4

Liaison: Act One

FIVE weeks before the December 15 war debt payments fell due, Stimson urged President Hoover to consult Roosevelt, until he yielded finally to what was for him an embarrassing necessity.

However, he crammed his message with his own ideas, so that, as Stimson noted in his diary, "It took away the simple and magnanimous tone which we had tried to get in the telegram. I'm afraid it will have a bad effect. Just by reciting all the difficulties and the attitude of Congress as meticulously as he has, it will scare Roosevelt away from any action whatever. In the second place, it will arouse a great deal of resentment abroad on the part of Great Britain and France." [1]

Hoover's message to Roosevelt implied that it might be advantageous to agree to reduce the debt if the British government compensated us by doing something which we desired. Perhaps, he suggested, we might ask it to return to the gold standard at a fair rate, or show greater vigor in urging general disarmament. He also requested Roosevelt to consider whether the representatives to be sent to the Monetary and Economic Conference should include some of the old or new members of the delegation to the Disarmament Conference, which was also soon to assemble in Geneva.

For then, he said, discussions about the debts, economic and monetary questions and disarmament could be better coordinated — and we would stand a better chance of getting some advantage for those we gave.

This message took Roosevelt by surprise. "We couldn't help," Moley recalled, "but appreciate the explosive nature of the package that had been left at his door." He urged the President-Elect not to allow himself to be drawn into any decision about the debts. The assertions of the debtors that they could not pay he did not regard as wholly valid; but even if they were, he conceived that keeping the issue alive might be a useful reminder to them that the United States would find it hard to finance another war in the United States.[2]

Roosevelt felt he had to respond to the call. But in doing so, he told Hoover that since the decision was the responsibility of those still having executive and legislative authority, he hoped they would confer with the members of Congress without his interposition. As though intent on differentiating his course from that of the President, he also said that in his judgment the several matters which Hoover wished to package together could best be dealt with selectively, even though some connection between what was done about each of them would emerge later.

While waiting for Roosevelt's visit to Washington, my colleagues and I, with minds bent to secure Mills's assent, wrote a simple reply to the British request for a postponement of the December payment which Roosevelt might be asked to approve. Its details have lost interest since. The President frowned on our production. He had just returned from California with the notion that he had lost the election in that state because of pamphlets and rumors circulated by his opponents stating that he had entered into secret agreements to reduce or cancel the debts. Moreover, he was chilled by a passage in the recent British note which could be taken to imply that in talks with former French Prime Minister Pierre Laval he had pledged the American government to wipe out much or most of the obligations. The sense that our debtors were using sneaky means of pressure upon him aroused his ire.

On November 22, Roosevelt streaked into Washington on his way to Warm Springs, Georgia. In this first encounter between the earnest President and his debonair successor, distrust and dislike poked out. Had Stimson been along he might have banished them. But the only attendants, Moley and Mills, were assertive antagonists.*

Moley had done what he could to keep the President-Elect on guard. He had written on cards questions to be asked of Hoover. One was certain to make him indignant. Was there any substance to the stories that he had given Laval and MacDonald secret promises that he would adjust the debts? On this card Roosevelt had scribbled in as a reminder to himself, a notation: "Secret agreements by Pres." [3]

Mills, on the other hand, had done all he could to prejudice Hoover against his visitor. Mills and Roosevelt had been classmates at Harvard and neighbors along the Hudson. A jealous rival for political power, Mills had made no secret of his opinion that Roosevelt was unqualified to be President and dangerously radical. Roosevelt, after he came out ahead, was amused rather than irritated by Mills's presumptuous ways.

Actually, the principles which Hoover told Roosevelt he thought should rule their response to the British government differed little in substance from those that the President-Elect had said he favored. Both men were against immediate postponement or cancellation; both were willing to hold out hope that the debt agreement would be revised. There were, however, two points of difference which partisanship rather than reality made appear important.

One was Hoover's sensible proposal that the Debt Funding Commission be reconstituted. This group, he suggested, might be made up of three Senators, three Congressmen and three presidential appointees. These last he would be willing to have Roosevelt name, or at least join with him in naming. Rather than repelling this suggestion himself, Roosevelt turned to the advocate at his

* Years later a common hatred of Franklin D. Roosevelt brought them together.

side. Why, Moley asked, could not the debt discussions be started through ordinary diplomatic channels? Had not the President the power to negotiate with foreign governments? Hoover did not bother to answer him.

The other point concerned Hoover's idea that the talks with our debtors be closely connected with talks about other international questions by conducting them through an interlocking directorate. Whether Roosevelt himself had any real convictions about this procedure is doubtful. But he allowed Moley to make objections to it, animated by his belief that the United States should not get itself enmeshed.

Roosevelt seems to have taken this meeting lightly, to have felt that he had shown polite deference to the President but avoided the trials of office before he had to assume them. His one remark about Hoover that came back to us was complimentary; that his review of the debt situation was thorough and interesting.

When Stimson asked how the meeting with Roosevelt had gone, Hoover told him that they spent most of their time educating an ignorant but well-meaning young man. But he thought some progress had been made.[4]

Hoover was disappointed because Roosevelt had refused to ease his task by complying with his proposal that Congress be asked to create a special agency. For he reckoned that any recommendations of such a nonpartisan group would be accepted by many Democratic members of Congress who would object to any that he might make. The President-Elect, it may be surmised, did not want to risk trouble with Democratic members of Congress whose cooperation he was going to need for his domestic program.

Since the two could not subscribe to a single joint public statement about their meeting, it was agreed that each give out his own. While these were being written, twisted accounts of what had been said found their way out of both camps. Some companions of Roosevelt chortled as they told newspapermen of the way he had ducked Hoover's attempts to lure him into responsibility for this touchy question of debts. William Castle, an intense partisan of Hoover, hinted to other newspapermen that Roosevelt had promised Hoover that he would in his statement support the idea of asking Congress to reconstitute the Debt Funding Commission.

Early next morning when Stimson went to the White House, the President and Mills were writing the statement of their views which they were going to give out. Although one is left to wonder how and why they could have gotten that impression, Hoover and Mills thought that Roosevelt had promised the night before that he would come out in support of Hoover's statement, but had begun to fear that he was now going to "welch." [5] That same morning Hoover explained to a group of Senators and Congressmen what the situation was and what he proposed doing. He sought their support for the main points in his statement and told them he thought it might be advisable to permit Britain to make the December payment in sterling. But Stimson noted: "The gentlemen who met us were a pretty hardboiled lot in regard to this proposition." [6]

It had been arranged that Mills should take Hoover's statement, along with the notes to be sent to our debtors, to the Mayflower Hotel and give Roosevelt the chance to look them over. When Mills did, Roosevelt merely glanced at them and nodded.

The President-Elect's statement was prepared on the train on the way to Warm Springs in consultation with Moley and Bernard Baruch. He expressed agreement with the principles which Hoover insisted should govern any discussion with our debtors, including the notice that we would deal with each individually and not as a group. But he dissented from Hoover's proposal to re-create a special commission as an agency to conduct the discussions with our debtors. They could be carried on through regular diplomatic channels, he thought, more expeditiously and flexibly.

Moley found the outcome gratifying. No retrospective comment has ever been more displaced by subsequent events than one he wrote in 1939: "It" (Roosevelt's statement made in connection with Hoover's statement) "maintained the integrity of the debts as living obligations which, from that day to this, have prevented the use of the United States as a war treasury by Europe, and have done more to stave off a general war than a dozen alliances or a score of diplomatic notes." [7]

In contrast to Moley's contentment with the outcome of this meeting, my own spirits drooped. I had tried over long months to persuade the leaders of the Hoover administration to adopt a more conciliatory and farsighted policy in dealing with our former allies; now it was apparent that the task of persuading the incoming administration might be as tiresome.

Still, there was Henry Stimson, the Secretary of State, to cling to. He had not forgotten that he was one of the group of influential Republicans that in 1919–1920 had remained in the Republican Party despite its opposition to our entry into the League of Nations, believing that his party would be able to cooperate more effectively with our former European associates than could the Democrats. His readiness to continue to do what he still could to make that belief come true had been displayed in connection with the replies we proposed to make to the British and French governments about the debts.

The notes which Hoover and Mills compounded were cold and forceful, even though Stimson managed to persuade them to tone them down. The British and French governments were notified that the December 15 payment could not be forgone, for reasons often explained. Any connection between reparations and debts was denied, the reply stating that "Reparations are solely a European question in which the United States is not involved," and "Debts must be treated separately from reparations claims arising out of war."

Stimson presented this answer to the British ambassador, Sir Ronald Lindsay, on November 23, the day after the Hoover-Roosevelt meeting. By way of preface Stimson said the British government had made it pretty hard for those who were fighting its battle because of the language in which its own note had been couched; it seemed to impute bad faith to the President. That kindly but lumbering man — a sympathetic friend of the United States — became "terribly broken up. He said it seemed as if we were deliberately trying to rub it in by our summary of American policy in the most bitter way." [8] He confided to Stimson that while in London he had been the main author of the note to which we were replying, and he avowed that he had not intended it to have the meaning which was being read into it. He thought the answer that had been given him to transmit would offend his colleagues, greatly lessen the chance of arriving at a compromise, and further harm the whole international situation.

Stimson was moved. Although fatigued and fretful, he went back to the White House and made another plea for a more yielding response. His earnestness induced Hoover to eliminate most of the combative historical summary and the rebuttal of the British (and French) imputations, and to soften some of the language. But the sting was left in — the refusal to recommend to Congress that the December payment be postponed. The revised version was given to Lindsay at seven o'clock that evening.

During the following weeks at Warm Springs, Roosevelt gave thought to his future program and appointments. Meanwhile, Hoover smoldered in the White House and Mills raged impotently. Stimson shared his anxieties with his group of close subordinates in the State Department, hopeful despite all signs that before he left office something positive could be done to repair the international situation.

To this end my own effort mainly centered on the arrangements for the prospective international Monetary and Economic Conference. The need to decide whether to go forward with preparations for the conference led to a revival of the effort to maintain liaison with the incoming administration. The American representatives on the Preparatory Commission of Experts, Day and Williams, had reported to the State Department on November 30 that in their opinion it would be futile to go on with preparations for, and convening of, the conference unless (1) a settlement of the intergovernmental debt question was in sight, and (2) it was understood that one of the prime aims of the conference should be to restore stability in the foreign exchanges, especially of sterling. As the delegates developed their views regarding the depressing effects of these two unsettled issues, Stimson and Mills were impressed. The

Secretary of State perceived that the prospect of doing anything effective at the conference was at stake. As I recorded in a memorandum of this discussion: "He [Stimson] walked to the window, waved his arm, and said it was just about time that someone had some guts in this matter. The opening has already been made by the President in his statement, with the suggestion that the American representatives to the Economic Conference should act as a debt commission. Why shouldn't the President follow this up in a special message to Congress? Secretary Mills leaned forward as he said, 'You will get the depression by the throat.' "

Stimson also fell in with Mills's view that President-Elect Roosevelt should be similarly briefed by Day and Williams. Thereby they hoped that he would be brought to realize that any conference held before March 4 must fail, and that no effective advance planning for a conference after March 4 could be made unless he took an interest in defining American policies.

The President had received these ideas favorably and said he was willing to act accordingly. He assented to the proposal that an effort should be made to arrange to have the President-Elect ask Day and Williams to come to Hyde Park.

It did not prove easy to get Roosevelt to receive these technicians and listen to their analyses and recommendations. He was being cautioned by Moley against being drawn off his course and involved in argument with his supporters. For Moley had been alarmed by what he learned of the program proposed by the committee of experts, correctly considering it to mean that the American government would be required to keep the dollar on the gold standard at its existing value, to reduce intergovernmental debts, and to adopt other measures of international cooperation. All these he deemed incompatible with the domestic program which the New Deal was to inaugurate.

George Harrison, head of the Federal Reserve Bank of New York, was at this time becoming greatly perturbed over the potential effect on the financial and political condition of the whole world if the debts should fall into default amid acrimony. He told Stimson and Mills on December 2 that he thought another attempt ought to be made to gain Roosevelt's cooperation; and whether or not the President-Elect responded, the President should call upon Congress to take some action. Stimson, though eager, was wary; he was afraid of stirring up a hot and paralyzing affray. He did not want to repeat the mistake Woodrow Wilson had made when he tried to drive Congress, though Harrison tried to convince Hoover this was the lesser of the risks he faced.

But it was to no avail. When Stimson and Mills followed Harrison to the White House, they gathered that he was regarded as that dreaded character a cancellationist. Still, they decided to telephone Ambassador Mellon and have him ascertain whether Britain was going to default or not. Mills was told he might keep an engagement to attend the Army-Navy football game in order to signify by his presence that all was calm in Washington.

Harrison went ahead on his own. He telephoned Rear Admiral Cary Grayson, who had been Woodrow Wilson's physician and was a friend of Roosevelt's, with whom he was lunching that day at Hyde Park. He asked Grayson to urge Roosevelt to invite Day and Williams to visit him at Warm Springs so that they might review the whole international situation as they saw it. But Roosevelt answered, "Let them talk with Moley."

When Moley talked with them, professional kinship apparently prevailed, for Moley told Roosevelt that he thought he should see them as soon as possible. Perhaps he reckoned that the President-Elect would alert his visitors to the fact that if their ideas remained unchanged when the new administration took office, it would either replace them or reverse the decision to participate in the conference. In any case, and with whatever reservations, Roosevelt agreed to see them.

When told of this we were cheered, not only because it might make it possible to proceed with preparations for the conference, but also because it might lead to a resumption of liaison with Roosevelt and even be the start of cooperation.

Before Roosevelt received Day and Williams, the debt situation took another and helpful turn. From Stimson down, all had pleaded with the British government to pay up in December, feeling that they were serving not only Hoover but also Roosevelt. We had urged Sir Ronald Lindsay to do his utmost to secure the consent of the British cabinet. Norman Davis in Geneva had pleaded with Prime Minister Ramsay MacDonald, at whose behest, braving criticism, the members of the cabinet agreed to make the payment even though they knew it would cause a sharp fall in Britain's gold reserves. But the British government, when it informed us it would do so, stated that the system of intergovernmental debts payment could not be revived without disaster. It served notice that this payment should not be regarded as a resumption of the annuities stipulated in the existing agreements.

While the prospect of receiving this payment was a welcome relief, the British note caused contention and apprehension. The blunt assertion in the note that this one payment must be regarded as exceptional, and as a prelude to re-examination of the obligation, aroused fears of a renewed outburst in Congress. To avert this the President, Stimson and Mills all thought it necessary to make and publish an immediate rejoinder. Our acknowledgment made on December 11 stiffly asserted that the Secretary of the Treasury had no authority to accept payment except under the terms of the original debt accord and could not approve the conditions which the British government wished to impose on the payment. Neville Chamberlain, Chancellor of the Exchequer, resolved the dilemma by a speech at Birmingham which began, "I don't think we need quarrel with the reply of Secretary Stimson to our note. We don't ask that our proposal be accepted at this stage, but we have reserved the right to put it forward when discussions begin." Thereupon the British government proceeded to make the payment in gold.

It did so in the hope of easing later adjustments and to help Stimson's efforts. For the predominant British view of the debts was expressed by John Maynard Keynes. "There are not now, and never were, any profitable assets corresponding to the sums borrowed. The medieval Church was wise to make a financial distinction between usury and a share in emergent profits. The war debts are a case of pure usury. Mr. Hoover's point that we bought food for civilians who were occupied in war tasks as well as actual munitions does not alter the case. We borrowed nothing except for purposes of war . . . [Moreover] the value received at the time was far less than that represented by the principal sum today. . . .

"What is our wisest course next Thursday? When one reads what Congressmen say to reporters, one's impulse is to bring things to a head at once. But patience is still the course of wisdom. We should agree to pay what is now demanded so as to give America time for reconsideration. But, above all, it is essential that we should declare plainly, and at once, that, failing a settlement which we consider satisfactory, this must be the end." [9]

The French government defaulted on its payment. Last-minute attempts failed to avert that and the imminent fall of the cabinet of Premier Edouard Herriot. The Premier pleaded with the Chamber of Deputies to authorize him to make the relatively small payment due (about twenty million dollars). But after an excited debate lasting almost through the night of December 13, the Deputies, by a large majority, refused to accord him the authorization. Some were most vehement in the statement of their belief that the debt was not a true or just obligation and never had been. Others deplored the way in which American influence had been exerted to deprive France of the reparations due it from Germany — in order, they alleged, to salvage the short-term loans of the American banks in Germany and long-term bonds owned by Americans. Still others rested their case on the fact that the real burden of the debt to the United States had become much harder to bear than in 1926 when France had been coerced into signing the debt accord.

On the morning of December 14 the Secretary of State was advised by Herriot that his government had fallen and that the Chamber of Deputies had refused permission to make the payment due. Similar notices of default were received from the Belgian, Polish and Hungarian governments.

Mills, throughout these days, was assertively active. I can still see and hear him saying, in one drafting session devoted to the answer to the British note, after the text he had written was turned down, "Well, here goes the best draft into the fire." Whereupon he tossed into the fireplace not only his own composition but the original British note.

Yet now that the climax had come, to my surprise Mills seemed unperturbed. Whether because of the reflection that at least the President and he had been spared the ordeal of wrangling with Congress, or because of the thought of the unsettled mess which Roosevelt would inherit, I did not and will not venture to surmise. But Secretary Stimson and those under him did not share Mills's calm, fearing the impact on all the other matters which were under discussion with European governments. In a memorandum dictated for my own benefit on December 14, I noted: "The newspapermen are flying around like a crowd of buzzards to see what new shape the conflict may enter, what weapons of retaliation may be employed. To a large group on the stairs I shouted, when held up and asked what I thought of the situation, that I thought it 'unnecessary, not inevitable, and too damn bad.' "

The situation sent a tremor among the diplomats who filed past the President on the night of December 15 at his annual reception for the diplomatic corps. His handshake with ambassadors from the countries who had refused to pay was limp, and his words of greeting were modulated. This was the President's formal farewell to the diplomats. The mood of depression throughout the country seeped into the occasion. The talk was also tinged with a note of regret at the prospective personal partings. Many working associations had turned into friendships. The decorations jingled, but not gaily as in more prosperous times; the gold braid glittered, but not as brightly as in merrier times.

During this fortnight of strain, Day and Williams had been waiting to be summoned to Warm Springs or Hyde Park. Before they were, Roosevelt received another message from Hoover. In this the President once again proposed that the three questions — intergovernmental debts, the matters to be discussed at the Monetary and Economic Conference, and disarmament — be given coordinate consideration by a unified American delegation to be appointed jointly by himself and Roosevelt.

Before dispatching it, Hoover telephoned to Colonel Edward M. House and told him what he was about to do. House said that he agreed with Hoover in every way and that he would tell Roosevelt so at once. Thereupon the message was sent off.

On December 18, the day after Hoover dispatched this telegram, Roosevelt received the two experts. Rexford G. Tugwell was in attendance. Roosevelt said that he wanted the opening of the conference to be postponed in order to give him a chance to get his domestic program for recovery well started. Day and Williams agreed readily, since they thought that little or nothing could be achieved in the near future. They left Hyde Park with the firm intention of getting the authorities in Washington to assent to their wish to delay their departure for Geneva and to set a later date for the convocation of the second meeting of the commission of experts, which had been fixed for January 19.

The next day Hoover, having heard nothing from Roosevelt, went ahead and sent a special message to Congress. Its leading feature was the reaffirmation of his ideas about procedure. He also inserted the opinion that one of the first and fundamental points of attack on the world-wide depression was to "re-establish stability of currency and foreign exchange." The next sentence was among those which I had managed to smuggle into the message — called good-naturedly by Stimson "Herbert's heresies." It read: "It must be realized, however, that many countries have been forced to permit their currencies to depreciate; it has not been a matter of choice." Heavy expenditures on arms, the President's exposition continued, was one of the causes of political and monetary instability. So were the intergovernmental debts. Although exaggerated in relative importance, in some cases they did weigh heavily on the balance of external payments. Therefore, all had best be discussed and settled concurrently.

That afternoon Stimson held a long special press conference to describe the background of the President's message to Congress.

After explaining its main points he said, "It is an honest attempt to put Mr. Roosevelt in a position in which he would be grateful to be, the President hopes, in regard to information and preparedness as regards the situation."

But perhaps the President-Elect thought this was a snare to commit him to the policies of the group he was superseding rather than his own. He was still unsure whether an attempt to connect negotiations closely on these subjects would be productive or skillful. In any case, in his answer to Hoover he stated that in his opinion *permanent* economic programs for the world should not be submerged in conversations relating to disarmament or debts. He recognized a relationship but not an identity. Therefore, he thought that each would require "selective treatment" and should be dealt with by different officials and in different ways. Thus he and Hoover remained at odds over this empty question.

Roosevelt also took occasion to make it clear again that he thought it would be "unwise to accept an apparent joint responsibility when he, Roosevelt, would not have real authority and could not share in the naming of the commission which Hoover proposed to establish." He would regret it, he added, if the outgoing administration initiated actions which might set policies which the incoming administration might find wrong. He saw no objection to informal discussion and preliminary economic studies. In short, he was willing to have talks start but he did not want decisions made until he was in office and had time to consider what to do about American foreign affairs.

Everyone in our small working group when it assembled in Stimson's office found it hard to see how to proceed. Roosevelt had evaded Colonel House's attempt to talk to him. He had spent three hours with Owen Young, who had been persuaded by Ogden Mills to seek the interview, but this renowned emissary had failed to make the President-Elect more pliable. This caused Stimson to remark at the end of the meeting in his office, in which no one managed to make his way clearly through the murk, that "all the wires to Albany are now down."

Hoover tried once more. On December 20 he sent still another

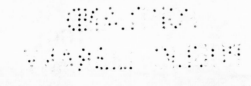

message to Roosevelt, in which he attempted to convince the President-Elect that he was not trying to convert him but merely seeking to set up essential advance arrangements for the proper and coordinated consideration of all three questions. "I realize," he wrote, "that your solutions of these questions of debt, the economic problems and disarmament might vary from my own. These conclusions obviously cannot be attained in my administration and will lie entirely within your administration. I wish especially to avoid any embarrassment of your work and thus have no intention of committing the incoming administration to any particular policy prior to March 4."

To Roosevelt and the men closest to him this assertion was not convincing. It was made even less so because Hoover went on to say that he would be glad if Roosevelt designated Owen Young or Colonel House or "any other man of your party possessed of your views and your confidence" to sit with officials then in Washington in an effort to see what steps might be taken to avoid the loss of precious time and the injury that would ensue. Moley correctly construed this as a hint that the officials in Washington would not be pleased at the thought of having to deal with him as Roosevelt's representative.

Before Roosevelt's next answer came, another thought occurred to Stimson's associates. They learned that the attractive young Congressman from Arizona, Lewis Douglas, had recently spent a weekend with Roosevelt. He was regarded by Mills and Stimson as well informed about international questions. So Stimson took Douglas out to Woodley and had him telephone Roosevelt from there. The President-Elect said he would send Moley to Washington to talk over the next steps to be taken in regard to intergovernmental debts and the international economic conference. But when Hoover was informed of this proposal, he took offense. He thought it was below his dignity and the dignity of a Secretary of State to treat as an equal an individual who was in so subordinate a position.

The wires thus remained down.

CHAPTER 5

Liaison: Act Two

THAT day, December 21, cheerful because I was leaving the worries of Washington behind for a while, I took the train for Cambridge. A farewell dinner was being given for that generous and helpful Harvard professor who had been my teacher, Edwin Gay.

On the morning of December 22, while gazing at the sooty snow that covered the lawns of the gambrel-roofed houses along Brattle Street, I telephoned my friend Felix Frankfurter, then a professor at the Harvard Law School. He told me that he had had a wire from the President-Elect asking him to spend that very night in Albany. I thereupon gave him as full an account as I could of the need for genuine liaison between the incoming and outgoing administrations. We agreed that the only possible mediator would be Stimson. We had faith that Roosevelt would recognize that the Secretary of State was concerned only with the general welfare and was open-minded enough to realize that policies other than those advocated by Hoover might be worth consideration.

Sometime during the conversation between Roosevelt and Frankfurter that evening, the President-Elect remarked, "Why doesn't Harry Stimson come up here and talk with me and settle this damn thing that nobody else seems able to?"

Whereupon Frankfurter called the Secretary and told him if he would telephone Roosevelt and ask whether something could not be done, the President-Elect would invite him to come up to Hyde Park the day after Christmas. Frankfurter also remarked that he thought there was a mixup; Roosevelt felt sorry that all attempts at cooperation had broken down. Stimson replied that he and his colleagues were also regretful over the impasse. They had formed the impression that Roosevelt had his own plans and did not want their cooperation. Let Frankfurter, he asked, think over the possibilities and telephone him again the next day.[1]

Of these events I knew nothing. But that afternoon, while on the train returning to Washington, I read the public statement which Roosevelt had issued in retort to Hoover's comment, and it seemed to me to leave the way open for a renewal of relations. It could be construed as signifying that despite his lively rebuttals, Roosevelt wanted to indicate that he was disposed to cooperate, provided a way of doing so could be found consistent with his own policies. I got off the train at Manhattan Terminal and sent a telegram to Allen Klots, Stimson's special assistant, asking him to pass on my impression to the Secretary.

Stimson, as I was later to learn from his diary, had already told Hoover about his talk with Frankfurter and of Roosevelt's invitation. Hoover thought he should refuse it. So did Mills. The President said the gate could be reopened only if Roosevelt sent to Washington two or three people of proper eminence to talk with him and Stimson and Mills. Hoover, Stimson thought, was still angry about the appearance in the press of unfavorable reports of his previous personal talk with Roosevelt — for which he blamed Roosevelt's entourage. Stimson did not then press the matter.[2]

What I learned the next day confirmed my belief that unless Roosevelt and Stimson could be brought together, an even thicker curtain of confusion would fall upon all our foreign relations. Norman Davis, the American representative on the organizing committee for the Monetary and Economic Conference, had been taken over to the White House by Stimson. Davis had chided the President in a semihumorous way about getting involved in this row with Roosevelt. But Hoover had not been amused. He was, in the phrase which Stimson wrote in his diary, "quite on the rampage." Stimson himself was irritated because Hoover had sent him a letter about Roosevelt's invitation which he thought quite superfluous.

After their sterile talk in the White House, Stimson and Davis returned to the State Department. Stimson asked Allen Dulles, then Legal Adviser to the American delegation to the Geneva Disarmament Conference, Harvey Bundy, Pierrepont Moffat and myself to hear what Davis had to say. Davis reminded us that he had obligated the American government to continue with the preparatory work for the conference. Therefore, it was imperative that Day and Williams return to Geneva for the second meeting of the experts, scheduled to start on January 9.

Day was still loath to go, thinking it a futile task under the circumstances. We told him that the impression must not be allowed to spread that the American government was no longer in favor of going on with the conference. If he and Williams did not return as planned, and/or if the meeting was postponed, the American government would be blamed and lassitude would set in. Day could not stand out against the combined insistence of the Secretary, Davis and myself; we all felt as Stimson did, that "although the experts have a pretty hard job to find anything definite under their present instructions, yet this must be done; and I have hopes, like the character in the novel, that something will turn up." [3]

That evening Frankfurter sent me a wire from New York, asking me to telephone him there. When I did so, he confirmed my impression that the latest statement which Roosevelt had given out was intended to convince American and foreign opinion that he wished to cooperate with the Hoover administration, provided he could do so without hindering his own future program. Roosevelt, Frankfurter reported, had expressed a high regard for Stimson. Then he gave me four messages from Roosevelt which he asked me to pass on to the Secretary. The first was — and this seemed to me to mark a change of mind — that he agreed it was advisable to have Day and Williams return to Geneva in time for the January 9 meeting of the experts, although he wished the determination of the final program for the conference to be postponed until after March 4. The second was that if the British government would send one or two of their economic experts to the United States, he would be glad to talk with them personally. Third, while he had not yet decided who was going to be his Secretary of State, and while for many purposes he thought Norman Davis would be useful, he would like to warn Stimson not to try to use Davis as a substitute Secretary of State in the meantime. And fourth, one of his clear prime purposes was to show the world that he wanted to cooperate with the Hoover administration in the interregnum.

I passed these messages on to the Secretary, who was dining at Woodley with Norman Davis. Thereupon Stimson telephoned Frankfurter. Respecting Hoover's ruling, he said that he could not go to visit Roosevelt. Gratified as he was that the President-Elect had such a pleasant opinion of him and wanted to talk with him, he could not see that at this time any good would come of their meeting. Stimson felt constrained to remark that for the present relations seemed to be "shut off"; the only way that he could see by which they could be renewed would be for Roosevelt to send down two or three persons of proper standing to confer with Hoover.

But Frankfurter still would not give up. On the next day — the day before Christmas — he called Stimson back. He said that after their talk the previous evening he had once again spoken to Roosevelt. The President-Elect, he reported, was genuinely eager to see the Secretary after his return from the trip on which he was about to start. He would be in his house in New York during the first half of January. If it would not be convenient for the Secretary to come there, Roosevelt would be passing through Washington later in January on his way to Warm Springs and would be glad to stop overnight to talk with Stimson.

Stimson was touched at Roosevelt's advances. His sense of his duty to try to assure continuity on our foreign policy rose to the top. There were many matters, he thought, which ought, in the national interest, to be talked over with Roosevelt: the Far Eastern and European situations, the questions before the Disarmament Conference, the program for the Monetary and Economic Conference. It seemed to him almost inconceivable that President Hoover should want to continue to deny the man who was going to succeed him the essential information which they could give him. No longer should the suspicions of the President and Mills be permitted to prevail. He would, he resolved, tell Hoover so in strong terms.

After James Grafton Rogers, an esteemed assistant, confirmed this opinion, the Secretary telephoned Frankfurter again. He asked him to repeat the messages from Roosevelt which had been relayed through me. Frankfurter, after doing so, went on to assure Stimson that Roosevelt was entirely sincere in his wish to talk with him, adding, "You know I'm an enthusiast. You also know that I am an accurate lawyer, so I want you to trust my accuracy on this matter." [4]

Roosevelt, thinking that Stimson might feel more sure of the sincerity of his wish to confer with him if told so directly, wrote him a letter. In this he said that he wanted to keep in touch with the Secretary, and told him that he should feel free *in person* to keep him informed of the course of events and discussions about international affairs, and to phone him at any time.

Thus, as Christmas came round, one transmission line was being strung. Over it an effort could be made to reach an accord that might ease or dissipate the pall of economic trouble that hung over the nation.

But could this line of liaison stand up against the strains upon it? Stimson and his subordinates in the State Department were required to give thought not only to the realities revealed in every incoming message, but to devising proposals that would be acceptable to both Roosevelt and Hoover. The good nature of the President-Elect could be counted on, we thought. But what of the slant of his ideas and the propensities of some of his advisers? Would President Hoover allow this line to be used? He would never understand why the economy had not revived under his ministrations. Moreover, it was natural for him to feel hurt because men under his command were becoming responsive to his victorious opponent.

Yet signs appeared which gave grounds for hoping that the line of communication might not only work but bring the main figures into personal touch.

Roosevelt followed up the letter he sent to Stimson by asking Tugwell to bring Day and Williams to Albany on December 27. Norman Davis was coming to visit him and this would provide the chance to get everyone in accord on the program for the Monetary and Economic Conference. But Davis said he wished to talk with Roosevelt alone so that he might also review situations in Europe with which the economists were not concerned. I have found no record of their talk. But after it ended Roosevelt told Tugwell that he saw no need to meet with Day and Williams again, that coordination could be achieved if the four — Tugwell, Davis, Day and Williams — met in New York. Day and Williams, after doing so and upon being informed that Roosevelt wanted them to return to Geneva for the second meeting of experts, became more cheerful about their mission. They were enjoined, however, to insist that the date for the conference meeting be set further forward.

Moley, having been in Cleveland, did not take part in any of these discussions. He may not have been aware that Roosevelt and Stimson were in touch. He attributed the signs of the President-Elect's willingness to cooperate with those still in office in Washington to Norman Davis's cunning and persuasiveness. Moley regarded Davis as a dishonest associate of selfish financial interests; as the agent of a conspiracy to involve Roosevelt in the debt question. About that it may be remarked that there was no need to involve Roosevelt — he couldn't possibly escape being involved sooner or later.

On Wednesday, January 4, Frankfurter learned that after talking with Hoover the previous night, Stimson thought that a meeting could be arranged if Roosevelt would write or wire the President. He might simply say that if the President had no objection, he would like to discuss certain matters affecting the State Department with the Secretary of State. Such a request would be in a settled tradition. For example, when Hoover had been President-Elect and had wished to confer with the incumbent Secretary of State, Frank

Kellogg, he had written to President Coolidge and asked him whether he was agreeable to such a meeting.

Thereupon Frankfurter phoned Roosevelt and gave him a summary of this talk with the Secretary of State. The President-Elect found the formalities amusing. Frankfurter remarked that it resembled an eighteenth-century minuet; Roosevelt said that it was eighteenth-century all right, but he did not know if it was a minuet. He would gladly write Hoover if Frankfurter would tell him what to write. "Dictate a letter now and write what you think I ought to send him." Frankfurter did so over the telephone, repeating what Stimson had told him he thought should be in the letter. Roosevelt took it down and then told Frankfurter that he would put the letter to Hoover in the mail that night. He asked Frankfurter to let Stimson know that he would be glad to have Stimson lunch with him at Hyde Park the coming Saturday or Monday. If he took an early train they would have ample time.

Frankfurter, trying to assure that the meeting would be congenial, reminded Roosevelt that Stimson was a "very different fellow from Hoover." Roosevelt responded, "That's been very evident throughout this affair." Then, since Roosevelt had had in the past only a few casual meetings with Stimson, Frankfurter went on to tell the President-Elect to bear in mind that Stimson was "rather slow-minded, methodical and single-tracked, like Woodrow Wilson," rather than quick and darting, and therefore Roosevelt should give him enough time to expound everything that was in his mind. Roosevelt promised that he would.

As soon as this talk ended, Frankfurter reported to Stimson again. The Secretary was much pleased. Yet he still seemed rather apprehensive about the meeting with Roosevelt and asked Frankfurter for any suggestions he might have about how to manage it. Frankfurter said the important thing for Stimson to remember was that Roosevelt really had confidence in him and merely wanted to be informed; that he should therefore go in a relaxed frame of mind and talk with the President-Elect as two men who cared about the same things and trusted one another. Roosevelt, Frankfurter continued, had a very friendly and boyish nature and Stimson should meet him in that spirit. Stimson in a serious voice said, "I am very glad to hear that." Frankfurter realized clearly that Stimson was still perturbed by all sorts of nonsense which his Republican associates had spoken about Roosevelt.

One other passage in their talks was to prove more prophetic, I think, than either of them at the time realized. Frankfurter said to Stimson that he expected the Secretary would continue to have considerable influence on international relations during the next four years, living as he would at Woodley in Washington. Out of office, Frankfurter ventured, he might have more influence with the new administration than he had with the present one. Stimson laughed and added, "You always were an optimistic fellow." Frankfurter replied, "These are terrible days and I suppose that determination and optimism are not offenses but needs." [5]

Neither of them could possibly have foreseen that seven years later, as the wars that were being fought in Europe and the Far East began to threaten our own national destiny, Roosevelt would ask Stimson to become Secretary of War; and that Stimson, although by then feeling his three score and ten years, would accept, and bear the heavy burdens of his office more sturdily than many a younger man.

CHAPTER 6

Liaison: Act Three

ON January 9 Stimson went to Hyde Park, where he and Roosevelt conversed for six hours. Their talk ranged over every important foreign problem before the American government, among them the Far East, disarmament, the economic conference, and debts. Roosevelt made good use of his chance to be instructed about the issues discussed, and Stimson made good use of his chance to acquaint himself with Roosevelt's ideas about each of them.

Stimson's diary entry tells that the two men found themselves to be in rapport. "The Governor did everything to make the interview pleasant, and his hospitality was very agreeable. I had never had a talk with him before, but we had no difficulty getting on. We both spoke with the utmost freedom and informality. I was much impressed by his disability and the way he paid no attention to it whatever. While we were finishing our luncheon the press were allowed in and the photographers. We had agreed on what we should say beforehand, and the Governor said it. He told them that he had had a very pleasant interview with me and that we had talked over the matters in the State Department and the foreign relations of the United States. When pressed by the reporters as to what foreign relations, he said we had discussed them all. I told them I had a very delightful luncheon and visit and I confirmed what the Governor had said about the nature of our talk. . . . When these reports came out in the press afterwards, they were perfectly proper and everybody in Washington agreed with me that it had been perfectly done. I was very much pleased because none of the President's forebodings was realized, and even he did not have a word of criticism." [1]

Most consequential was the section of their talk about the Far Eastern situation. Just a few days before, when the Japanese ambassador had tried to minimize recent advances in North China and said "that in any event Japan had no territorial ambition south of the Great Wall," Stimson reminded the ambassador "that a year ago he had told me that Japan had no territorial ambitions in Manchuria." Whereupon the ambassador had become greatly flushed. Then, after the ambassador remarked that in all frankness he must tell the Secretary "that no Japanese Cabinet which advocated a compromise of the Manchukuo question could survive in Japan; that must be regarded as a closed incident," [2] Stimson had said that in that case he could see no other course than for Japan to get out of the League of Nations and the Kellogg Pact. [3]

Poor Katsuji Debuchi. He was a person of gentle spirit and sincere address, and he really regretted the necessity of defending actions of his government which he too disliked. When next I went to dinner at the Japanese embassy I could not but note his dolorous expression, and I felt all the more regretful in the company of Madame Debuchi, his gentle wife, who was as charming an adornment of the embassy as the cultivated shrubs and trees on the lawn.

Stimson reviewed for Roosevelt the history of his actions, of which this was merely the most recent incident. He said that he was confident that in the end China would resist this attack as it had so many others in the past. Roosevelt agreed that Japan would ultimately fail. Then, as Stimson set down in his diary:

"I [Stimson] described the function of the American fleet at Hawaii and how necessary it was for it to remain there. . . . He seemed to fully agree with me, and I remember when I said that

Japan had sought to get the fleet removed, he asked me if it was possible that Japan had been rash enough to attempt to dictate the policy of the American fleet. He told me a story of his own action as Assistant Secretary [of the Navy] in getting out the 'Orange Plan' of the Navy against Japan in respect to the defense of the Philippines and how surprised he had been to find that, under the plan as it then stood, the fleet was to leave the Philippines and the Army in it unprotected and return to the American coast. I told him that was not the plan now as I understood it and I pointed out to him the strategic effect of the Hawaiian position in stabilizing the situation against any attack either on our own coast or the Philippines.

"I described the present militaristic group which holds the power in Japan . . . a temporary reversion by Japan to the old position of a feudal, military autocracy, and to this he agreed. I told him of the present ticklish situation at Geneva and the likelihood that it might be advisable for me to make another statement as to this government's position. I said to him, 'I do not wish to ask any commitments from you but I certainly do not wish to make any such statement and then have you immediately afterward come out with a contrary position or statement.' He replied, 'You need have no fear of that.' " [4]

Stimson, to anticipate, took Roosevelt at his word. A few days later he warned the Japanese ambassador not to think there would be any change in American policy. He also sent a message to the same effect to Sir John Simon, British Foreign Secretary, who was about to leave for Geneva to attend a special meeting of the Assembly of the League of Nations. But from Simon's answer he got the impression that although the Foreign Secretary was ostensibly welcoming his cooperation and telling him that the Assembly would surely approve the report of the Lytton Commission, he was indifferent to the non-recognition policy. [5]

Then, on January 17, while American officialdom was speculating about what would happen next, the President-Elect, without consulting Stimson again, issued a public statement in which he said that "American foreign policy must uphold the sanctity of international treaties." This was correctly taken to mean that he aligned himself with Stimson's policy. Pierrepont Moffat happened to be in the office of the Secretary when Stimson learned of this and observed that "It was like lifting a heavy weight off his chest." [6] Gratefully Stimson telephoned Roosevelt to thank him. Roosevelt said he was very well satisfied with their teamwork.[7]

When Moley reproached him, Roosevelt put an end to the comment by recalling that his ancestors used to trade with China. Moley quotes him as saying, "I have always had the deepest sympathy with the Chinese. How could you expect me not to go along with Stimson on Japan?" [8] When Tugwell tried to alarm him by saying that our course might draw us into a war against Japan, Roosevelt said that such a war might better come then rather than later.[9]

This indication that the new administration would continue Stimson's policy caused the will of the British and French governments to stiffen. The emergence of Hitler as Chancellor of Germany on January 30 also disposed them more openly to sponsor the doctrine that treaty obligations should not be cast aside.

A month after Roosevelt had publicly spoken up in behalf of Stimson's policy, the British asked whether the American government would continue to cooperate with the League of Nations in regard to the Sino-Japanese situation, and also whether it would make a public statement of approval of a proposed resolution of the Assembly adopting the report of the Lytton Commission. Stimson assured the British government that American cooperation with the League in this matter was well anchored. He told D'Arcy Osborne, the British chargé d'affaires, that the issuance of a public statement by the American government before the Assembly acted on the report would be highly unwise. It would surely be seized upon by the Japanese authorities as evidence that the United States was behind the whole movement within the Assembly and was seeking to impose its will upon the Assembly.

The Secretary of State also allayed Hoover's fears by assuring him that the American government would not be asked to become a member of the League committee contemplated in the League resolution to follow up its recommendations unless, as was unlikely, the resolution was accepted by both Japan and China. The

President thereupon assented to Stimson's proposal that the American government associate itself with the Assembly after it had passed a resolution adopting the report. It would then state that the findings of the Assembly corresponded to those of the American government and that the Assembly's stand conformed to the policy of non-recognition for which the American government had stood since 1932.

But at the last moment Hoover was unnerved again by a warning from Joseph Grew, our ambassador in Tokyo, that the situation in Japan was dangerous. The President wanted to include in the statement which the American government was to issue the point that under no circumstances would the American government resort to sanctions. Stimson noted in his diary that "it was his [Hoover's] old habit. He thought that would relieve the tension in Japan. I told him I didn't think it would do this, and I thought it would give all the other nations who had with difficulty followed it up to this point the idea that we had let them down. Finally he yielded to my argument and did not press the matter further; and I could not help but feel that it would be a horrible thing to make a statement which would be so much of an anti-climax to what the League was doing on this great day when for the first time in history the united group of nations had condemned morally another great nation." [10]

Stimson had shown the draft of the statement to Senator Cordell Hull of Tennessee, who he knew was to succeed him as Secretary of State, and secured his approval. On February 25, President Hoover glanced over it and said it was all right. It was mimeographed and put out to the press, and telegraphed to Geneva.[11]

Stimson had been regretful but not surprised when, on February 24, after the Assembly had adopted the report of the Lytton Commission, the head of the Japanese delegation, Yosuke Matsuoka, had read a declaration which said that the Japanese government "has now reached the limits of its endeavors to cooperate with the League of Nations in regard to the Sino-Japanese differences." He had then led the Japanese delegation out of the conference room. This was the same excitable and voluble individual who, fervidly admiring Germany and hating the United States, was to become

Foreign Minister in the cabinet of Prince Fumimaro Konoye in 1941 and was more responsible than any other civilian for bringing the United States into the war.

Stimson construed Matsuoka's dramatic exit as meaning that Japan would soon leave the League of Nations. Stimson had been inclined to believe this would not make any difference. But still he became disturbed as he grew more aware of the extent to which the Japanese action worried the British, French and other governments who still relied on the League to restrain aggression in Europe. The British government had let its anxiety become known through the addresses made by the British ambassador in Tokyo. Sir John Simon had gone so far as to assure the House of Commons that "under no circumstances will this government authorize this country to be a party to the [Sino-Japanese] conflict." At about the same time Winston Churchill, in a public lecture, manifested a similar wish to soothe Japan by remarking that "We do not want to throw away our old and valued friendship with Japan."

Roosevelt was, a fortnight hence, to inherit this unresolved situation in which Japan was defying the judgment of the whole Western world.

CHAPTER 7

Liaison: Act Four

I HAVE run past other stations in the tunnel of liaison. When Stimson talked with Roosevelt at Hyde Park on January 9, they arranged that Roosevelt should see Hoover again, when next he would be passing through Washington. Here was a longed-for second chance to secure the needed accord. So in advance of that visit we in the State Department tried to make the President and Mills more amenable.

On his return from Hyde Park, Stimson had informed us that he got the impression that Roosevelt's views regarding the debts and the Monetary and Economic Conference were in flux. He had told Roosevelt that almost all the experts — American and foreign — regarded the debts as a barrier that should be surmounted before the conference met; and they also thought that stabilization of currencies (especially of sterling) was the first step to recovery. "In general," Stimson wrote in his diary at the end of this sector of their talk, "my attitude was to prevent him [Roosevelt] from being over-confident about the Conference and dismissing it from his mind as something which did not require important attention." [1]

The President-Elect had taken pains to make Stimson understand why he would not agree to Hoover's proposal that they appoint jointly, or that he alone designate members of an interlocking group to prepare for and conduct the discussions about the debts, disarmament and the conference. He thought everyone would assume that the individuals selected would be members of his cabinet; but he was not ready to choose them. Moreover, he believed he could get Congress and the country to accept a debt readjustment if he personally made and sponsored it. In that connection Roosevelt had wondered whether the British government might send over someone like Stanley Baldwin, then Lord President of the Council, who could talk with him and do the spadework about the debts. Stimson had demurred, saying that he thought it unlikely that Baldwin would come, and if he did come he would not be alone because of the cleavage between the British Treasury and others of the British cabinet. But he had ended by telling Roosevelt that while he saw great difficulties it might be possible to arrange such a visit. Uppermost in his mind were doubts whether Hoover would be willing to have him try to do so, since the President might be offended by the effacement. A mistake at this point would break the liaison again beyond mending.

Hoover, however, responded to the suggestion by setting down in a memo how he thought an invitation to the British government ought to be carried out. Roosevelt's presumptive line of negotiation seemed to him to disclose the fact that the President-Elect had not yet comprehended the problem with which the world was confronted. Hoover still believed that for our promise to adjust the debt agreements we should try to extract from Great Britain a pledge to make adequate efforts to remedy world economic conditions and change the course of economic deterioration in the United States. For such large purposes, he concluded, a visit of merely one representative of the British government to talk only about the debt would end badly. What was needed was a prolonged discussion between all the best British and American minds that might eventuate in a general program to reverse previous economic failures. This program the two governments — American and British — could present jointly to the Monetary and Economic Conference.

If Roosevelt, then, would select the persons he would like to have do the preparatory work, Hoover would be glad to appoint them, "If they are men of understanding in these questions." In any event the British group should not arrive in the United States before March 1 or until the new Secretary of the Treasury and Secretary of State were appointed. For otherwise, if negotiations were attempted jointly by the outgoing and incoming administrations, they would be harried by every partisan newspaper and politician. "However," Hoover wound up by saying, "if the Governor wants an Englishman to come over, and if *he* will do all the negotiating, we can facilitate it." [2] In other words, the existing administration would act primarily as a committee on arrangements.

Stimson telephoned Roosevelt that evening and faithfully transmitted Hoover's ideas and opinions. He said that he thought that Roosevelt, before agreeing to a debt settlement, would like to be sure that Great Britain was going to cooperate with us at the Monetary and Economic Conference. In the light of what occurred later, the sequential passage in Stimson's record of what he said to Roosevelt and what Roosevelt said to him has a special interest: "I pointed out, for example, that the United States would wish to secure the assurance of Great Britain that she would stabilize sterling as a means of raising world prices . . . this could be a great advantage to us unless our nation proposed to join in the race for national inflation which is now going on among the nations, which, of course, I assumed Roosevelt would not want to do. He at once said that of course he did not want to join in such a race." [3]

Stimson also repeated what he had told Roosevelt when he visited him at Hyde Park — that the British government would want to send several men, not merely one. Roosevelt remarked that he hoped we could keep the number down; he did not want the British to send too many.

Stimson then made it clear that while the officials in office would do all they could to clarify the matters to be discussed and ascertain the views of foreign governments, they would not be able to conduct negotiations. Roosevelt said he realized this was so. In view of this and other considerations, Stimson said he thought the

British should not arrive before the first of March, by which time Roosevelt would have selected his Secretaries of State and the Treasury. Roosevelt agreed.

By this shift in the scope of the talks contemplated, in the size and character of the British group to be invited, and in the time of their arrival, the President-Elect in effect accepted future responsibility for the whole negotiation.

In this conversation Stimson also tried to mark out the guidelines for an agreement between Roosevelt and Hoover when next they met. At the end of a long record which he made in his diary, he wrote, "Bundy and Feis listened in on the auxiliary earpieces which I had in my study [at Woodley] and were very much pleased with Roosevelt's attitude and with the outcome of the talk." [4]

CHAPTER 8

Liaison: Act Five

ALAS, Stimson's efforts to moor this second talk between Roosevelt and Hoover so securely that they could not drift apart were again washed out.

Roosevelt left for Washington early on January 19, Moley, who came along, was disturbed because Norman Davis was also on the train. He was afraid that Davis would interfere with his own determination to dissuade Roosevelt from agreeing to what Hoover and Stimson were going to propose. The matters about which he fretted were phantoms — in the sense that although they might be conceived, they could not be materialized, no matter what Roosevelt or Hoover said or did. For example, the debtor governments could not be prevented from linking the debts with those matters which were to be considered at the Monetary and Economic Conference.

While Roosevelt, on his way to Washington, was listening to Moley, Hoover was hearing Stimson's report of his most recent telephone talk with Roosevelt. The President seemed to be content with the positions Stimson had taken and less bothered than he had been about the way in which the Secretary was working along with Roosevelt. The British ambassador was informed that progress was being made in bridging the gap between the two. Stimson asked him whether it would be possible for the British government to send someone over to begin discussions with the President-Elect. Lindsay said it was quite possible.

So after lunch Stimson set off cheerfully for the Mayflower. Roosevelt's first remark after his greeting was, "We are getting so that we do pretty good teamwork, don't we?" Stimson laughed and said yes. They were referring to the conjunction of their statements on the Far Eastern situation. As their talk traveled, the Secretary again counseled Roosevelt against entering into negotiations about the British debt except in connection with other matters of interest to us, especially a promise to stabilize sterling. With or without warrant, Roosevelt now seemed to him "wobbly" about the strategy.

The President-Elect at this juncture asked Moley and Davis to join them. When Stimson then proceeded to review the whole range of subjects he and Roosevelt had talked about on the telephone, he got the curious notion that both Davis and Moley "cordially and vigorously agreed with me on every point; and this seemed to bring Roosevelt round so that . . . I came away with the impression that he was in full accord." [1]

The next morning — January 20 — Stimson and Mills arrived at the White House just as Roosevelt, Davis and Moley were being ushered into the Red Room. The President sat on a sofa with his back to the window. Roosevelt was on his right in a comfortable chair. Stimson and Mills were seated on a nearby second sofa; and next to them Davis and Moley on chairs, making a circle.

Of the many confused scuffles it has been my professional pleasure to study, the one that ensued is the hardest to relate with confident accuracy. It was reminiscent of a naval engagement on a foggy night between two opposed fleets, each ship firing whenever a gun flash was seen, being quite as likely to blow up a friend as an enemy. In this instance as well, the proponents were shooting at shadows and hitting the air. The course of the talk is explicable only on the supposition that each of the two groups suspected the other of secret purposes. The record indicates clearly that one prime aim which Hoover and Mills had in mind was to induce Great Britain to stabilize sterling and return to the gold standard, thereby averting the possibility that the United States might go off the gold standard. Is it not probable that Roosevelt perceived that acceptance of the Hoover-Mills-Stimson strategy might imperil his future freedom of action?

Hoover started the talk by observing that the British government was waiting to be advised when discussions regarding the debts were to take place. Roosevelt confirmed his wish that these discussions be held in abeyance until after March 4. Hoover and Mills assented.

Next, the argument about whether debt discussions were to be conducted separately or in connection with other questions set in. Hoover repeated his conviction that since the debt question was but a segment of the whole international situation, it should not be discussed separately and that compensation must be secured for any reduction in the debts. Moley did not wait for Roosevelt to object. Fearing that Stimson and Davis might have persuaded him, Moley, to Stimson's surprise, "jumped in as the opponent of any attempt to connect the debt negotiations with assurances as to the economic situation in general. It seemed to me such a reversal of Moley's attitude of the evening before, where he had been helpful on the subject, that I could not understand it." [2]

Stimson, Mills and Davis all spoke up in support of Hoover's view and tried to down Moley. Up to this point, Roosevelt — who, Moley thought, was enjoying the tussle — said nothing. Now he affirmed that he thought it best that debt discussions be carried on separately. His idea was that the British government might send someone to the United States to talk about debts, and that other questions might arise naturally in the course of their talks. Whereupon Stimson rose out of his chair and took up a stance before the mantelpiece. It was imperative, he said, that he, who would have to make arrangements with the British, know precisely where the President-Elect stood on the matter. Would we or would we not keep open the chance to seek compensation in return for concessions on the debts by linking all questions of interest in a unified negotiation? The British would want to know; for if the discussions were to be inclusive, they would want to bring over a bevy of qualified officials, not merely Treasury representatives.

From then on the listeners got a more, not less, contradictory impression of what was said and decided. Moley thought Roosevelt "Firmly, unequivocally . . . indicated that discussions of the debts and other matters must be separate." [3] But Stimson thought Roosevelt acquiesced in the idea that, although the two sets of discussions must be conducted by different groups in different rooms, they would be very closely related. Roosevelt spoke of them as "being twins." [4]

Hoover then concluded, as recorded in a memorandum he wrote about this conference, that "it was now a question of saving the Governor's face in view of his public statements, and I stated that often enough these were questions of a formula and we might try to arrive at a formula." [5] So the President wrote one which marked the separateness of the two subjects by putting each in its own sentence, and yet recognized the connection between the two. It read:

"The British government has asked for a discussion of the debts. The incoming administration will be glad to receive their representative early in March for this purpose. It is, of course, necessary to discuss at the same time the world economic problems in which the United States and Great Britain are mutually interested, and therefore, that representatives should also be sent to discuss ways and means for improving the world situation."

Hoover thought the result was "to state our appearance of separation to the public but a consolidation of them in fact to the British delegations." [6]

Roosevelt probably thought the wording made little difference. In any case he made no objection to the inclusion of this formula in the press release given out following the conference. Moley thought it meant "there was to be a clear demarcation between the two sorts of discussion with the British." [7]

It is hardly to be wondered that the whirligig of argument started again that afternoon when Stimson, after talking with Hoover, set about writing the aide-mémoire to be given the British ambassador. It was understood this was to be cleared with Roosevelt. Either because he was leaving immediately for the South, or because he was bored or indifferent, or wanted to use Moley to fight out the issue, Roosevelt asked that assiduous assistant to meet with Stimson and pass upon the text.

Stimson, however, tried to settle the matter without getting into another tangle with Moley. He telephoned Roosevelt, who was just about to leave the hotel for his train, and held him long enough to read the draft to him. Roosevelt made two comments. He thought Stimson's draft did not make it clear enough that the two sets of discussions were to be kept separate. And he was afraid that Stimson's language implied that the American government was accepting a commitment to reduce the debts. Moley, he said, would visit the Secretary at the State Department to straighten out these points.

Stimson reworked his aide-mémoire to prevent any possible interpretation that the American government was committed to debt reduction. Moley called upon him and was joined by Tugwell. When I entered the Secretary's office after lunch I found him gazing at Moley and Tugwell with an air of perplexity, while they showed signs of irritability. Moley thought that Stimson's draft still retained a more definite connection between the two sets of discussions than Roosevelt had approved. Stimson thought otherwise. Becoming admonitory, he began to lecture them, to warn them that if they failed to secure compensation for any reduction in debts they would be in for trouble.

But Stimson kept using his pencil until Moley thought the text acceptable. While Moley was still in his office, Stimson read it to both the President and Ogden Mills, explaining that it was the best he could do under the circumstances. They did not grumble over it. Moley for his part thought that the document definitely distinguished the two sets of negotiations and that the battle had been won. He probably believed he was saving the President-Elect from himself. Neither he nor Stimson seemed to realize that the battle they had been fighting was a sham one. It was much ado about nothing.

As soon as Moley left, Stimson asked the British ambassador to call. He said that he had now been formally authorized by Mr. Roosevelt to extend an invitation to the British government to send a representative (or representatives) to the United States early in March to discuss the debts owed to the American government. Then he read aloud a paragraph from the aide-mémoire which Moley had approved. "Mr. Roosevelt wishes it understood that any discussion of the debts which the British government may wish to bring up must be concurrent with and conditional on a discussion of the world economic problems in which the two governments are mutually interested, and therefore that representatives should be sent at the same time to discuss the ways and means for improving the world situation." Lindsay asked him whether those other matters included gold — presumably meaning the question of whether Great Britain was to return to the gold standard. Stimson answered that he thought they did, but he could not interpret Roosevelt's words.

In a meeting with reporters immediately thereafter, Stimson remarked that while the proposal first made by Hoover would have meant an earlier beginning of negotiations, out of deference to Roosevelt's wishes only preparatory work would be carried on until after March 4. This remark, although offered only as background information, may have contributed to the spurt of partisan comment during the next few days. The gossip that reached my ears at the time was that Hoover was giving out stories about his meetings with Roosevelt which cast a poor light upon the Democratic participants. Journalists, among them Arthur Krock of the *New York Times* and Frank Kent of the *Baltimore Sun,* were suspected of trying to supplant Moley by Davis; and probably they were.

Moley telephoned Roosevelt at Warm Springs and told him of these stories. He told the President-Elect that if he preferred to have Norman Davis — that bogeyman — take over the work on foreign affairs, he would relinquish it. Roosevelt laughed at the idea and suggested that the stories which worried Moley had probably been given out by supporters of Davis who hoped he might be made Secretary of State. He then went on to soothe Moley further by telling him: "I am through with Norman Davis. The incident is closed so far as I'm concerned. When he got off the train we said goodbye and no mention of a future appointment was made. In the matter of debts, you are my sole representative . . . I also want you to go ahead and get Rex [Tugwell] and two or three others to begin preparing the stuff I'll need for the preliminary economic discussions with the foreign representatives after March 4." [8] But Moley was to learn that Davis would not easily be chased out of Roosevelt's circle.

Stimson was not released from his trouble even overnight. President Hoover began to insist that the French government be called on once more to pay up. The Secretary thought that Hoover was not thinking so much about the welfare of the world as about his own personal record and party advantage. The presentation of another dunning note would be a futile and irritating gesture. Moreover, he had the impression that Roosevelt did not want this issue to be pressed, and he feared that if it were, the new collaboration might be broken.

He went over to the White House on January 21 and explained his misgivings about the note; the President and Mills were inflexible. "We had," he wrote in his diary, "some pretty hot words, the President getting more irritated than I had seen him for a long time. I spoke pretty freely myself." But Hoover calmed down, and when Mills produced a shorter and more conciliatory text, he accepted it with the remark that eventually he was going to send the long note with all the counts of indictment against France and a rebuttal of the allegation that he had promised Laval to cancel the French debt.

On the following day Stimson again tried to dissuade the President from sending the short note. To no avail. After an argumentative talk on the telephone, the President asked him if he was going to send it; Stimson answered that he would if the President directed it; the President said that he requested it. He and the President hung up their telephones, mutually angry. [9] Stimson with great misgiving sent off a letter to Roosevelt telling him what he was going to do. The President-Elect thought the decision about the note to

France had better be deferred until he could observe the reaction to the invitations to discuss their debt obligations that he wished sent to those debtor governments which had paid up in December. But would Stimson please make clear that each would be dealt with separately and at Roosevelt's early convenience?

On January 24 the British ambassador brought in a reply to our invitation. This seemed satisfactory to Stimson. After reciting it over the telephone to Roosevelt, Stimson said he had told Lindsay again that he thought Roosevelt would wish to have some assurances as to the attitude of the British government on some other subjects before he gave up any debts. The President-Elect said he warmly approved of the attitude which Stimson had taken.

So round and round went the liaison, more like a tumbleweed than a vine. While Roosevelt and Stimson had been working together, Mills had been seething.

On the morning of January 26 he summoned Harvey Bundy and me to his office and stormed at us for two hours. He said he resented the way in which Stimson was giving out material for Roosevelt and in a sense acting as a temporary Secretary of State for him. He averred that Hoover had told him he had never been so humiliated in his life. Saying that he was expressing Hoover's reaction as well as his own, he fumed at the implication in the British note of acceptance to our invitation that the British were going to insist on a great cut in their debts because of the great shrinkage in the reparations they were receiving from Germany. He predicted that this meant that the two governments would collide head on in the discussions after March 4, and that consequently the American government would be called on to renounce the position it had held for twelve years.

The prediction that they would collide was, it seemed to me, likely to be true. I thought a collision could only be averted if we agreed to write off most of the debts. But Mills thought they could still be collected or traded; and like Moley he thought if they could not be, it would still be useful to keep them alive as a cause of alienation between the United States and the defaulters. He wanted

Hoover to send Roosevelt a note warning him that there was trouble ahead; the American people would not allow any administration to cancel the debts. This seemed to us an attempt to put Roosevelt on the spot — which he would resent. But after a long and disorderly conversation, Bundy and I agreed it might do no harm if Roosevelt were merely advised that there seemed to be a serious difference of intention between the American and British governments, and that unless this was abridged before the British debt mission arrived failure lay ahead.

I reported this talk to the Secretary. He asked Bundy and myself to prepare a letter in this sense to be sent to Roosevelt. We did so reluctantly, preferring to wait until Roosevelt showed that he wanted our advice.

But Mills would not leave any blank pages in the written record which would prove to partisans and posterity that he never failed to try to get our money's worth. Persisting, he composed a memorandum to be sent to Roosevelt. Hoover reintroduced into it all his own views about the way in which the debt negotiations should be conducted. He sought, while instructing Roosevelt, to protect his own administration from criticism if Roosevelt refused to follow his advice and trouble occurred.

By this time I could only sigh wearily over the way both groups were clinging to untenable positions. So I found myself telling Mills that I had often had the privilege of differing with one administration, but this was the first time I had ever had the privilege of differing with two simultaneously.

Moley, who was in Washington this same day, told Senator Cordell Hull of Tennessee, who he had learned was to be Secretary of State, the story of his difficulties with the Hoover administration. The few comments of this "gaunt inarticulate man" indicated neither agreement nor disagreement with the course Roosevelt and Moley had followed. There was about him, Moley thought, "an H. B. Warner air of infinite patience and long suffering." [10]

It will appear that Hull, after he and Moley were both installed in the State Department, allowed his subordinate to take charge of the discussions with our debtors, sitting by as they ran their dreary course.

Stimson, having read the Mills-Hoover memorandum which they wished him to send Roosevelt, suggested that it might be received with a more open mind if he telephoned Roosevelt and let him know that they were mailing it down to him. Hoover told him to go ahead. Before the afternoon was over Stimson talked with Roosevelt, while Mills and Bundy listened in. The Secretary explained that not only Hoover and he but the British ambassador as well feared a head-on collision about the debt question. He then told Roosevelt that the President had formulated his ideas on the subject, that they were very clear and good, and that he thought Roosevelt should consider them; so he was proposing to send them down to Warm Springs. Roosevelt said, "All right, send them to me."

But another way of dealing with the situation occurred to Stimson. That very morning the British ambassador had said that his government had asked him to return to London for consultation, and that he would probably sail the following Tuesday, January 31, on the *Europa*. This, the Secretary suggested to Roosevelt, offered an excellent opportunity for an informal message which might avert the collision toward which the two governments were apparently drifting. Roosevelt asked whether it would not be useful if he talked personally with the ambassador before he left. Did Stimson see any objection? None, Stimson said; if he were in Roosevelt's place he certainly would do so even if there was a statute in the way. Roosevelt then said that if Sir Ronald Lindsay wished, he might fly down to Warm Springs the next day, joining Mrs. Roosevelt, who would be passing through Washington.[11]

Hoover did not object. Lindsay accepted the invitation gladly. But Mrs. Roosevelt said there would be no room on her plane. So the ambassador went down to Atlanta by commercial plane and motored out with her to Warm Springs.

The talks between Roosevelt and Lindsay came to nothing. The report that circulated in the State Department was that the President-Elect had told the ambassador that although interest payments might be reduced, the principal was untouchable. The two parted, mutually puzzled and discouraged. It was rumored that the British government was considering sending only two subordinate Treasury officers to Washington.

At this juncture, Day and Williams appeared on the scene again. It will be recalled that before their departure for the second session of the committee of experts they had regarded their errand dubiously. But on their return they spoke rather hopefully. In Washington on January 31 they outlined the elements of a general settlement they believed to be obtainable. The United States was to reduce its claims against foreign debtors; Great Britain was to promise to keep the value of the pound stable; France was to give assurance it would eliminate quotas for imports; and Germany was to end its control over payments to foreigners. To secure such a settlement, they urged the American government to suggest that the Monetary and Economic Conference be convoked at the earliest possible time — during May. I spent much of that day arguing with them because I did not believe that this was a negotiable bargain. In a bulldog speech which the Chancellor of the Exchequer, Neville Chamberlain, had recently made, he disavowed any intention of giving anything in return for a cut in the debts, and declared that Great Britain would not pay to the United States more than it could collect from Germany and other European debtors.[12] This utterance had evoked harsh rejoinders by those stalwarts of nationalism, Senator Borah and Senator David I. Walsh of Massachusetts.

But Day and Williams evidently persuaded Moley, and Moley evidently persuaded Roosevelt. For when he telephoned Stimson on February 3 to let him know that he was going off on a sailing cruise, he asked the Secretary to tell the British government that he would be pleased if after March 4 it sent over to Washington representatives authorized to discuss not only debts but tariff policies, gold, the control of foreign exchange and armaments.

And so off went Roosevelt on Vincent Astor's yacht *Nourmahal*. He may be excused if he left the men in office to struggle by themselves a little while longer with the spreading bank crisis, the darkening depression, the cramping debts, the tangle over other international economic and financial affairs. Moley had sent him the final report of the Preparatory Commission of Experts for the prospective world conference. No note tells whether Roosevelt read it or even glanced at it as he sailed and fished in the southern waters. He left it to Moley and Tugwell to ponder these questions along with those of us who had been dealing with them.

I had been busily working along on the hopeful but unconfirmed supposition that I would not be tossed out of the new administration. My position was deemed only advisory. I had to bow before the judgment of the decision makers. They had to take responsibility for acting on my advice when they thought it was good, or rejecting it when they thought it was bad. I was not a presidential appointee and I did not know of any member of Congress eager to have some political protégé take my place. During the two years I had been in Washington I had had little contact — other than social — with members of Congress; and the few I knew well were friendly.

For a long time I had lamented that the Hoover-Mills policies would neither remedy our economic and social troubles nor restore relations with our former allies to amity. The two men did not seem to me to know what was occurring in the country and the world, much less why. My views and recommendations for months had been more akin to those of the New Deal than to those of standard conservative Republicanism. Hoover had been kind to my wife and me because of her old family relations. But I found him awkward company.

Roosevelt I still had not met. Yet I was pleased by his verve and vitality. Although slightly disturbed by signs of slovenliness of thought, I was inspirited by the evidence of his positive wish for reforms and innovations, and his awareness of prevalent distress. I looked forward like millions of other Americans to the time when the authority would pass to him from the "old gang" (except Stimson) — the little mentally and financially shut-in group. So I was gladdened by a letter which Felix Frankfurter had written me on

February 10 to tell me that he had had a talk with Moley about me; he had assured Moley that although he had found me always at Stimson's side, still I was professionally detached and capable. Then he informed me that it was probable that I would be asked to stay on in my present post, and he urged me to stay. Although Moley had a very different temperament from Stimson, wrote Frankfurter, "of his general right-mindedness and his eagerness for the things you and I care about, I have no doubt."

Within a few days there was direct confirmation that Roosevelt was willing to have me stay on, and that I would be accepted as a member of the group working on the measures to be discussed with the foreign missions which had been invited to come to Washington and on the program for the Monetary and Economic Conference.

On February 19 I was in New York to see my mother, who was mortally ill. Tugwell urged me to stay overnight. Stimson gave me his permission to do so. I was asked (I think by Tugwell, although my notes are not definite) to join in a discussion in Roosevelt's home on 65th Street the next morning. The President-Elect was cordial but the talk was desultory. Probably his main purpose in having me come was to get a personal impression of me before giving approval to my continuation in my job. He wanted me to help on the many economic and financial problems which were bedeviling the world. I said I gladly would. So I knew that I would be kept in my position, preserve my title, continue to receive my salary and to enjoy my comfortable, spacious office with its fireplace and balcony. My satisfaction would have been complete could I have forgotten the implacable flow of telegrams from abroad and of memoranda. These kept me reminded of the depression which, like a virus, was draining the energies and wasting the capabilities of the American people.

The news that I had been in Roosevelt's presence preceded my train back to Washington. That afternoon Kay Bundy, Harvey's wife, was giving a tea party. She had asked my wife to pour. As Ruth entered the drawing room Kay shouted gustily (the gusto was passed on to the sons), "Oh, Herbert has been to see Roosevelt — it's all over the front page of the afternoon papers." Harvey, gen-

tlemanly friend though loyal Republican, congratulated Ruth.
When she told me this on my return, I merely grinned and said
Franklin D. Roosevelt had a fine face that showed character and
thoughtfulness. But nothing was fully settled; I was tired and fuzzy
— as fuzzy as the situation!

I realize that in these preceding pages I have assimilated my own
experience with the process of liaison. The excuse must be that I
was, I think, the only senior individual in the State Department,
except for a few foreign service officers temporarily on duty in
Washington, who stayed on in the new administration.

Tugwell was in and out of Washington the next fortnight seeing
Hull, Stimson, myself and others. For the first time, during a day-
long excursion into Virginia, I was struck by his advocacy of various proposals which would necessitate dictation and control by the
federal government. His cold idealistic purpose and intellectual distinction made their mark upon me. But at the end of the day I
could not shake off the impression that he cared too little for individual liberties and had too little tolerance for individual inclinations, faults and follies.

Tugwell told me that Roosevelt, Moley and he were still in favor
of creating an advisory committee for the conference. They wished
me to be executive (initiatory) secretary of the group. Hull approved and agreed to assign rooms in the State Department where
the group could work. The arrangement was never carried out. No
group in which permanent officials systematically merged their
thoughts with those of the newcomers was activated before Roosevelt's entry into office. Nor did we receive instructions from him or
make reports to him. He was too busy selecting his subordinates
and assistants and considering the many divergent ideas and proposals for national action aimed at reversing the course of our domestic affairs.

CHAPTER 9

Liaison: The Rancorous End

ON FEBRUARY 17, on land again, Roosevelt phoned Stimson. The Secretary asked him to set a date to talk with the British ambassador, who was due to arrive in New York shortly. Roosevelt said that he would see him the very day he arrived.

It is noteworthy that he did not suggest that Stimson advise Hull to sit in with him. This led Stimson to infer that Roosevelt was going to be his own Secretary of State. After talking with Hull several times, Stimson noted in his diary that he had intimated as much, and had "apparently knuckled under." Hull struck Stimson as "gentlemanly, rather slow and a little 'senectified!' [sic]." [1]

Sir Ronald Lindsay had nothing helpful or new to convey. When he called on Stimson on February 23, the Secretary of State found him "evidently discouraged by the situation which he now envisaged from both sides." Stimson, however, was the gloomier of the two because of the wilting economic and financial situation — so despondent that he said to Lindsay that now even an accord on debts would cause only a brief shower of optimism. Of Roosevelt's blitheness one might think either that he did not grasp the firmness of foreign resistance to resumption of payments and so remained confident that he would find terms acceptable to both the debtor governments and Congress; or that he had decided that the debts could not be collected and his main object was to make sure that the foreign debtors would be blamed for the default, not himself.

During the last fortnight of the Hoover regime, the efforts to secure Roosevelt's cooperation shifted from foreign affairs to our own domestic crisis.

In the course of that telephone talk which Stimson had had with Roosevelt on February 17, he had stepped beyond his official domain. He had remarked that he supposed the President-Elect knew of the banking troubles which were sweeping the country. Roosevelt said "The Texas gentleman of the R.F.C. [Jesse Jones] had fully apprised him of it." Stimson had gone on to say that the situation seemed to him so grim that it could not be managed merely by intermittent contact between Roosevelt and himself. It called for continuing conferences day and night between the officials in office who were trying to stem it, and those who would be responsible after March 4. Roosevelt responded breezily. He said that he realized the importance of such cooperation and would try to let Stimson know within a few days the names of the new men who would take on the assignment.[2]

This conjured up the prospect of an immediate joint effort by the two groups to prevent the banking crisis from becoming nationwide. But oh so briefly! For Hoover sent a letter full of ingrown thoughts which Roosevelt virtually ignored. This missive, written by hand, Hoover dispatched on February 18 by special messenger with orders to place it in the hands of Roosevelt himself. The agent located the President-Elect at a banquet in the Astor Hotel given by New York City political reporters and gave the letter to him, explaining where it had come from and his instructions.[3]

Meant as a desperate appeal, it was marred by its defensive and admonitory tone and tenor. Hoover began by saying: "A most critical situation has arisen in the country of which I feel it is my duty to advise you confidentially." He then went on to allege that "The major difficulty is the state of the public mind, for there is steadily degenerating confidence in the future which has reached the height of a general alarm. I am convinced that a very early statement by you upon two or three policies of your Administration would serve greatly to restore confidence and cause a resumption of the march of recovery."

What Hoover urged Roosevelt to do was to clarify "the public mind on certain essentials which will give renewed confidence. . . . I do not refer to action on all the causes of alarm, but it would steady the country greatly if there could be prompt assurance that there will be no tampering with or inflation of the currency; that the budget will be unquestionably balanced even if further taxation is necessary; that the government credit will be maintained by refusal to exhaust it in the issue of securities." [4]

When a copy of this letter was shown me, I sniffed. Its ideas and words were echoes of those of Mills and the big bankers. None of them would face the fact that their own policies during the previous decade had fostered the depression. They were taking refuge in the belief that the soundness of their policies and actions would be proven if only the President-Elect and the inflationist members of Congress and other groups would stop scaring the American people.

This interpretation of the causes of the debacle was becoming a certitude to Hoover — as stated, for example, in a memo which he sent on February 20 to Republican Senator David A. Reed of Pennsylvania in an attempt to guide him in his persuasion of his Democratic colleagues. The President, after repeating his explanation of the cause of the spreading bank panic and the export of gold, wrote: "These movements [of gold currency and the flight of capital] are, however, symptomatic and very disturbing. Considered with the very much larger question of currency hoarding they show an alarming state of public mind. That state of mind is simple. It is the breakdown in the public confidence in the new administration now coming in. The American people do not wait for a known business event; they act to protect themselves individually in advance." [5]

That Hoover was fully aware of the import of what he was pleading with Roosevelt to do is shown by another paragraph in the same memo to Reed: "I realize," he wrote, "that if these declarations be made by the President-elect, he will have ratified the whole major program of the Republican Administration; that is, it means the abandonment of ninety per cent of the so-called new deal. But unless this is done, they run a grave danger of precipitating a complete financial debacle. If it is precipitated, the responsibility lies squarely with them for they have had ample warning — unless such a debacle is part of the new deal."

Despite his perception that Roosevelt was being, in effect, asked to desist from going forward with his own program, Hoover became more convinced that Roosevelt was shirking responsibility and intentionally making it impossible for him to salvage the situation. In a cabinet meeting on February 21 he bemoaned Roosevelt's refusal to speak out as he wanted him to. The silence of the President-Elect, he opined, was sending quivers of fear throughout the country. Moreover, it was preventing any effective action to deal with the situation because Congress would not pass required emergency legislation unless Roosevelt urged the Democratic members to do so. The next day he remarked to Stimson that he thought Roosevelt's conduct was really that of a madman.[6]

Roosevelt had not yet answered Hoover's last plea. Whether his delay was accidental or deliberate is a matter of conjecture. Roosevelt, when he did reply, explained that it was unintentional and that he had "mislaid" Hoover's letter. Moley recalls that during that dinner at the Astor Hotel, while the raucous stage show was going on, Roosevelt passed the letter to him under the table, signaling him to read it. He remembers also that after the dinner three or four of them went back to Roosevelt's house, where the letter was passed around and discussed. Roosevelt seemed to him to be by all appearance unmoved.[7] However, the President-Elect did have William Woodin, whom he was going to appoint Secretary of the Treasury, inform Mills on February 23 that he would not make any such statement as Hoover suggested.

About a week later, since nothing more had been heard from Roosevelt and since in Stimson's phrase the "situation was rapidly going to the devil," he and Mills urged Hoover to write to Roosevelt again. This time the President did not repeat his request that Roosevelt make a public statement in regard to his fiscal, banking and monetary policies. He merely described the rapid deterioration in the situation during the week past — the terrible bank crashes in Detroit and Cleveland, the closing of one of the banks in the District of Columbia, and the rumors that the New York banks were in trouble.

Roosevelt's formal answer to Hoover's earlier letter was received. It was mild. But while saying that he was as concerned as the President with the gravity of the banking situation, he dissented from Hoover's explanation of the causes of the situation and remedies for it. "The real trouble," he said, "is that at present values very few financial institutions . . . are actually able to pay off their deposits in full, and the knowledge of this fact is widely held. Bankers with the narrower viewpoint have urged me to make a general statement, but even they seriously doubt whether it would have a definite effect." [8]

Hoover to the very last of his years thought otherwise, despite the fact that the many public statements which he had issued in order to reassure the business and banking community had failed to reverse the downward trend. He based his opinion on the belief that almost all the banks would prove to be sound if the panic could be arrested.

On his last day before leaving office Hoover made a final effort to enlist Roosevelt's help. George Harrison telephoned Mills that morning. He said that the Federal Reserve Bank could not pay out gold and currency at the rate of the past few days. But if it did not — and ceased also to support the value of the dollar in world markets — it would be equivalent to abandoning the gold standard. Then the value of the dollar might go anywhere, even though the Federal Reserve System still had a gold reserve of more than 40 per cent of its obligations.

The board of directors of the Federal Reserve Bank of New York reached a consensus that: (1) the most desirable step would be the passage that very night of legislation that might protect the banking situation; (2) if that could not be done a national bank holiday should be declared; and (3) if that were not done, gold payments should be suspended.

Harrison so advised Mills and Woodin. They said that there was practically no hope of enactment of remedial legislation that night. Harrison was informed that the President was considering whether to invoke the Trading with the Enemy Act, which had been on the statute books since the First World War, in order to declare a national bank holiday.

The Federal Reserve Board, according to Hoover's later account, declined to recommend this action to him or to Congress. Thereupon the board of directors of the New York Federal Reserve Bank on March 3 passed a resolution asking the Federal Reserve Board to urge the President of the United States to proclaim Saturday, March 4, and Monday, March 6, national bank holidays. This resolution was read to Eugene Meyer, chairman of the Federal Reserve Board, and Secretary Mills over the telephone. After it was transmitted to the President he spoke to Harrison. Why, he asked, was Governor Lehman balking over declaring a bank holiday for New York State, as had been requested by Mills and Meyer? Harrison told the President that he and the other directors of the New York Federal Reserve Bank thought a national holiday preferable. But Hoover, without stating definitely that he would not declare a national holiday, asked Harrison to try once more to get Lehman to act. Though loath to do so, Harrison did try again, and Lehman said he would comply if he were asked not only by the Federal Reserve Bank of New York but also by the large New York private banks and by the superintendent of banks of the State of New York.[9]

It is probable that it was after this conversation (though it may have been before it; the available records do not make the point clear) that Hoover telephoned Roosevelt. The President now tried to persuade the President-Elect to get Lehman to declare a state bank holiday. Roosevelt refused to press the governor since this might involve him in responsibility for the situation at the last hour. He suggested that Hoover should call Congress together at once and ask it to pass a joint resolution declaring a national moratorium. This, Hoover thought, was not necessary, since the situation could be dealt with by invoking the emergency powers available under the Trading with the Enemy Act. But Hoover said he had qualms about using the act because of doubt of its legality. He asked Roosevelt whether, if he took this step, the President-Elect would approve it publicly. Roosevelt said he did not think his approval essential; Hoover could act on his own.

Hoover was sure that Roosevelt wanted the collapse to be complete, that he was intent on having the situation as bad as could be before he took office. For then he could act the hero who would rescue the nation — like the handsome actor in old-time melodramas who hauled the lovely maiden off the railroad tracks to which she had been roped by the villain just as the cowcatcher on the express train was about to toss her into eternity.*

Thus the attempt at liaison between the outgoing and incoming Presidents ended rancorously. But some of the subordinates of both remained on good terms and worked with each other to master common misfortunes.

---

* Hoover's suspicion that Roosevelt might be deliberately welcoming the disturbances and panic subsequently was to grow into a bitter certainty which he bluntly avowed in his memoirs. Thus, in *Memoirs*, Vol. 3, p. 216, he wrote, "I may repeat that the event of March 3rd was a hysteria among bank depositors induced by Roosevelt's own conduct. Early in January he could have prevented it by ten words in reaffirmation of his promises, then only two months old. Or by a little co-operation, he could have prevented even a temporary closing of the banks." In an even more accusatory passage in the *Memoirs* (p. 357), "Every collectivist revolution rides in on a Trojan horse of 'Emergency.' It was a tactic of Lenin, Hitler and Mussolini. . . . This technique of creating emergency is the greatest achievement that demagoguery attains. The invasion of New Deal Collectivism was introduced by this same Trojan horse . . . the wholly unnecessary panic of bank depositors which became Roosevelt's basis of emergency. He created it himself by refusing to co-operate."

Hoover convinced himself that this opinion was correct because subsequently banking institutions that held about 98 per cent of the banking deposits paid them off. His thought would never admit the possibility that this was facilitated, if not made possible, by the "collectivist" policies upon which the President-Elect was about to engage.

CHAPTER 10

The Defeated Depart

WEEKS before its term of office ends, a defeated administration is displaced in the public mind. The newspapers and radio are crammed with reports of new appointments. They tell little of the acts and plans of those about to leave.

I have among my papers a copy of a letter from a State Department colleague written about this time. "The Captains and the Kings depart or get ready to pack their bags. There is a general sense of demoralization and decay in the old crew. The President barks occasionally from the White House. The Secretary has a lame ligament and spent energy. We are trying to clear our desks. There are new banners on the horizon — strange dreams and rumors of raids or rallies. I am restless to have it over and give my seat to a stranger."

As I walked each morning from our home in Georgetown to the old and ornate State Department building across the street from the White House I noticed the progress from one day to the next in the erection of the wooden grandstands along Pennsylvania Avenue. I wondered what thoughts flowed through the minds of President and Mrs. Hoover as they watched the carpenters at work on these structures which were to be the platform of honor for another President.

For all those fortunate enough to have a chance to share in the public affairs of Washington the spectacle of the passage of power should be a lesson in humility.

Early in February my wife and I went to Woodley to have dinner with the Stimsons, just the four of us in the dining room overlooking the terrace and the meadow, now white with snow. John and Ellen McCloy had been there before dinner, and they always cheered up the household. During the meal and afterwards, the Secretary talked genially of his long-past holidays of camping and mountain climbing in the West. But Mrs. Stimson seemed on edge. She said their personal plans were fluid. She was naturally anxious as to how they would fare in the era about to begin. This was, she remarked, having no second sight, "the end of public life for Harry."

The Secretary of State had taken the defeat of his party with his usual courageous fairness. As related, he had done his utmost to assure a smooth and steady continuation of the policies he had been pursuing to restore and maintain the bases of peace in international economic and political affairs. His acts and attitudes were the expression of a noble spirit disciplining disappointment. He loved the conduct of public business and the sense of serving the public good. His attachment to his law firm had remained deep, and his friendship with his former partners was undimmed by time. Still, in talking with him one could detect regret and dejection over the prospect of returning to the practice of private law.

Among the circle of close subordinates and assistants that worked for him in the State Department he had inspired an enjoyable sense of unity and common friendship. That small group had lived almost literally in each other's pockets — seeing one another morning, noon, evening and not seldom in the office in the late hours at night. Now the circle was about to be broken and the group was about to scatter. The nature of the association is illustrated by the entry which Pierrepont Moffat, usually unexpressive, made in his journal on March 2, two days before the end: "Went out and played a final game of deck tennis, for this Administration at least, with the Secretary, Bundy and Feis. It was cold, with a raw Northwest wind blowing, but we all enjoyed it to the full, and still more a talk-fest in front of the open fire afterwards."

To lift the pall of sadness over parting, Assistant Secretary Harvey Bundy and his wife Kay gave a farewell dinner for the Secretary at their home on the evening of March 4, after the inauguration. No one could foresee that in the next decade Bundy would become special assistant to Stimson, who would then be Secretary of War, and a confidant in regard to the progress of the development of the atomic bomb; or that one of his sons, McGeorge Bundy would become the coauthor of *On Active Service in Peace and War,* Stimson's memorable account of his years of public service and later Special Assistant to another young man from Harvard, John F. Kennedy.

We gathered at the Bundys' at eight. Harvey was his usual easy self, and Kay sprightly enough to dispel any note of sadness on this occasion. There were Allen Klots, Stimson's junior law partner and Special Assistant, and his wife Mary; James Grafton Rogers, who had been Stimson's closest associate in dealing with the crisis in the Far East, and his warmhearted wife Cora; Under-Secretary of the Treasury Arthur Ballantine and his wife Helen; and a brother of Kay Bundy's named Putnam. A small company. Everyone seemed to share the sense of sweet, almost merry companionship all evening. Any somber thoughts the Secretary may have had gave way to his enjoyment of the occasion.

Harvey proposed a toast to the Secretary at dinner's end. Then he read a poem — anonymous, but written by my wife.

TO THE MASTER OF WOODLEY

Official parting is not farewell
For those who have known his vivid spell.

He still will have his lovely acres,
The mellow woodland, and rolling lawn.
He still can hear the lark at dawn,
And watch the cardinal's dart of color,

> *And smell the fresh-cut odorous grass.*
> *He still will push the logs from his fender*
> *With boots mud-splashed from a country ride;*
> *And throw the deck-ring harder and straighter*
> *Than other men less quick to decide.*
> *He will look at his law, and enjoy his tea*
> *With a lady in bittersweet velvet near him —*
> *While all the rest of us men and women*
> *Are going about our duties, alas!*
> *With a little ache that the daily tasks*
> *Aren't shared or planned or captained by him.*
>
> *Mayn't we come and warm our hands*
> *Occasionally at this genial fire*
> *That burns and always will burn higher*
> *Than other fires less beneficial?*
> *Than other fires in other lands?*
>
> *Official parting should make amends*
> *In that we lose, yet find, our friends.*

The ladies and gentlemen separated. I was informed later by one of the ladies that the talk among them about those who were to grace official drawing rooms in their place was waspish. But by the time they joined the gentlemen downstairs in the recreation room their feelings had apparently been relieved by being freely expressed. Rogers from Colorado pounded the piano and, with his good ringing voice, sang songs of the West like "The Santa Fe Trail" and then we all joined in singing college tunes. The champagne kept coming round, and presently all of us felt sentimental and witty — a sense of gaiety misting over the natural sadness of a farewell.

All the others present were devoted and ardent supporters of the Republican administration and were leaving Washington. I alone had been asked to stay on, being immured in my post as a technician supposed to serve all superiors with fealty. None of these colleagues gave me a sign of being either envious or critical. The Stimsons showed their support and acceptance of my decision by inviting us to come out for dinner the following night at Woodley. That was for us the most touching moment of the whole evening.

PART II

Roosevelt Takes Charge

CHAPTER 11

The New Group

BETWEEN election and inauguration Roosevelt had devised his program with an almost Churchillian flair. The financial crisis and the momentous decisions ahead did not awe him. Our plight was calling forth the daring and determination he had shown as Assistant Secretary of the Navy in the First World War, and after paralysis had struck him down, and during his long period of recovery and self-discipline. The weight of work did not cause him to sag any more than did the ten-pound steel brace which he had to wear.

What a different appearance and demeanor he had when he took office, I cannot help remembering as I write, from the stricken man I was to see for the last time after his return from the Yalta Conference in 1945; then his eyes, gray with fatigue, looked out vaguely from the shrunken flesh of his face, and his hands so shook that he could not light a cigarette, and he did not seem to grasp what was being said. At Yalta, finally, he had met difficulties too heavy even for him to bear, and I think he suspected it.

March 4, 1933, was a blustery day, a pale sun brightening the dark gray clouds at intervals. Before the ceremony all members of the new cabinet and their families accompanied Roosevelt and his family to the simple, harmonious church near the White House, St. John's Episcopal Church. Roosevelt had worshiped there when Assistant Secretary of the Navy. The service was conducted by Endicott Peabody, headmaster of Groton, where Roosevelt had gone to school, tutor and model for well brought up young men of socially esteemed families.

Secretary Stimson had given Ruth and myself two excellent tickets to one of the stands right under the semicircular inaugural platform at the Capitol. Wearing winter clothing, around noon we wove our way through the crowds to find our places. The better to see and hear, I stood astride two benches. An announcer droned on, telling the crowd of the preliminary proceedings. He heralded the approach of the outgoing President and the incoming one about a half hour before they could be seen coming down the ramp. In the small group close to them were to be glimpsed Mrs. Roosevelt in "Eleanor blue," Mrs. Hoover and Mrs. Woodrow Wilson. Roosevelt walked chin up and slowly on the arm of his son. His profile and presence were impressive as he stood before Chief Justice Charles Evans Hughes and took his oath to "protect and defend the Constitution of the United States, so help me God."

He spoke his inaugural address in a clear, resonant tone, with excellent diction. His voice carried to all of those in the stands below. Of all the passages in the speech we were hit most squarely by his epigrammatic statement that "The only thing we have to fear is fear itself." So were many others to whom we spoke. More sobering was his statement that in order to deal with the grave economic and financial emergency in the country he might have to ask Congress and the American people for powers equal to those which were accorded the President in wartime. The audience, although impressed by the affirmativeness of the address and the prospect of bold action, remained grave and quiet. They did not break into his speech with loud applause but seemed rather to want to think it over before they expressed themselves. There were only a few exultant shouts. The auditors heard excited hip-hip-hoorays only later when they turned on their radios and listened to the broadcasts of the inaugural ceremony that poured out of the receivers many an hour.

Almost everyone remained in the stands while the new President, his family and intimates walked down the long ramp to the automobiles which were to take them to the White House. Our own fancy was caught by the small graceful head and figure of Roosevelt's granddaughter, his only daughter Anna's little girl, who was being carried down the ramp on the shoulders of her father. On returning to my desk, where work awaited me, I still found myself cheered and assured by the positive spirit which animated the address and the man who had given it; and wondering what changes his coming might bring in my assignments. We did not watch the inaugural parade, not being among those who had contributed to the outcome of the event.

On returning home that evening before going to the Stimsons', I found a telegram from two old friends that read: "Who cares what bank failed in Yonkers as long as you have the kiss that conquers."

For the readers of cables or dispatches in the State Department it was not easy to worry less than before about the way in which the international scene had darkened during the days before and after the inauguration.

As will be told later, a few days previously the Japanese government had given notice that it was going to get out of the League of Nations. This confirmed the impression that it intended to pursue without heed of outside opinion its attempts to extend domination by the aggressive will of the military leaders. On the day after the inauguration the German Reichstag accorded absolute power to Adolph Hitler. All news from Germany told of growing maltreatment of all whom the Nazis wanted to punish or displace, and of the alarming rate at which the German army and Nazi military formations were being enlarged and equipped.

However, during the spring and summer that were to follow almost all Americans were so engrossed in their own troubles that only a few to whom these events abroad had penetrating personal meaning — Jews and liberals, some diplomats and journalists, scholars, ministers, bankers — concerned themselves greatly about them.

To almost every American, man and woman, what counted most was whether the bank in which they had their savings was going to be allowed to reopen; whether they would be given a chance to postpone payments on their mortgage and so retain possession of their house or farm; whether the stocks they held would recover their value; whether the prices of wheat and corn and cotton and tobacco and hogs they raised would improve enough to maintain their family and pay their debts; and above all, whether factories would resume operations and they would again have paying jobs. These and other phases of the domestic situation were to the forefront of America's thoughts, the primary focus of activity on Capitol Hill and in every city, town and village in the country. It was only later in the spring when the foreign missions arrived, headed by eminent officials whom Roosevelt had invited, that public attention turned to international aspects of the situation. Even then these commanded only the margins of it.

Of the senior officials of the new administration, I knew few and those not well. I had been introduced to Secretary of State Cordell Hull on March 1, when he spent the day in the department getting acquainted. He was cordial. Soon thereafter he asked me to report to him on the work that had been done in preparation for the prospective international Monetary and Economic Conference, and said he would read with interest the small group of memos I carried in my hand. In a talk that rambled somewhat with a downward beat, he recalled how, in the Senate, he had been a strong advocate of American membership in the League of Nations and how sad he had been when that was defeated; and that during all his official life he had tried to convince his fellow legislators that trade barriers between nations not only inflicted economic injury and sustained monopolies but were one of the chief causes of war. His reminiscent remarks were tinged by a sense that he had had so little company in past efforts, which later came to seem to me a sign of inner personal loneliness, relieved by the loving companionship of his wife.

At the end of my first two long talks with him I was pleased at the thought of working under so kindly, reflective and idealistic a man. But I wondered whether his mind would be incisive enough and his will strong enough to deal with the harsh forces that were gathering around us. At the end of March, after sitting in a spiritless conference about debts which he and Moley had with the British ambassador, I noted down that his was "a ruminative mind which has pondered long on the political history of the United States and on international economics. But one which is not flexible within this sphere and vague outside of it. He no longer gathers ideas from others, and when confronted with the obstacles and difficulties to his good intentions, does not analyze them and figure out ways of licking them; he preaches against them." And again, "Hull operates in a vacuum of his own making, repeating his generalities but leaving all action on any point to Moley, who regards him as a voice crying in the wilderness."

The one condition which Hull had made on accepting the office of Secretary of State was that the Under-Secretary should be a person of experience who knew the diplomatic world. This led to the selection of William Phillips and the elimination of two rivals for the post — William Bullitt and Raymond Moley.

Phillips was a distinguished and courteous foreign service officer. But he and Hull did not work together with ease. They were too different in temperament, and Phillips, being an old friend of the President and having grown up in the same circles, had an easier personal relationship with Roosevelt than Hull ever developed. Being diffident, Phillips never took advantage of his intimacy with the President to push his personal opinions or fortune. But he had to be reminded by his assistants from time to time to urge the President to invite Hull over to the White House for a talk or an informal luncheon.

I found it pleasant to work with and for the new Under-Secretary. His presence provided signs of continuity in the State Department; his dress, gentlemanly manners and direct talk reminded me of what I had found admirable in the upper reaches of Boston society when I was a student at Harvard — reaches where my social activity rarely took me but which I could glimpse on the days of the great football games and commencements and occasional dances to which I strayed and during my period of training in the naval reserve where my fellow apprentices were virtually all Harvard Bostonians. Phillips's assignments in other lands made him feel closer to people of another race, religion or color than the usual members of the Boston society to which he belonged.

Whether the President decided to place Moley in the State Department as inducement for him to stay in Washington, or in order to have a personal representative in that department who might sympathize with his views more than the staid career officials, I do not know. The appointment as Assistant Secretary of State was to cause grief for everyone. Moley has since averred that he balked at the suggestion because to him Hull "personified the philosophical opposition to New Deal policies" but that out of devotion to Roosevelt and the New Deal he yielded to his importunities. The President dictated to him a brief statement of his duties. They were to include the handling "of the foreign debts, the world economic conference, supervision of the economic adviser's office and such additional duties as the President may direct in the general field of foreign and domestic government." [1] In fact, Roosevelt turned to him for many other matters in the domestic sphere. He was called on to give direction to and review the work of other presidential assistants and idea men, to aid in drafting of speeches and legislation, and to act as liaison with members of Congress in regard to some measures. Apparently the President did not consult Hull in advance about this definition of Moley's realm of duty, for on his first visit to the State Department the incoming Secretary of State remarked to a few of us that Professor Moley was to have the room that had been occupied by Assistant Secretary of State Rogers, and that Moley had distinct ideas as to what his functions were to be but had not told either himself or Phillips any details. Nor did Moley later make it a practice of telling Hull about the errands he was performing for the President, or what he was saying to foreign diplomats (nor did the President, until the denouement, instruct him to do so; but that should not have been necessary).

One of the entries in Pierrepont Moffat's journal, made before Moley even entered the department, was prescient: "The newspapermen all tell me that Moley will hang himself within a few months, that he has already earned the unreserved enmity of the press, of Sumner Welles, of Norman Davis and most important of all, of Colonel Howe." [2] And certainly William Phillips heartily reciprocated Moley's dislike and disdain.

Nevertheless, Moley was Roosevelt's most active factotum. The permanent staff of the State Department soon learned that he was too busy with headier tasks and contacts to give either intellectual leadership to, or drudge within, the designated area of his nominal assignment. It became speedily apparent that his spasmodic initiatives in foreign affairs would become entangled with those of the Secretary of State and other members of the department. The confusion over jurisdiction and policy was incessant. It would have been so even had Moley been a considerate, placatory and gifted diplomat. But he was not. I myself had reason to be grateful to him and every wish to be helpful to him, for I understood that it was at his behest that Roosevelt had decided to let me continue as Economic Adviser in the State Department. Moreover, I had the sense that my views on domestic affairs were akin to his. I did not comprehend until later how strong was his nationalist bent and how variant his conceptions of what American foreign policy should be.

Despite the fact that we were supposed to be working on many of the same problems, I did not see him often or long enough to get to feel that I really knew him. On such occasions as I did see him, in and out of the department, my admiration for him waned. His manner and his mind seemed to me to warp under the great power which suddenly he had come to exercise during those first few months of frenzied New Deal activity. He treated all his associates in the State Department from Hull down to the desk officers offhandedly. Once, for example, having concluded that he ought to know some of his senior division heads, I made an engagement for him to see James C. Dunn, then chief of the Division of International Conferences and Protocol and a career officer who concealed beneath the conventional polished exterior of the old type of State Department official an astute mind and industrious habits. Moley barely bothered to say hello and goodbye.

In conference with foreign ambassadors Moley was often guarded and gruff and seldom troubled to prepare for his discussions with them. In his rooms at the Hotel Carlton, from which he carried on so many of his operations, his demeanor and his voice over the telephone were those of a triumphant political general, a rough mover and shaker, a General Patton of the State Department command with an epithet on his hip.

But these impressions were formed on the run, for he was always running, and I was always panting, during these days. After three weeks of observation, I hurriedly jotted down: "[Moley] An interested mind, which only exposes itself in jumps. A mind which does no systematic solutions or even systematic procedure, but catches at ideas, or measures how they fit into the combat of political forces and ideas. He sometimes asks others to think through; he does not do so himself. He is too blithe on important matters, too disposed to pass over them with a jest. Yet in this spirit he believes that international relations can be kept in good shape — seeing their importance less clearly because no American political interest forces them on his attention."

Moley's suspicion of and opposition to the outlook of Wilson-Hoover-Stimson-Hull became centered on Norman Davis. A fellow-Tennessean, Davis was an always sympathetic intimate of Hull, called in by him to discuss every worrisome problem. He had close associations with large banks and investment firms in New York City, bonds of friendship with those leaders of the Democratic Party that remained faithful to the Wilsonian aspirations. Thus, when Roosevelt told Moley that Davis was "out," he must have meant merely out of Moley's hair and hearing. For the President gave Davis a commission as roving ambassador, and late in March he lit off for London with authority to discuss with Prime Minister Ramsay MacDonald and other British officials the schedule for the Monetary and Economic Conference. Later he served as American representative in the disarmament discussions at Geneva, an assignment which brought him in constant colloquy with leading figures in European governments. Davis's expositions and pleas were aimed to persuade Roosevelt and Hull that the American government should associate itself with the governments of Western Europe in plans for disarmament, the maintenance of peace, and commercial and monetary cooperation. Thus, by Moley and other New Dealers, he continued to be regarded as an underminer of the New Deal, a smooth diplomat who was again trying to subject American policy to the control of Wall Street and the lackeys of European society. Before very long the break between the two was complete.

Moley protested to the President because Davis, while in London, talked with MacDonald and Simon about the debts and the program for the conference. The President sent a note to Hull asking for information and telling him to instruct Davis to abstain from further activities in these realms. Moley stormed angrily into Hull's office and went to the verge of accusing the Secretary of duplicity since he was acquiescing in Davis's initiatives. Hull was disturbed by this personal affront. He seemed only then, when telling me of this, to wake up to the fact that Moley really expected to be in sole charge of the debt questions and the program for the Monetary and Economic Conference, dealing directly with the White House and not through him and Phillips, and without ever feeling obliged even to keep them advised. They felt themselves faced with an unmanageable situation and suspected that Moley intended to build up a personal organization within the State Department. Yet it was not Hull's way to make a decisive issue of the challenge to his authority and insist that the President curb Moley. He just smoldered, complained to his staff, and waited for Moley to fall into the boiling pot of circumstances.

Rexford Tugwell, now Assistant Secretary of Agriculture was more intent than Moley, less volatile and less eager to stay close to the presidential presence. I was struck by the handsomeness of his face and the gracefulness of his bearing. His mind was active and bold, his care for the general good genuine, his talk and methods direct and upright. Still he shocked me, for he was so disposed to advocate plans not only for agriculture but for every branch of American economics that would bring them under government organization and control. I do not remember ever having any really thorough talks with him. But I think in retrospect that he had come to the conclusion during the depression that the American economy could and would not recover well and operate steadily unless government assumed comprehensive direction. His concern for the general welfare did not seem to be matched by sympathetic feeling for individual men and women in their plight. For instance, when late in February I had remarked to him that the bank closings were causing great anxiety to many millions of innocent depositors, his only and curt response was, "Let them bust — then we'll get things on a sound basis."

One other newcomer in the Roosevelt entourage puzzled me, even while he attracted me. That was William Bullitt. Having failed to be named, as he had hoped, Under-Secretary of State or ambassador to France, he made temporary shift as a Special Assistant to the Secretary of State. I did not know at the time how genuine was his jovial friendship with Roosevelt, who had sent him as his special reporter on three confidential trips to Europe. Therefore I did not know whether his zestful accounts of talks with such heads of state as Prime Minister MacDonald and Premier Herriot and with the heads of the Bank of England and the Bank of France were imaginative or true, as they were. He was a fluorescent sort of fellow, to whom diplomacy was an incessant drama. Its lurid scenes, strange characters and bold possibilities incited his imaginative interest. His interpretation of personal behavior was, I think, affected by his earlier association with Sigmund Freud. At first his jocund manners, his aura of habitual intimacy with great men and great events, his hasty rush to what seemed to me inadvertent conclusions, threw me off. But I came to respect his quick and incisive intelligence and enjoy his verve and faithfulness in friendship. Hull also began to enjoy having him about as he got to know him better. While waiting for some assignment suited to his ambitions, he did odd jobs of drafting and intelligence. His chance was to come later when Roosevelt used him to prepare the way for the agreement with the Soviet government that opened the way to recognition, and then appointed him our first ambassador to the Soviet Union.

The member of the cabinet I had met first was that "curmudgeon" Harold Ickes. This grumbling, thrusting man had been in Roosevelt's office on East 65th Street the same morning I was there discussing plans for the coming conference. It was then that Roosevelt had asked him to be Secretary of the Interior. It happened that we walked out of the house together and discovered we were both headed downtown, he for Grand Central Station to take a train for Chicago, I for where I was staying. Then an event took place which, if not without precedent or repetition, was certainly not routine. In what must have been his evident excitement at the prospect of a cabinet career, he invited me to lunch at the Roosevelt Hotel. I did not know at the time what a singular gesture this was, for among his other traits, one that I presume went along with his scrupulous management of public money, was his miserliness. And yet on this day he bought me a lunch — albeit watching my choice of items on the menu with a sidewise glance. I remember noticing one afternoon at his house in the country how, as he was paying off some men who had been doing gardening work for him in crisp new dollar bills, he would run his hands over the surface of each bill before parting with it, as though he couldn't bear to give it up.

In contrast I found myself quickly drawn to the man from Iowa who was to be the new Secretary of Agriculture, Henry Wallace. He was brought to our house in Georgetown by Tugwell, perhaps a few days before the inauguration. He looked self-reliant but trusting. His talk was a little hesitant, puzzled, but illuminated by lofty purpose. I could not but note that the shoes he wore were still the same as those worn by farmers in small towns in Iowa, and that his hair was cut as the barbers in these towns cut hair. The back of his neck was red and creased like those of men who spend long days under the sun behind a plow or on a tractor seat. Happily we formed a friendship which was not hurt by the divergence of my judgment from that of his chief assistant, Tugwell. I was to feel during the next year that Tugwell and I were engaged in something of a duel for Henry Wallace's judgment and support — not a duel for personal influence, but a duel between an advocate of a policy for American agriculture resting on dominant government controls and direction indifferent to its effect on our foreign relations, and an advocate of a less regulated policy.

In view of the later boohoo about Wallace's mystic beliefs, a note among my papers, written after a talk we had with Hull about clashing trade policies in the course of which the Secretary of State's comments faded out in obscure confusion, is amusing. Secretary Wallace remarked to me at the time: "I think the Secretary of State is gradually reaching the state of Nirvana."

Although I did play a small part in the discussion of monetary and banking measures during the first month of the new administration, I had merely a slight acquaintance with the new Secretary of the Treasury, William Woodin. One could not but be attracted by his kindly air and responsiveness to any glimpse of the public interest. The way in which he accepted and carried forward the novel monetary and banking measures that were taken soon showed that his gentleness of manner did not mean that he was timid or unimaginative. However, he was modest and had little positive vigor; in and about him were intimations that it was probable that others, not he, would make the decisions in his area of responsibility. His real flair and greatest interest was in music, as an appreciative auditor and composer. Indeed, his real wish had been an appointment as ambassador to Germany because of his admiration for that country's excellence in music.

I came to know Henry Morgenthau, Jr., well only some months later, after he was appointed Secretary of the Treasury when Woodin was forced by illness to relinquish the post. He was a person of basic good will and kindly intentions, but his mind was slow, his self-knowledge little and his sense of humor adolescent. He was at once shrewd, gullible and suspicious. Two purposes were to dominate his thought and actions: a wish to serve and please his neighbor, friend and boss, Roosevelt; and a determination to down the Nazis. In both aims he was importantly successful.

Despite our differences in temperament and his rasping push, Morgenthau and I got along rather well in almost daily dealings for quite a long time, for we had many views in common. But then he grew more and more dissatisfied with Hull's prudent conduct of foreign affairs and began to replace, with men of his own, the financial representatives in foreign posts whom I had chosen. And gradually he became more and more influenced by the viciously assertive staff that assembled around him, led by Harry White. They used him and he used them and — here I am leaping far beyond the chronology of this narrative — many years later I had to ask Hull to be relieved of my role as liaison with the Treasury because I did not want to have to bear their disagreeable assaults any longer.

The new Under-Secretary of the Treasury, Dean Acheson, was a long-time resident of Georgetown whose caustic wit, graceful mind and lively friendliness I had known and enjoyed before. I was to work closely with him in later years after he entered the State Department, but again — to allow my narrative to leap the years — his eventual assumption (along with Adolph Berle, Jr., Myron Taylor and others) in the closing years of the war of responsibilities in foreign economic affairs was one of the reasons why I decided to resign. I had had enough by then of compounded jurisdiction and superior interference, and I was very weary.

In trying thus to give the residue of contemporary impressions of these men who were to figure so daringly in American history during the next few years, I have exceeded my title. Not all, but many were intellectual roustabouts and I felt at home with them. I was glad to have the chance of sharing in their endeavors.

CHAPTER 12

The Dollar Goes Off Gold

DURING the first hundred days, Roosevelt's handling of domestic economic affairs was dazzling; of foreign economic affairs, dizzying.

The measures which the new President employed for reopening the banks were in fact similar to those which Hoover's group had worked out, and he sailed along from day to day, enjoying the irony of his role as rescuer of our financial and banking system. When on the afternoon of March 8, as the main features of his emergency program were being settled, Felix Frankfurter entered his office, Roosevelt's first words of greeting were, "Well, Felix, they'll make a banker of me yet."

An admirable job was done — first of salvage, then of recuperation. The new administration had to choose between saving the relatively sound banks and letting the weaker ones go or trying to put them all back in business. Though this left their depositors in distress, the administration decided to leave the weaker banks to an ordeal of later examination. By doing so it conserved government credit, a policy that won the respect even of conservative financial interests.

Banks judged sound even at current debased value of their assets were reopened; those judged almost sound were financially assisted. By the end of March banks holding over 90 per cent of the country's deposits were again doing business as usual. The funds thereby freed were greatly needed to provide depositors with means to procure essentials. The credit of the national government rebounded as indicated by the steep drop in the interest rates on its short-term bills.

Industry and commerce began to revive and employment rose. The prices of farm products advanced, though still held in the depths by the weight of surpluses. Many, many farms and homes which were in jeopardy because of debts were rescued. Millions in need were given relief, though on far too mean a scale. Plans were made to employ men and women who could not find jobs in private economic enterprises or in projects financed by the government — but in an amount far less than should have been allocated for the purpose, since Roosevelt was still in the stage where he believed a balanced budget essential to national health.

As observed by Marriner Eccles, whom Roosevelt was later to appoint chairman of the Federal Reserve Board, "The naked rusted girders of the Department of Commerce Building in Washington stood for a month as a token of Roosevelt's resolve to balance the budget." [1] Could the fact that the structure might be considered a monument to Hoover (Secretary of Commerce before being elected President) possibly account for the willingness of the new neighbors to let it stand in its naked emptiness?

New legislation was presented to Congress, bringing industries under codes in order to sustain the prices of products and the wages of the workers (the National Recovery Administration, NRA); a complex program was devised for the purpose of supporting and gradually improving prices of farm products (the Agricultural Adjustment Administration, AAA); and work was begun on legislation to regulate the sale of securities and the conduct of the investment business. Through these measures, and beyond and above them, belief in our powers of recovery was restored. Men and women, old and young, began again to think constructively about their future. Roosevelt, on being congratulated for these achievements by a visitor, was modest. He said that he had had the good fortune to enter office just as the crisis became so bad that the American people had in effect thrown up their hands and said, "Please lead — tell us what we can do." He was trying his best to push ahead as far as he could in response to their pleas.

The transformation was achieved without coercion. But the effects of some of the measures taken clashed with the effects of others. A few of the most important rested on suppositions not easily reconciled with the program being formulated for the conduct of economic and monetary relations between the United States and foreign countries. For example, the laws enacted to regulate and support agriculture and industry might make it harder for the United States to export its products and harder for foreign producers to compete in American markets; yet the American government was expressing favor for a worldwide program to reduce trade restrictions. In the discussion of what might be attempted at the prospective Monetary and Economic Conference, the idea that all governments might agree to expand public expenditures in unison was to the fore; yet the fiscal program which the Roosevelt administration presented to Congress was animated by the wish to economize. And most confusingly — as we shall shortly be telling — while the American government continued to pay homage to the idea of international monetary stabilization, the dollar went off gold and its value began to fluctuate.

Such contrarieties were at the time almost ignored. The attempts which were made to call attention to them while they were still latent were thought to be needlessly worrisome. As was, for example, a memo I sent to the Secretary on March 23 in which, after pointing out the indicated crisscross, I concluded that unless domestic measures were coordinated with agreements which we intended to seek with other countries there would surely be trouble and confusion. "This is," I explained, "not only a question of coordinating the substance, but even more important, of coordinating *the time element* in the development of different policies."

I ventured to make a proposal. Why not create an economic

policy committee of ten members, five from the cabinet or who were assistants to cabinet officers and five not in public life? This committee, I suggested, should be put in charge of the talks with foreign representatives who had been invited to Washington and should later serve as the American delegation to the conference.

This proposal was lost in the shuffle. Even if the President had read it, it is more than probable that he would not have wanted to turn this assignment over to any such groups. He wanted to keep it under his thumb. In this he was abetted by Moley, who was to be the thumb's thumb. When on the same day a group of us tried to lay out a program for discussion and submitted a list of those who should be asked to develop it, Moley said that this group must not be institutionalized and should be kept informal. He was proud rather than worried by the lack of systematic preparation, as may be illustrated by a remark he made to me when I told him that a lot of preliminary work would be required for an important meeting with the British ambassador. He waved my anxieties aside, saying humorously that an Irishman never needed to talk with an Englishman, and that his grandmother would roll over in her grave if he should do any preparing. When James P. Warburg, who was present, recorded this conversation in his journal for March 25 he added, "Poor Feis is totally unable to cope with Moley's playboy manner, and doesn't realize that Moley is quite able to take care of himself."

That I must have continued to make a nuisance of myself is indicated by another entry in Warburg's journal, for March 31, which I came across much later: "I went to the State Department and had a very full talk with Feis. I told him he was rapidly making himself impossible by his continual complaints about lack of organization and lack of policy. I told him that it was perfectly true that there was no organization and no policy, but the only way to make progress was to accept these facts and make the most of them."

The advantages which the President and Moley probably saw in this way of conducting business was that it left them freer to adapt their actions to circumstances. But the flexibility of procedure they preferred left the formulation of our policies more exposed to tem-

porary shifts in the wind of circumstances and the gusts of personalities.

However, we did manage in some way or other to formulate a
statement of policies before the foreign missions arrived. When on
April 3 we explained it to Hull item by item he said he was very
well pleased with it; at least it gave him something that he wanted
in the trade field. The President on April 13 also thought our ideas
in this area fine; he was enthusiastic about the first initiative we
were to take — the effectuation of a tariff truce during the conference — and he approved also our intention to propose (1) a hori-
zontal cut of tariffs by all countries and (2) trade treaties between
individual countries providing for reciprocal reductions of trade
barriers.

But except for such occasional consultation, the President contented himself with what he gathered from his conversations with a
few cronies, particularly Moley, Warburg and Bullitt. He seemed
confident that he could keep the talks with the foreign missions
rolling along a pleasant line.

Before their arrival, though, the United States went off the gold
standard and the international value of the dollar, like that of the
pound, was bobbing about. To grasp why and how the American
government took this step it is necessary to scan the prior turns in
the international monetary situation and the attendant circumstances in the United States.

Great Britain (and twenty-five other countries whose foreign
economic activities were mainly conducted in the pound sterling),
having returned in 1925 to the gold standard as too high a valuation of the pound sterling, had been compelled to leave it again in
1931. Thereupon it had allowed the pound to fluctuate. This depreciation of the pound had enabled Britain to regain its international balance and recover, but it made competition harder for the
producers in the United States and Western Europe.

The governments and financial controllers of France, Italy, Holland, Belgium, Germany and Switzerland were determined to maintain the existing gold value of their currencies. France, Belgium

and Italy, having been raddled by the great depreciation of their currencies in the years after World War I, were fearful of being forced to go through that sickness again. Germany, whose currency had become valueless in the early nineteen-twenties, was even more resolved not to repeat the experience. So its government exercised strict control over foreign exchange and German exports and imports.

These industrial and trading countries, known collectively as the gold bloc, were convinced that an international gold standard was the soundest basis for their national economies and for international commerce. They deplored any developments which might threaten it.

As the depression went on and trade fell and fear spread and only speculators thrived, their gold reserves had been subjected to erratic inflows and outflows. By 1932 even the dollar, which had hitherto been considered a safe repository of value, had become weaker. Americans and foreigners had begun to sell dollars and other currencies for gold, or for the currencies of the gold countries. Speculators against the dollar became bolder, the main centers of their operations being Paris, Amsterdam, Antwerp and Zurich — those bastions of the gold standard. This had been the trend, it may be recalled, when in May 1932 the British and American governments had agreed to convoke a conference to deal with international economic and monetary questions. As told, President Hoover and Secretary Mills had conceived that one of the primary aims of that conference would be to induce Great Britain and other sterling-currency countries to stabilize the pound and return to the gold standard. In a memo of mine at the time I had advised that the most satisfactory way to bring this about would be for all main currencies to be devalued in terms of gold preliminary to stabilization. For venturing such an abhorrent proposal I had not been reproved. But it had not been put up to the British authorities. Mills had made it plain that he mistrusted any project for an international conference as a threat to the American "hard money" position. Members of the Federal Reserve Board in Washington and the head of the Federal Reserve Bank in New York had been worried lest the conference lead governments to intrude on their operations and policies.

During the 1932 election campaign neither candidate for the presidency had admitted that he was considering or might be compelled to consider bold departures in a monetary sphere and/or changes in the gold value of the dollar.

Hoover, on the stump and in letters, had repeated over and over his opinion that fear over Roosevelt's intention to "tinker" with the dollar was one of the chief reasons for the continuation of the depression and the banking panic.

Roosevelt had avowed just as often that he was as devoted a supporter of "sound money" as Hoover, and that Republican charges to the contrary were false. On November 4, for example, Roosevelt had urged Senator Carter Glass of Virginia to refute charges that the Democratic administration was going to resort to reckless inflationary measures. He himself indignantly told the press that "It is worthy of note that no adequate answer has been made to the magnificent philippic of Senator Glass the other night in which he showed how unsound this assertion was. I might add, Senator Glass made a devastating challenge that no responsible government would have sold to the country securities payable in gold if it knew that the promise — yes, the covenant — embodied in these securities was as dubious as the President of the United States claimed it was. Why, of course, the assertion is unsound. . . .

"One of the most commonly repeated misrepresentations by Republican speakers, including the President, had been the claim that the Democratic position with regard to money has not been sufficiently clear. The President is seeing visions of rubber dollars. But that is only part of his campaign of fear. . . .

"The Democratic platform specifically declares, 'We advocate a sound currency to be preserved at all hazards.' That, I take it, is plain English."

It was plain English. But it had not had plain meaning either to me or to my professional colleagues. Several possible and very different conceptions of "sound money" were in vogue. As for the "rubber dollar," it could well be argued — as Roosevelt subsequently did — that the value of the dollar during the Hoover administration had been extremely elastic; that since its power to purchase necessities was much greater in 1932 than it had been in 1928, a sound dollar was one that would revert to its earlier real value.

In short, the semantics of monetary policy had been badly mauled in the political fray.

The American members of the Preparatory Committee for the conference reported after their return from the first session that all of the delegations except the British and the Japanese thought world monetary stability essential to general recovery and therefore urged a universal return to the gold standard. The British were demurring, contending that stabilization should be deferred until prices and money incomes had risen and international trade had increased.

The opinion about the primacy of stabilization which Williams especially espoused had been enthusiastically approved by Hoover and Mills. This was the start of a slide into a strategy for the conference which caused all the other measures which had figured in the original correspondence to pivot around a stabilization accord. It was not foreseen that this demand for stabilization would concentrate upon the dollar. Day and Williams, after having talked with the President-Elect and Moley, had left for Geneva to attend the second and final meeting with the impression that the new administration would adopt their recommendation that the American government would use its influence to cause the British government to return to the gold standard at a fixed rate, possibly in return for some reduction of its debt.

On January 19, 1933, I had addressed a memorandum to the Secretary of State in which I commented, "I am of the opinion in our discussions of the fields in which an effort must be made to work out a common policy with the British that relatively too much emphasis has been upon the question of sterling stabilization and too little upon other possibilities." The import of another memo which I sent along shortly after was that while there were reasons and tendencies that made the British government less resistant than before to stabilization, it was still likely that it would want to continue to watch the movement of prices and experiment longer with measures, national and international, of raising them before committing itself firmly to any rate for the pound.

By the end of January 1933, when Day and Williams returned to Washington again, the aim — to get the British government to stabilize sterling — had hardened still more in their thoughts. The impression left by my notes of what they told me is that the President-Elect acquiesced in that purpose and that even Moley fell in line with it. The all-around bargain visualized was that Britain would obligate itself to return to gold at a fixed rate; the American contribution would be a reduction in the debts due it; the French contribution would be an elimination of its quotas; and the German contribution would be an elimination of exchange controls.

This program was fallacious for one primary reason: the governments concerned were no longer in a position to carry it out even if they had so wished. The accentuation of the depression, the continued deterioration of the banking situation, the steeper fall in prices, all led to a coagulation in my opinion that there would have to be a revolution in the monetary positions of the United States and other main countries before stabilization of their currencies could or should be undertaken.

Accordingly, in still another memo, which I sent to the Secretary on January 29, I argued that the "underlying economic forces made this program impractical." It was predictable that the producers and the workers and the politicians in the United States and other countries were going to demand bolder monetary and banking measures and that this would make attempts to achieve stabilization on the basis of the present values of the dollar and franc premature. This led me into an angry intellectual brawl with my old associates Day and Williams. But their stand had not been shaken even when Neville Chamberlain, on January 28, said in a speech that Great Britain would return to the gold standard only when certain it would work well and when there was an international agreement on the fluid conditions under which it would operate.

Monetary reform, he said, would not in itself cause a satisfactory and lasting rise in prices and money incomes; it must be accompanied by united international action on the economic, financial and political factors that caused the crisis.[2]

The developing situation in the weeks before Roosevelt took office and the appraisal of its causes in financial circles is illustrated by the report which Harrison made to his fellow members of the board of directors of the Federal Reserve Bank of New York on February 23. Withdrawals of gold from circulation both by hoarding in the United States and through export, he said, had been heavier than in any recent similar period. Still he thought there was little foreigners could do to hurt our position. The real danger came from the actions of our own people. They were beginning to react badly to gold exports and the declining exchange value of the dollar, and to the excited fears of banking trouble and inflation. "This represents something more than a hoarding of currency, which reflects a distrust of banks," Harrison warned. "It represents in itself a distrust of the currency and is inspired by talk of the devaluation of the dollar and inflation. . . . The only way to stop it . . . is to revive the conviction that the currency was not going to be inflated or devalued." [3]

But confidence did not revive; it slumped further. And the volume of gold exports and earmarkings for foreign banks sped up.

Before Roosevelt took office I received an inkling that he might decide that the United States had better leave the gold standard.

In February 1933 Tugwell was in Washington on other business. He came out to our house for luncheon and there he told me that the President-Elect had asked him about a week before to look up the legislation under which President Wilson had, during the First World War, embargoed gold shipments from the United States. He asked for my help in securing the information. I could foresee that if the word spread that the President-Elect was likely to order a cessation of gold shipments the outflow would turn into a flood. So fearful that if I talked to Secretary Mills himself my inquiry would travel to the White House at once and possibly excite some sort of public statement, I turned instead to my close working associate, Daniel Bell, the Assistant Secretary of the Treasury. I told him in the utmost confidence what information was wanted. Within a few minutes he called me back and gave me what he said were the pertinent legislative references. Tugwell having come to my office, I turned over the citations to him. I suggested that he ought to advise the President-Elect to have his own legal counsel study the subject thoroughly. He at once telephoned Hyde Park and gave Roosevelt the information in hand, with the suggestion that the lawyers be asked to review it. The President-Elect instructed Tugwell to ask Senator Thomas J. Walsh of Montana, who was to be designated Attorney General in the new cabinet (he died on March 2, on his way to the inauguration), to look into the matter. But that able Senator was away from Washington, on a honeymoon with a young wife. Tugwell had to phone the President-Elect again. He was then told to turn for help either to Senator James Byrnes of South Carolina or to Senator Key Pittman, the silverite.

Tugwell hurried off to the Capitol to discuss the matter with one of them. Though uneasy, I felt obliged to refrain from telling even Secretary of State Stimson of Tugwell's request. I went about other business, but I was not allowed to let the matter slip out of my mind. Bell called on the telephone again to tell me he was sorry but the information he had given me was partly incorrect. I remarked at once that that was fine, just fine, and when he asked me why, I blurted out to him that it had already been sent "high, wide and far." When he asked me what that meant, I was called upon to tell him that it had been passed on to Hyde Park. Thereupon he exclaimed he thought it was necessary to tell Under-Secretary Ballantine what had happened, and ask him to come over to the State Department at once and bring along the Treasury lawyers. I asked him to wait before doing so.

Tugwell had told me he was taking the five o'clock train for New York. Looking at the clock I saw there was still a few moments before it would leave. I telephoned the stationmaster and asked him to inform Tugwell that it was imperative that he take a later train. A porter took off his bags while he telephoned me and we arranged to meet in Pittman's office. As he did not see any further need of consulting with Treasury officials, I phoned Bell and told him not to come to the State Department but rather to bury the subject in his mind. Then I phoned Ballantine and, though I could tell he was offended, pledged him to secrecy.

This was in a sense a silly injunction. For when I met Tugwell in Pittman's office they were already engaged in active pursuit of the information through lawyers in the Senate Legislative Bureau who might not feel obligated to maintain secrecy. After a brief talk I said I did not think that I could be of any further use at the moment. Pittman agreed and said he would complete the research and would phone Roosevelt. Before going out the door, however, I could not refrain from remarking again that if news of this action under consideration became public we might expect a great surge in the flow of gold out of the United States.

This inquiry and episode stimulated me to set down on March 3, the eve of the advent of the new group, my impressions of the international monetary situation. They were: (1) that only a handful of countries still maintained legal gold value for their currencies, but these included important countries such as France, Holland, Belgium and Germany, and they were fearful of being forced to abandon the gold standard; (2) that the recent fluctuation of currencies not on the gold standard had been large. For example, the value of the British pound in terms of the American dollar had recently swung all the way from $3.20 to $3.70; (3) that stabilization need not mean the end of depreciation of currencies in terms of gold. One appealing possibility was the devaluation by agreement of the currencies of all countries that thought it advisable; and (4) that perhaps the British government could be induced *after* general devaluation to enter into a stabilization accord provided it was subject to review if Britain should again find it too hard to balance its foreign accounts without suppressing domestic economic activities. The most recent utterances of Prime Minister MacDonald and Chancellor of the Exchequer Chamberlain seemed to me more pliable than their earlier ones.

Should the American government at this time commit itself to maintaining the existing gold value of the dollar, even temporarily, I queried? Would it not rather be well advised to develop a program for general devaluation and provisional stabilization that might or might not be presented to the British and other governments depending on future circumstances?

I sent copies of this memo to Stimson, Mills, Hull and Moley. I do not remember whether any of them read it and spoke to me about it.

One of Roosevelt's first actions on taking office, as already told, was to close all banks, and in that connection to make exports of gold and silver and the transfer of capital out of the United States subject to license. But this could be and was construed by many as merely one feature of a temporary emergency program rather than a deliberate monetary policy. Secretary of the Treasury Woodin explicitly assured the country on March 5 that the United States had not gone off the gold standard.

Within the next week Roosevelt submitted to Congress two major proposals. Both could be interpreted to mean that he intended to preserve the existing gold value of the dollar. One was the Emergency Banking Bill, which was intended to assist banks deemed sound enough to reopen. The Federal Reserve Banks were authorized to advance funds against the government bonds and other assets of the banks deemed good; and the Reconstruction Finance Corporation was enabled to subscribe to the stock of banks which needed more capital to operate. The other was entitled "A Bill to Maintain the Credit of the United States Government." Its main mover was former Congressman Lewis Douglas, the conservative-minded Director of the Budget approved by Roosevelt. This law gave the President authority to cut the salaries of government employees, and reduce pensions and payments to veterans. It was intended to assure the American people that the soundness of American currency was esteemed, and that the safety and credit of the American government was trustworthy. A week hence the government was going to have to obtain about one billion dollars to pay off securities falling due and other obligations. Moreover, the officials of the Federal Reserve Banks were asking for reassurance before they bought more government bonds to help out private banks.

A similarly conventional approach seemed indicated by a passage in a message which, on March 10, Roosevelt sent to Congress about his economy proposals. "Too often in recent history," he said, "liberal governments have been wrecked on rocks of loose fiscal policy. We must avoid this danger." [4]

On March 15 I was taken by Hull to tea with the President in the White House. James Warburg, consultant to Roosevelt about monetary policies, had been recommending that the American government maintain its virtual prohibition of gold exports and allow the value of the dollar to fall further in order to cause prices to rise and to avert other inflationary measures. He was of the opinion also that for the time being the question of whether or not to devalue the dollar ought to be left open; and that the government should set aside a large "stabilization fund" through which to manage and control movements in the value of the dollar. The President quizzed him about these views, with which I was in general accord. As recorded by Warburg in his journal, "The President finally said that he thought the suggestion had great merit and that he would like to see it pursued energetically at once." When Warburg told Moley of this conversation, Moley said he was delighted. But he was strongly opposed to consulting Harrison about the stabilization fund. Warburg proceeded to try to work out a plan whereby it would be operated by a foreign exchange division of the Treasury.

In anticipation of the scheduled talks with the foreign missions which were soon to flock to Washington, Warburg, with the President's knowledge and the approval of Woodin and Moley, had several talks about monetary matters with the British Treasury representative, Kenneth Bewley, the French financial attaché, Emmanuel Monick, and Paul Claudel, the French poet who was serving as ambassador. On March 30 Warburg reported to the President that they had agreed on many elements of a common monetary policy. Among these were: that the main countries should individually and collectively try to maintain stability of their currencies; that *ultimately* they should return to the gold standard; and that thereafter central banks should have a uniform rate of gold reserves against currencies and a supplementary one which could be in either gold or silver. Whether or not the dollar was to be devalued in terms of gold before this program was put into effect was left open.*

A few days later, April 4, when the President had spent almost the whole morning reviewing with Hull, Moley, Warburg, Bullitt and myself the program to be discussed with the foreign missions, Warburg read his memorandum about monetary and fiscal actions. Roosevelt said he liked it. Warburg asked him whether, in the provision for ultimate return to the gold standard, he wished the question of devaluation of the dollar to remain undetermined. The President said that was exactly what he wanted.

While these discussions were taking place, the clamor within the United States for inflationary measures of some sort became more vociferous and impatient. Few of their proponents were outspoken advocates of great and rapid expansion of public expenditure with a resultant budget deficit. Many of the schemes propounded were a heartfelt repetition of that cry which William Jennings Bryan had so vehemently made in his campaign for the presidency against William McKinley in 1896: "You shall not crucify mankind upon a cross of gold." The audiences of farmers, laborers and small-town merchants attributed their distress to the oppression of powerful financial interests in the East who wanted, they thought, to keep prices down and interest high.

By the spring of 1933 diverse organizations and groups were crying aloud for some kind of monetary inflation or devaluation, or both. Most effective, probably, was the Committee of the Nation. Among its members were prominent merchants, such as the head

* These points of policy, which were included in a resolution to be discussed with the visiting missions and presented to the Monetary and Economic Conference, were set down in a memorandum written by Warburg on March 30. After talking with Walter Stewart, myself and others, Warburg revised its language and slightly amended it.

of Sears Roebuck, some journalists, some Wall Street operators and some foreign exchange speculators. Their purpose was to get the United States off the gold standard and to bring about devaluation of the dollar from which they would profit either as speculators in foreign exchange or as businessmen. Another group, more conservative, who stood to gain by devaluation were those who had already exported gold or otherwise acquired liquid deposits in foreign banks. They conceived that they were merely protecting the value of their capital. More voluble and on the friendliest terms with the members of Congress were the advocates for the reincorporation of silver in the monetary system as an addition to monetary and banking reserves and the currency. These included such influential figures as Senator Key Pittman and Senator Elmer Thomas of Oklahoma. Their case for bringing back silver was spread among the populace by the broadcasts of the radio priest of Detroit, Father Coughlin, who, it became known later, was speculating heavily in that metal either on his own account or on that of the Church. Then there were the exporters — especially of farm products — who had been at a disadvantage ever since Great Britain had gone off the gold standard and the value of sterling had fallen much below its previous parity with the dollar.

And lastly — and this is not authoritative classification — there were students of public affairs who thought that the time had come to break — or at least to brake — the control of the Federal Reserve System over the amount of paper money in circulation, and that the government should issue directly or indirectly other types of paper money to pay its bills and promote business activity.

Believers in the necessity of resorting to any or all such actions circulated in the corridors of the Senate and the House of Representatives and sought appointments with the President and the Secretary of the Treasury. They even infiltrated into my subordinate office in the State Department in order to present their arguments that the United States must cast off at least temporarily the restrictive bonds of the international gold standard. Some seemed self-interested, scheming and ignorant, but basically I was in accord with their intent and inclination.

The American government was now actually on the verge of going off the gold standard. During March and early April the government had issued a few licenses permitting the export of gold. The exchange value of the dollar had been declining slightly. The foreign exchanges were in confusion as a result of the uncertainty that still surrounded the intentions of the United States Treasury with respect to gold exports. These had been becoming increasingly profitable on paper; and it was becoming probable that the occasional issuance of licenses to export small amounts of gold would no longer be sufficient to support the dollar. The wish to exchange it for gold or other currencies was stimulated by the combined demand for some sort of swift and drastic inflation which was breaking loose in Cognress. These impelled the President to end the pretense that we were adhering to the gold standard and assent to legislation which entrusted him with vast inflationary powers.

When the exchange markets opened on the morning of April 18, the dollar broke badly. The Treasury refused applications for licenses to export gold. The President had asked Secretary Hull to come to the White House that night to discuss the imminent conferences with the many foreign missions invited to Washington. The Secretary took Senator Pittman and me along. I went with the intention of using this fortuitous chance to plead with the President to postpone the Monetary and Economic Conference till midsummer, and preferably until the autumn. By that time, I thought, the American government would have more reliable knowledge of the extent and nature of actions required to stimulate recovery, and thus be able to determine with greater certainty what international engagements it might assume. But this intention was driven out of mind by what occurred.

When we entered the Red Room the President, seated, greeted us jovially. At his left, on a couch, Raymond Moley was bending forward, holding a small black notebook and a pencil (or pen). Warburg and Bullitt were there; our arrival evidently interrupted a lively conversation. Soon afterwards Secretary of the Treasury Woodin and Director of the Budget Douglas sauntered in.

The talk about the policies and proposals to be discussed with visiting foreign missions never got under way. For the President, with a chuckle, informed the assembled group that the American government was abandoning the gold standard. No more gold exports would be licensed; holders of paper currency would no longer be permitted to redeem it for gold. He averred that he had been impelled to take this action at this time because he had been informed — presumably by the Treasury and the Federal Reserve Bank of New York — that in order to maintain the existing value of the dollar in the face of withdrawals from the bank and a flight of capital, the American government might have to permit within a few days the export of one hundred million dollars or more of gold.* The American gold-supply position was, the President knew, as strong as it had been in many years. Our stock of gold was adequate for a much larger volume of credit and Federal Reserve currency. Still he was afraid if the American government remained obligated to defend the dollar, the drain of these gold reserves might become unbearable, and the government and the banking system would have to clamp down hard on tendencies to expand. Moreover, he hated to think of the unearned gain which speculators would reap.

This wish — to prevent further loss of gold due to the defensive and speculative demands for it — was certainly one of the precipitating causes of his decision. But it was not the only one. Going off gold would, he thought, cause a rapid rise in dollar prices of goods and an increase in money incomes, so crucially needed by producers and debtors. It might enable him to avert introduction of those kinds of inflationary measures being demanded. It might aid American exports, especially of farm products. And lastly, it would put the American government in a better position to bargain with the British and other foreign governments about the relative gold values of their currencies.

* Later the President said that he had information that as much as a half-billion dollars of gold might have been earmarked. See p. 245.

I was not startled by our departure from the gold standard. Nor was I upset, since I had shared Keynes's opinion that it was absurd that the state of national and international affairs should be vitally affected by the supply, and ebb and flow, of that sterile metal, gold. Nor was anyone else present disturbed (except Douglas). The President's announcement, in short, did not make a sensation among the auditors; it evoked comments of approval and conjectures about its consequences, but no ejaculations of astonishment or protests.

I was perplexed, however, because Prime Minister MacDonald, that decently purposed person, had not been told of our intention. He was being left to learn of it from a bulletin tacked on the ship's notice board. The President and Moley seemed to find amusement at the shock he, Montagu Norman (called by them "Pink Whiskers") and sundry other foreign officials were going to experience. They did not seem to me to be worried, as I was, over the chance that our action might capsize the prospective discussions with the British on other matters. On the next morning when I expressed this anxiety to the Secretary of State, who had remained almost mute during the evening session at the White House, he said he thought it would have been useless to protest a decision already taken, and that he did not want to dissipate his influence. Later on I came to wonder whether in reality the decision not to let MacDonald know in advance what we were going to do was not less harmful to his fortunes than would have been a decision to consult him about it. By our negligence he was protected against insinuations that he had connived in our action, or at least had proven ineffectual in preventing it.

The President, after the comments about leaving the gold standard trailed off, went on to say that he wished most of all to discuss with us another important matter which required immediate attention. Senator Thomas had informed him the previous day that because the Senate Agriculture Committee had come to the unanimous conclusion that the farmer could be saved only if the buying power of the dollar was greatly reduced, he had prepared an amendment to the Farm Bill.* This, he had explained, would give the President discretionary authority to take any or all of four actions: (1) to issue paper currency in whatever quantities the President might direct; (2) to order the recoinage and free coinage of silver at such ratio to gold as he might wish; (3) to reduce the gold content of the dollar; and (4) to organize a dollar stabilization board to regulate the value of the dollar and thereafter to stabilize its value.

In the same letter in which he transmitted this information to the President, Thomas had pointed out that the commodity purchasing power of the dollar was about two and a half times what it had been not many years before. He had also stated that when the amendment was discussed in the Senate he was going to exhibit samples of corn, wheat, cotton and oats. "At the present prices," he had continued, "farmers must produce one quart of wheat and deliver same to market to secure one cent. He must produce three-quarters of a quart of shelled corn to receive half a cent, and must produce and deliver to market one quart of oats to secure half a cent, and must produce enough cotton, ginned, to fill an average-size pillow to equal the sum of five cents." The Senator indicated that he regarded this amendment as a statement of principles and that it was subject to revision in detail.[5]

By the evening of April 18 this amendment had been set in print and was being studied by members of his committee and others. Moley had that morning discussed it with Bullitt, Woodin and Warburg, and had given Warburg to understand that the President was going to ask Thomas not to introduce this "resolution." [6] But the President now told us that he had let Thomas know through Byrnes that he would not oppose it — provided it was amended in important particulars. Moley seems to have remembered his next words, although I do not. He said, "Here, Ray, you act as clearing house to take care of this. Have it thoroughly amended and give them the word to pass it." And turning to the rest of us he remarked, "Congratulate me." [7]

When some of us began to expostulate, the President explained

* Title III of the Emergency Farm Mortgage Act of 1933.

that he had decided to go along with the Thomas amendment because if he did not do so Congress was likely to pass a mandatory law instead of a permissive one even over his veto. The latest draft of the amendment was read aloud. Since Thomas had sent his letter to Roosevelt, the authority to issue notes had been stretched; in this printed text of the amendment the Treasury was to issue notes in currency denominations not only to pay at maturity any outstanding government obligations and to buy such obligations in the market *but also "to meet current expenses."* That additional clause, the President said, he was going to ask Thomas to strike out; and he was also going to suggest the addition of a provision for an amortization fund to retire these notes of an amount equal to the interest on the government obligations which they were used to purchase. Therefore, the President remarked, these Treasury notes would be quite different from the notorious "greenbacks," and the United States would not be entering into another greenback era.

This observation did not, however, convince us. Warburg, Douglas and I — interrupting each other — argued that granting to the President this wide-open power to issue Treasury notes would swiftly stimulate fears of inflation. If it were used it would cause speculative inflation not only of the currency but also of credit. It might bring into existence a great excess of liquid banking reserves, which could be the basis for speculative borrowing — by those who sought to gain by borrowing while prices were low and the value of the dollar high and then paying off their debts when prices soared and the value of the dollar fell.

Warburg also contended that resort to this authority would prevent the Federal Reserve System from regulating the value of currency. The President rejoined that it would be difficult to expand the currency through the Federal Reserve System because the government did not control it. Was not the influential Senator Carter Glass of Virginia — who had refused the offer to enter his cabinet as Secretary of the Treasury — even then trying to take away the small measure of control over the system that the government had? When the dissenters next warned that if, once this power were used and the price of commodities began to leap because of fear, he might find himself compelled to issue more and more in order to prevent a relapse, the President said that they were seeing spooks and exaggerating dangers. He did not directly answer the assertion that the mere possibility that this power might be used would stand in the way of a revival of a market for bonds.

The talk went on awhile longer and touched the other sections of the amendment, but not significantly. Warburg's reminiscent description in the account (which he later entered in the Oral History Project at Columbia University) of the way in which those present looked and acted corresponds roughly to my own memory of the scene. "Moley was in one of his satanic moods when he was delighted by this dramatic move of the President and rather amused by my discomfiture. Bullitt ditto. Bullitt thought this was a wonderful show — and great stuff. Hull never opened his trap. Pittman made sure we would buy silver and enable us to raise the price of silver. . . . Feis looked as though he was going to throw up. . . . Lew Douglas went to bat with me and Will Woodin, once he got through his head what it was all about, which took some time . . ."

The President, having listened with unruffled good nature, closed the argument. He reiterated his opinion that since the authority granted was optional people would not be alarmed, especially since he intended to make a statement that this power would only be used with great judiciousness. He was sure, he repeated, that it was better to arrange for Congress to pass a permissive inflationary act rather than one which would compel him to take inflationary measures.

At half past eleven when we straggled out of the White House, there seemed little reason to think that the objections cited had made much impression on the President. But Pittman, foreseeing that some of the arguments made against the currency provision would reappear in the Senate debate, remarked that it might be wise to consider a limitation of the power to issue these greenbacks in order to avoid a filibuster.

I walked home to Georgetown somewhat disturbed but with a

sense that, in the end, the course actually followed would not be too impulsive or extreme. I learned later that Warburg and Douglas walked the streets for two hours, awakened Bullitt at five in the morning and continued to bewail the measures taken and to be taken.

The next evening Senators Pittman and Byrnes, Warburg, Douglas and Bullitt met with Moley in his room at the Carlton Hotel. They then redrafted the amendment in order to reduce the chance that it might incite an uncontrollable inflation. When Douglas reported to the President what they had done, he found him amenable and had no trouble getting him to agree to the more restricted range of delegated authority.

Thomas and his associates in the cause of inflation acquiesced to the limits imposed on the President's power to issue greenbacks. But they retained the provisions that looked toward devaluation of the dollar and upward valuation of silver.*

The presidential order, made effective at once, forbade the export of gold, except for amounts earmarked to the account of a foreign government. The value of the dollar dropped thirty cents in terms of the pound sterling. The quotations for wheat and cotton rose abruptly. The price of common stocks leaped upward.

People on the whole seemed pleased that the dollar had been detached from its fixed gold anchor. Whole some members of the American financial community regarded it as permanently destructive of the international monetary order, other conservative elements responded calmly, even favorably. Thus the *New York Times* wrote: "This action was deemed by his advisers to be a constructive step from both a domestic and international viewpoint, in that it would tend to raise commodity prices in this country and, by putting the United States on an equal monetary footing

---

* Finally enacted on May 12, it authorized the President to direct the Secretary of the Treasury to issue up to three billion dollars of United States notes (greenbacks) to meet maturing obligations and purchase interest-bearing obligations of the United States. The other delegated powers were more precisely defined, and the lowest limit to which he was authorized to reduce the gold content of the dollar was 59 per cent of its former content.

with most of the other countries of the world, increase the chances of all governments getting together on a more stable monetary basis following the world economic conference."

The officials of the Federal Reserve System were reconciled to the action after Harrison explained to them why the President thought it essential. There was no question, he said, but that the country was "right on the edge of the precipice of wild legislation and something had to be done to prevent Congressional excesses." [8] They even leaned favorably toward the President's wish to have the system make substantial further purchases of government bonds in order to lessen the chance that he might have to use authority granted under the Thomas amendment to pay off government bonds in greenbacks.

Some British authorities and journals accused Roosevelt of having made Britain the victim of a rough trick. Most American commentators denied it. They did not think that the British, who had been off the gold standard for two years, should set up a chorus of complaints from one end of their isles to the other now that the United States had followed suit. Little concern was felt at the time over the chance that as a result of our action France, Holland, Belgium, Italy and Germany might in turn be forced off the gold standard and have to revalue their currencies. As will be recounted, their missions, which were soon to visit Washington, were reassured that our action was merely a response to special and urgent circumstances and that the dollar would be stabilized again as soon as possible.

CHAPTER 13

The Flurry of Foreign Missions

WHEN those of us in the State Department and other departments had first learned how many missions were going to come to Washington, how important were the officials who went to lead them, and how wide the portended scope of the talks was to be, we had been taken aback.

It had all started on March 16, when the President had said to the British ambassador that he thought it be a good idea if the Prime Minister himself came to Washington. Sir Ronald Lindsay had said that he could not possibly come without talking about the debts. The President had said, "Why shouldn't he come and talk debts?"

To those of us who knew what special pleading had been required to persuade the British government to make the December 15 payment, the chance that Roosevelt and MacDonald would agree about the debts seemed slim. And if they did not agree, the chance that plans for the Monetary and Economic Conference would founder seemed real. Moley had continued to oppose any and all suggestions that the President ask Congress to authorize postponement of the payment due the coming June, since it might run him into a fight with the influential Senators. Hull had thought it best not to involve himself by espousing any suggestions.

On March 30 the Prime Minister and Foreign Secretary Sir John Simon had told Norman Davis that they thought it important, on account of world conditions, that the conference should meet as soon as possible. The date they had had in mind was the latter part of May. Moreover, the Prime Minister had explained that he thought the best course would be to leave the debts in the background for the time being and to concentrate upon ways and means to achieve recovery; if the two governments could show that they were working closely together on a promising program for the amelioration of conditions, there might then be some change in American opinion about the debts.

A few days later Davis had met not only with MacDonald but also with his most important cabinet colleagues: Baldwin, Simon, Chamberlain and Walter Runciman, president of the Board of Trade. Davis had thought that MacDonald wanted him to learn directly from his colleagues the objections that were being raised to his acceptance of the President's invitation to come to Washington. The Prime Minister had again reviewed the difficulty he would have to face if the debt payment, which might fall due while the conference was in session, was not deferred; and both Baldwin and Chamberlain, clearly unenthusiastic about having MacDonald go to Washington, had said they felt the British government would be drawn into futile acrimony or, in an effort to avoid it, would be induced to give semipromises which the British government could not keep.

Davis had persisted. Although he could not hold out any hope that Britain would be relieved of the June 15 payment, he had said, "there were many more important questions in which both countries were vitally concerned and . . . naturally the President, who was fully alive to their difficulties as well as his own, would not encourage a visit from the Prime Minister if he did not think it might hold out possibilities of serving a useful purpose." [1]

The debt question having thus been fuzzed up enough, MacDonald's cabinet colleagues had agreed that the Prime Minister might go to Washington as chief of a large British mission. On so learning, Roosevelt had instructed Under-Secretary Phillips to call in the ambassadors of numerous other countries and tell them that the heads of their governments would also be welcome. The prospect caused consternation in the State Department, for the diplomatic representatives of many smaller countries were also angling for invitations. The entry which Pierrepont Moffat made in his journal on April 6 was a restrained expression of anxiety: "The President's general idea of cheerfully welcoming anyone that wants to come is not without danger and I have not seen a disposition on the part of anyone to warn him."

First the British mission was to come, and next the French, and after them the Canadians, the Argentines, the Italians, Germans, Chinese, Mexicans, Brazilians, Japanese and Chileans. Discussions with these specially appointed foreign missions were to be interspersed with talks with the diplomatic representatives and technical advisers of a score or more other governments that had responded to our circular invitation.

Of the first few talks with the most important missions, which began on April 22, the President took initial charge. These meetings were alternated with others in the State Department. With the missions sent by the more important countries there were six, eight, or even ten consultations. As these preliminary exchanges of views strung along, the extremely busy President left the task of exposition more and more to officials of the State and Treasury Departments, and one or two members of Congress. Each was sometimes summoned at the last minute to come to the rescue of his colleagues and repeat his lines. For several weeks the reception rooms of the State Department were crammed with foreign visitors waiting their turn (or return) to listen to the exposition of American aims and views and to expound those of their government. The movement in the corridors of that old building was at times as animated as the rush in a railway station at commuter time.

Moley was at the President's side whenever he could be. Hull presided over some of the discussions in the State Department with a benign air and tireless repetition of his belief in the remedial effects of free trade. Bullitt was here, there and everywhere. My staff and I were usually trying to be in two rooms at once. The chiefs of the geographical divisions shepherded the visitors from their part of the world and made records of what was said. In one consultation, with T. V. Soong, the Chinese Minister of Finance, Senator Key Pittman took the lead, since the main topic was the future of silver and its price, present and future.

What a medley of ideas and desires emerged from these talks — and without ever being arranged into a thoroughly considered program! Regarding the ends to be sought, there was general agreement; but decisions about measures needed to achieve them and their timing were left for the conference to decide. This caused the discussions to seem so unreal to some of us subordinates that the statements issued to the press by the heads of missions and the President echoed hollowly.

The President talked with MacDonald about the debts, but they could make no progress towards an accord on this troubling issue. Both ardently wished to prevent it from separating the two countries on other issues and from halting the convocation of the conference; this may be discerned from the careful language of the joint statement they issued on April 25: "During the day the Prime Minister and the President have discussed the problems of the debt of the British government to the United States government. Both have faced the realities and both believe that as a result they lay the basis of a clearer understanding of the situation affecting the two nations.

"It would be wholly misleading to intimate that any plan of settlement is under way. . . . The point to be emphasized is that with the most friendly spirit progress is being made." [2]

The President also talked about debts with the French mission which came to Washington immediately thereafter. Headed by Edouard Herriot, who was no longer Premier but still a leading figure in the Chamber of Deputies and who had continued to advocate resumption of payments, this mission, too, was inconclusive. Roosevelt and officials under him tried to persuade the French mission that France should take some steps toward repayment if only to lessen the obstacles to solidarity with Great Britain and the United States. Herriot replied that French sentiment, as reflected in the Chamber of Deputies, was still so hard set against payment that he had only the faintest hope of securing authorization.

But the joint release signed by the President and Herriot on April 28 after the end of their talks did not dwell on this difference. The exchange of views was described as "free and cordial," which it was. The two governments were stated to be in full agreement that the Monetary and Economic Conference should meet promptly and that its object must be "to bring about a rapid revival of world activity and the raising of world prices by diminishing all sorts of impediments to international commerce such as tariffs, quotas and exchange restrictions, and by the reestablishment of a normal financial and monetary situation." But again what, precisely, each of the participants was expected to do in order to achieve these ends was left for future registration. Sound but platitudinous observations were made to take the place of definite obligations, as in the following statement: "The questions which are before the world today are for the most part, in our opinion, intimately bound up with one another. They constitute the separate elements of a single problem, the sound and permanent solution of which should be sought in an international collaboration supplementing the indispensable domestic efforts of each country."

As the procession of foreign visitors continued during April and May, the formulation of American policies seemed to me to become looser rather than firmer. But the announcement gave the contrary impression. This was not intentional deception. It was due mainly, I think, to the contagious optimism which President Roosevelt generated. It was sustained by the plausibility of the expositions of American policies and intentions which were made by all of us, expositions which minimized the domestic political and economic pressures on both the American and visiting authorities.

These were half forgotten in the rush and gush of consultation, and the eager will to believe.

One set of talks, those with the German mission, headed by Hjalmar Schacht, president of the Reichsbank, took a much sharper turn than any other.

Because of my deep resentment at the way in which the Germans had allowed Hitler to gain control of their destiny, I had refused the dinner which the German embassy gave in honor of the mission and also an invitation to lunch at the White House with Schacht. Shortly before the first talk with him about economic affairs in which I took part, James MacDonald, who was soon thereafter asked by the League of Nations to become High Commissioner for German Refugees, told me that Hitler had said to him, "I've got my heel on the necks of the Jews and will soon have them so they can't move. I am only doing what other countries would like to do."

The meeting with Schacht took place, as I remember, in Hull's office the morning of May 8. Having been on another assignment, I found the discussion well under way when I entered the room. The Secretary of State was sitting quietly behind his desk. Senator Pittman and Mr. Bullitt sat in chairs to his right, and I sat down next to them. The Germans were in a semicircle in front of the desk. Schacht did all the talking for them. He spoke with voluble assurance akin to that of a schoolmaster lecturing to his pupils. His gray, mean face was pinched above his high, stiff collar, and his pale eyes gleamed sharply behind unrimmed spectacles as his glance darted about from person to person.

Schacht dwelt on the difficulties, real enough, which the Reichsbank was having in securing foreign exchange — dollars, pounds and other currencies — to pay for needed imports and to meet German debt obligations. He suggested that countries to which Germany was in debt ought to give preference to German trade. Moreover Germany, he said, would be justified in treating preferentially those of its creditors that bought a large volume of its goods.

He also said that Germany ought to be given easier economic access to the colonies of other countries. Although all these points were contestable, no one made an issue of them.

Then Schacht went on to serve notice, almost as though it were merely incidental, that the German authorities were going to stop all transfers of payment in foreign currencies on all German external obligations. He averred that the decision to cease transfer had been made some time previously but that on receipt of the invitation to visit the United States it had been suspended out of what he called "courtesy." It can be assumed that he knew, as did the American group, that this action would be a hard blow, not only to large American banks but to the many thousands of Americans to whom German federal and local governments and industries had sold their bonds during the decade of exuberant financing in the 1920's.

Before anyone responded to Schacht's suave notice, the group adjourned for luncheon at the White House. But when talk was resumed in the State Department that afternoon Schacht repeated that this portended action was made necessary because the Reichsbank did not have the required foreign funds. The German government, he said, in taking this action without previous consultation with its debtors, thought that it would be easier for everyone concerned to be faced with an accomplished fact. Still no response from the Americans.

The German government apparently intended that the numerous private investors who had bought German bonds should learn the hard news from the morning newspapers. But greater consideration was apparently to be shown to the banking group which had made loans to the Reichsbank and other German government institutions and banks. For that evening, after the dinner at the German embassy, Schacht confided to Warburg (whose long-established and esteemed family bank in Germany would soon be compelled to close) that the move he had in mind would apply only to debts outside the standstill agreement, which covered mainly debts due to foreign banks. He intended to call a meeting of this group of creditors and to secure their consent to suspension of transfers. The next morning, alone with Warburg, he confided to him that he had cabled Berlin to go ahead and expected to hear shortly that action had been taken.

Bullitt and I agreed that this German decision should be challenged and that if, nevertheless, the German government took the action of which we had been forewarned, it should be reprimanded. The loss that would be suffered by American creditors of Germany would retard our own recovery. Moreover, in view of the fact that President Roosevelt had, in his campaign speeches, criticized the reckless way in which foreign securities had been purveyed to the American people with exorbitant profits for the bankers who sold them, they and Congress might well conclude that the President had assented to this refusal of Germany to continue to pay in dollars. Still further, there was reason to fear the effect of the German action on other debtors who had less reason to honor their obligations than had Germany.

When the President's attention was called to these considerations, he at once postponed the appointment with Schacht he had arranged for that afternoon. All of us, headed by Secretary of State Hull, trooped over to the White House. Although it is quite possible that Roosevelt had received from Schacht a previous hint of his intention, now the President spoke with indignation about it — especially concerning the highhanded manner in which it was going to be taken. Bullitt and Pittman had hastily written out a brief memorandum to be given to Schacht; it said that the American government was "profoundly shocked by the action which the German government was going to take." Warburg objected to the word "shocked" and suggested we say, instead, that we were "greatly disappointed." But the rest of us wanted "shocked" and it stayed in. The President canceled an engagement with Schacht for that afternoon and suggested that Hull receive him instead and give him the "aide mémoire."

I do not remember any other details of the presidential comment. But William E. Dodd, our ambassador to Germany, recorded in his diary the President's account to him of what he had said to Hull.[3] According to this account the President had sug-

gested to Hull that when Schacht came to see him he should pre-
tend to be deeply engaged in reading documents and should pay
no attention to his visitor while he was left standing for about three
minutes. Hull was then to look up without showing any surprise at
Schacht's presence. He was to find among his papers a note from
the President stating our serious opposition to the German default,
and give it to Schacht. The President thought that Schacht's arro-
gance both invited and justified such rude treatment.

As I was not present when the Secretary of State received
Schacht that afternoon, I do not know whether he acted out the
pantomime which the President had suggested. But after his talk
with Schacht he informed the rest of the group that he had behaved
as coldly as he felt. Schacht was obviously taken aback, perhaps
because he had told the President before of Germany's decision
and the President's manner had remained cordial. Now abruptly he
was confronted with a vigorous protest. That evening, in talking
with Warburg, Schacht raged over the situation. In telling us of
Schacht's remarks, Warburg said he thought it probable that
Schacht had advised Hitler after his earlier talks with the Secretary
of State and the President that the German government could proceed to suspend payment without fear of retaliation. Now he was
obviously worried about what would happen when he told Hitler of
our objections.

This episode did not terminate the talks which Schacht had in
the State Department and with the President during the following
days. These were repetitive dialogues. In the meeting on the morning of May 11, Pittman and I made a stern effort to make Schacht
understand the reasons why we thought the action he had in mind
was unfair and unjust. We pointed out, among other matters, that
the failure to remit dollar payments would injure many thousands
of American bond holders; that the American government had not
demanded reparations payments from Germany at the end of the
war as it might well have done; that American officials and banks
had mediated in bringing about a reduction in the reparations payments from Germany, and had facilitated the acceptance of reduced schedules by aiding in the flotation of large German govern-

ment loans (especially those known as the Dawes and Young Plan loans); that these and other American investments had enabled Germany to get through difficult postwar years and to reconstruct its economy; that after the depression had set in, President Hoover, by bringing about a temporary moratorium on the payment of all intergovernmental debts and reparations, had helped to preserve the German state at a critical period; and finally that the Reichsbank would be able to accumulate the means of making substantial payments if Germany spent less on imports used for rearmament.

Schacht paid some heed to these protests and arguments. In deference to our show of resentment at his intention to act without advance discussion with or notice to the creditors, he said he would postpone action until he had entered into consultation with them. That he intended to act at once was revealed not only by his original statement but by what his assistants confided to other American officials. Now he said he would try to consult with all American creditors speedily. But he added that while he could get in touch with the American and other foreign banking interests and invite them to come to Germany at once, he did not know how to reach the many thousands of American bond holders. He asked for suggestions as to how this might be arranged. The Secretary of State said that the American government could not get involved in these private debts, but that perhaps the Treasury or the Federal Reserve System might be able to suggest a procedure for arranging consultation with the bond holders. Schacht concluded by saying that he would try to work out ways of consultation with the creditors, but he reiterated that time was of the very essence and very short.

During the last day of Schacht's visit, Hull, having been urged to do so, warmed up to the German a little in order to obtain his country's cooperation in the tariff truce we were proposing. The farewell interview with the President seems to have gone off pleasantly, and the customary deceptive joint statement of good resolutions was issued. The introductory sentences read: "In our conversations we have been guided by the hope that the World Economic and Monetary Conference may be successful. Quick and far-reaching solutions are necessary to save the economic life of the world. We are convinced this cannot be achieved unless, along with economic disarmament, there is military disarmament."

This series of wide-ranging talks with Schacht and his colleagues confirmed my impression that no matter what might be proposed or agreed upon later at the conference in London, there was little chance that the Hitler government would relax its controls over the German economy, over German foreign trade and foreign monetary transactions. All of the American group, I think, shared my impression that Schacht was a sleek, possibly self-deceiving but certainly self-preservative servitor of Hitler — a most skilled banking technician without heart or morals.

The conferences which followed with many other missions and foreign embassies added nothing to what had been discussed with the few more important ones.

Each of the missions carried away some conception of what the American government wished the conference to accomplish, and what it presumed to be a reliable summary of pertinent American policies. By then the American expositors had repeated their ideas so often that had they been punched on a paper roll they could have been played on a pianola — or, to be more up to date, spewed out of a computer. There was no time for second thoughts, since almost at once the delegates had to get ready to leave for London.

For the one irrevocable decision had been to fix the place and time for the World Monetary and Economic Conference. It was to open in London on June 12. While in Washington, MacDonald again said he thought the conference should be convoked as soon as possible in view of the miserable international economic situation. The auditors surmised he had more explicit reasons in mind as well. One was his hope, which turned out to be a shrewd one, that if the conference were in session on June 15, when the next payment of the British debt to the United States came due, the impending uproar over any refusal to continue to pay might in some way be quieted. Another was the possibility that the value of the dollar might decline further and faster, to the disadvantage of British commerce, and so alarm the gold bloc countries as to doom the conference to failure in advance. MacDonald's idea of procedure at the time was that the conference should meet for a week or two for a general exchange of views; then the chief delegates would depart, leaving six or seven committees to work on until autumn. Then if the prospects were good, the full conference could reassemble.

Towards the end of a meeting in the White House between the President and MacDonald and their advisers on April 25, after taking a deep breath, I ventured to ask whether, since is was quite possible that the economic and financial outlook and policies of both the United States and Great Britain would still be so unclear in June that neither government would be able to give firm undertakings about its future actions, it would not be advisable to defer decision about the date for convoking the conference. But the Prime Minister summed up again the reasons why he thought postponement would be harmful. The President, who not so long before had wanted to put off the conference until his domestic program was well on its way, now seemed as eager as the Prime Minister (and Herriot) to hurry into it. The joint statement issued the next day affirmed that "It is the hope of both governments that it may be possible to convene the Conference for June."

Between the departure of the missions and the convocation of the conference, the discussions about the debts and the conference meandered. They were overcast by the darkening political scene in Europe and the Far East.

CHAPTER 14

We Agree to Discuss Stabilization

AT the same time that we were conferring with the visiting foreign
missions in Washington, talks about stabilization of the dollar had
been going on. It was hard to tell what the President wanted. His
ideas veered and waffled. Even now, with many records opened, it
is not easy to trace their gyrations.

In the discussions with the British and French missions, Roosevelt's comments as well as those of his chief associates led these
missions to infer that the stabilization of the dollar in the near future was a genuine possibility — almost a probability — even
though he was not ready yet to determine the precise time when the
American government might agree to take action, or what the relative rates for the several currencies would be.

Certainly such an intention was implied in one startling proposal
which the President allowed Warburg and Bullitt to make to the
visiting British and French monetary and financial experts. On
April 26 Warburg asked the French financial experts if (repeat, if)
the American government was willing to experiment with stabilization, what method could they suggest? What about creating a three-
country stabilization fund? Charles Rist, adviser to the French mis-

sion, said that the matter would have to be considered. After this talk Warburg, Moley and Pittman went to the White House. Warburg wrote in his journal, "I stated the case and the President very quickly saw the point. He said that with the necessary reservations as to our right to change the figure if it proved incorrect, he was not unwilling to suggest a discount of the dollar from its former gold value of between 25 to 15 per cent. I told him that in my judgment anything above 15 per cent would be both dangerous and costly; that by nature the dollar belonged at par; and that the balance of payments would tend to put it there unless we took arbitrary measures in our domestic program." Warburg, in effect, was fighting the battle again about use of the powers granted the President under the Thomas amendment.

With or without sufficient reason, he thought he had convinced the President. This entry in his journal continued, "After full discussion we were authorized to set a discount of 15 per cent as a hypothetical figure." That same afternoon Warburg told the three French financial experts, Rist, Monick and Jacques Bizot, that the American government would join the British and French governments in an attempt to stabilize the dollar at that rate while reserving the right to change it if necessary. The attempt was to be made by a stabilization fund which the three would operate jointly. Sir Frederick Leith-Ross, Chief Economic Adviser to His Majesty's Government, was similarly advised.

The American proponents of this proposal thought it would be taken up at once. But it was not. The next morning Rist said it would be very difficult to get the Chamber of Deputies to authorize a contribution to a joint stabilization fund, since it might be used up in buying dollars and a loss be incurred. Warburg then said it had been proposed only because the French government was determined to have the dollar stabilized. It was indeed! The French were saying that they could not even agree to enter into a tariff truce for the period of the conference unless assured in this regard. Rist said that Paris would be consulted by telephone.

On April 26, after the visiting French group had their final conference with the President, Warburg told him that the French financial experts had said they might get some news that night in New York before they sailed. But they heard nothing.

Leith-Ross had responded to our overture by professing to be shocked at so low a valuation of the dollar. On April 30, the British government demurred. It was opposed to any attempt deliberately to drive down the value of the dollar — since it would not help us and would cause all Europe to go off the gold standard and defeat the Monetary and Economic Conference — and therefore it could not cooperate in holding down the value of the dollar; nor would it agree to stabilize sterling until the British balance of payments was in equilibrium, a debt settlement reached and tariffs lowered.

President Roosevelt seemed to be relieved. He told Warburg he was delighted that "from having been on the spot we have now put the French and British on the spot as regards exchange disorder." [1] Unlike some of his advisers, he was pleased rather than troubled by the fall in the value of the dollar that was taking place. He was neither afraid of a reaction nor alarmed by the possibility that France, Belgium, Holland and Germany might also suspend gold exports. He was willing to let the French and British authorities worry awhile longer. He thought that only if they became more troubled would their complacency fade and would they become disposed to accept a compromise on rates acceptable to the American government.

Shortly afterward, while reporting to the President about the course of discussion with the Argentines, I referred to some of the difficulties due to the decline in the value of the dollar. He said that his guess was that if this continued for the next few days, there would be a worried fire alarm from the French — and then we would get the stabilization terms we wanted. Warburg and Bullitt, who had been the sponsors of the provisional stabilization proposal, agreed to this forecast. But I remained dubious of it, predicting gloomily that is was more likely that the French and other governments would stop gold exports and let the franc decline and that the Mark would just crumble. Both they and I were wrong, but I was the more wrong.

And yet — and yet — the President still gave out that he favored an attempt to work out a stabilization accord when, at the end of his conference with the Italian Minister of Finance, Guido Jung, he approved a joint press release that included the statement: "We are in agreement that a fixed measure of exchange values must be re-established in the world and we believe that this measure must be gold." [2]

On May 7 the President announced in his second fireside chat that the American government would not validate the clause in its bonds enabling owners to redeem them in gold coin "of the present standard weight and fineness." He justified the measure on the ground that there was not enough gold in the world to enable it to fulfill this contract. The gold value of the dollar at the time in international markets was about 83 per cent of its former value in terms of gold and the gold franc. Although this decision was fair under the circumstances, bond holders — domestic and foreign — resented it. In this same speech the President explained that his aim was to reduce the real burden of debt — public and private — to the level of 1926 by, in effect, restoring the price and money income levels of that period. This would mean that debtors, as he stated, would be able to pay off their debts in the same "kind of dollar" as the one in existence when most of the debts were incurred.

Although I still thought it unlikely that the American government would determine the relative value of the dollar until domestic recovery had gone much further, my belief was obscured by the haze spread by presidential statements. This is illustrated by an extract from my exposition of American policy to the Polish ambassador on May 15. "This fluctuation in currency values is having an abnormal effect on the flow of international trade. It seems essential that this fluctuation be ended and that the value of the various currencies be stabilized. . . . The United States believes in the gold standard. It looks forward to the eventual establishment of an international gold standard. It realizes that the time is not yet ripe for such action and that progress in that direction must necessarily be slow. It is ready at the present time to contemplate a *de facto* stabilization providing such stabilization includes all major currencies. This *de facto* stabilization would be a temporary arrangement where by a definite relationship in terms of gold would be established between currencies." [3]

In a passage in the notable message which the President sent on May 16 to the various heads of the governments represented at the Disarmament Conference — of which I have told elsewhere — he remarked that "The [Monetary and Economic] Conference must establish order in place of the present chaos by a stabilization of currencies, by freeing the flow of world trade, and by international action to raise price levels." [4] Roosevelt must, or certainly should, have realized that he might be called upon sooner than he might wish to translate this profession of necessity into action.

On this same day, May 16, the French government tried to retrieve the opportunity it had lost because it had not responded at once to our proposal. Monick told Warburg that he was now authorized to accede to our suggestion of a joint stabilization fund. Warburg asked him whether that would be on a risk-sharing basis. Monick said it would be, with certain reservations. Warburg and Monick seem to have agreed on the main features of the proposed accord: the dollar was to be stabilized at a 15 per cent discount from its former ratio to gold and to the gold franc; the central banks were to cooperate to keep rates near those agreed on by undertaking to buy up the *five hundred million dollars of the currencies of the other two countries*. But relative exchange rates were to be tentative and subject to change after due notice. Warburg anticipated that economic forces would keep the value of the dollar up and that the chief task of the fund would be to support sterling and the franc, which could be done without shipping gold out of the United States.

With the President's assent Warburg informed the British Treasury representative of the recent exchanges with the French, cautiously adding, however, that the American government had not yet made up its mind how to respond. On the next day the French ambassador left a memorandum in the State Department which said the proposals made by the American experts during the Washington conversation apropos of a tripartite cooperation had been studied in Paris with great interest. It then went on to state that "the French Government is firmly convinced that the work of the Conference greatly depends on what will be done in order to remove the uncertainty which exists today as to the future of the two currencies as important as the pound and the dollar. It is very much concerned in the matter and believes that in order to enable the Conference to arrive, in the course of its first meetings, at the establishment of sufficient accord concerning the indispensable stabilization of the pound and the dollar, conversations should start immediately between the American, British and French Central Banks." [5]

French gold stocks were at the time very large. But in partial explanation of the anxiety of the government of Edouard Daladier, it should be recalled that it was disunited and upset by the coming of the Nazis into power. Its main supporters were middle-class people who were frightened by signs that working millions were moving politically to the left. They were afraid that France also might be forced off the gold standard, and that then the value of the franc would decline, as would that of their savings and pensions; moreover their ownership of small stores, workshops and farms might be menaced by the rise of a revolutionary proletariat, made more discontented by a rise in the cost of living.

The President did not think these French fears warranted. But he remarked offhandedly to his advisers that he was willing to reach a stabilization accord provided he could get a good bargain, and also provided that it did not interfere with the creation of new purchasing power in the United States and the course of recovery. The President's idea of a good bargain was evolving. He now envisaged a dollar worth no more than $4.25 to the pound sterling and one quarter less than its former gold value, hoping that commodity prices in the United States would rise correspondingly.[6]

Hull did not try to anticipate the terms of the accord when, as instructed, he informed the French ambassador in Washington on May 19 that American representatives would "be glad" to join in talks with the French and British governments and their central banks. He said that they would be in London in about two weeks (*i.e.,* just before the conference met), at which time they would be ready to discuss these important matters wholly independently from the program of the conference. A similar message was conveyed to the British authorities.

Geroge Harrison of the Federal Reserve Bank of New York and Montagu Norman of the Bank of England were both being told by officials of the Bank of France that "nothing could be accomplished at the World Conference until some agreement had been reached for monetary stabilization between England, France and the United States; that the Bank of France believed conversations should be held as promptly as possible and before or at the very outset of the World Conference and that these conversations should be participated in jointly by the governments and Central Banks." [7]

On the morning of May 29, after the President had run through with Moley and Warburg the instructions which he was going to hand to the whole delegation to the Monetary and Economic Conference that night, Warburg asked how he wished the discussions about stabilization handled. [8]

Oliver Wentworth Sprague, former adviser to the Bank of England, who had been persuaded to accept the job of Assistant to the Secretary of the Treasury, spoke up. He said they could best be carried on by Eugene R. Black, the new chairman of the Federal Reserve Board, as representative of the Treasury, and by George Harrison, since the subject was not within the purview of the conference. Roosevelt said that seemed all right. He confirmed Warburg's understanding that if the British or French financial officials raised the subject with him in London — where he was to be financial adviser to the American delegation — he was to explain that special representatives were being sent over for this particular purpose. But, Roosevelt added, he would be glad to have Warburg send on his views. Soon thereafter Sprague himself was asked to go in place of Black.

The reasons for the decision to keep discussions about stabilization clear of the deliberations of the conference were several. Only a small number of countries would be engaged in them compared with the many who were to be at the conference. The officials of the central banks of the United States, Great Britain and France were alarmed at the idea that their policies and actions might be subjected to the scrutiny and direction of political representatives. The President, though, as indicated by his comments anent the Thomas amendment, was not satisfied with the independence of the Federal Reserve System and not really pleased by its policies; but at this time he needed the cooperation of the banking community, which thought the Federal Reserve System its own.

The Secretary of State was not consulted about these arrangements. But he was relieved rather than hurt by the fact that the question of currency stabilization was fenced off from his jurisdiction. Whether this was because of canny suspicion of trouble ahead, or because of a lack of interest in and knowledge of the subject, I do not know. Before leaving for London, Sprague asked Phillips to allow Warburg to join in the discussions. Phillips so notified Hull after his arrival in London. Hull thereupon informed the President that the delegation thought it important to have Warburg act as liaison between the group that was to discuss stabilization and the delegation. The President assented to this request. Warburg participated actively in the discussions from the outset. Through the delegation office he communicated with the Treasury and directly with the President.

As far as is known, President Roosevelt did not give Sprague or Harrison or Warburg definite or written instructions. According to Moley, he merely told Sprague to go ahead and see what he could do about negotiating some sort of arrangement to steady the exchanges.

The subject having been excluded from the jurisdiction of the delegation, I did not feel called on at this time to express my contrary estimate of the probabilities. True, my impressions of the highflying special agents selected left me skeptical. Harrison was an estimable person, but more of a mediator than an originator. Sprague had been impressive and lucid as a teacher — when I sat in his classroom at Harvard — but he now struck me as somewhat pedantic. Warburg was experienced in the banking world and shimmering bright, but almost too quick and self-assured. And Moley, who would be passing on what was done, was by then overbusy and too attracted by the glamour of great men and affairs.

Still, I was borne toward hope by Roosevelt's buoyancy and resourcefulness. I was too glad to be going along to London to issue any more gloomy advance prognostications. I was too eager to be present at the spectacle and see whether constructive order might be brought out of the confusion. And I was ready to work hard to contribute to it. The ambiguity I let stand.

CHAPTER 15

Meanwhile, Fission in Europe

THE talks in Washington glozed over the political disruption going on in Europe. You might well call this "political fission," because ultimately it brought atomic weapons into being.

Germany was the explosive center of the disruption. In January 1933, the weak and ramshackle cabinet headed by General Kurt von Schleicher had been forced to resign. In the new cabinet formed within forty hours Hitler had been named Chancellor. Captain Hermann Goering was Minister of Portfolio in charge of the vital Ministry of the Interior, and the notorious schemer Franz von Papen was Vice Chancellor and Reich Commissioner for Prussia. Baron Konstantin von Neurath, a mediocre career diplomat, was made Foreign Minister, an appointment correctly construed as designed to lull the West. The main support for this new cabinet were the National Socialists, but they were joined by two smaller reactionary parties which wealthy industrialists and vocal military figures supported. This menacing coalition of diverse extremists had been fostered by a common fanatical nationalism and hatred of democratic governments and the parliamentary system.

The German banking and business community was submissive,

thinking that they would have influence enough to keep the new regime within safe bounds or at least cause it to spare their interests. This expectation had been transmitted to Washington and American business interests. Schacht, for example, had assured our chargé d'affaires in Berlin, Alfred Klieforth, a few days after the new regime had taken office, that "in the field of economics and figures the Nazis will make no attempt to carry out their well-known demagogic reforms, and they will not be permitted to engage in experiments likely to jeopardize big business and banking in Germany and that American business in Germany had nothing to fear and that all big business viewed the new regime with sympathy." [1]

George Messersmith, American consul-general in Berlin, was more dubious. In a letter to me on February 4 he had written, "[Hitler] too is a patriot but he is no longer the leader of the movement which he started. He and his associates in their drive for power promised everything to everybody and now . . . he has arrived at the Chancellorship, consented to by the President [Paul von Hindenburg] certainly against every wish and prejudice he has. He was accepted as Chancellor by the President only when assured that Hitler had been bound by restrictions which would keep him and his associates within reason. But Hitler and his associates actually do have the power and it is a grave situation as to what influence Papen can have and what [Alfred] Hugenberg and his party [the Nationalists] can eventually do to restrain him."

It had been expected that this coalition government led by Hitler would wait until the elections, due in early March, were over before resorting to drastic measures to subdue all opposing elements and individuals. But (as the saying in the Caribbean goes, *"But* is a conjunctive") the new regime had resorted quickly to terrorist measures, infecting more Germans with its insane spirit of hatred and nationalism. Late in February, after the burning of the Reichstag — which the National Socialist government had itself arranged — it had drastically suppressed all political opponents. Hitler and von Papen had badgered the senile President Hindenburg into issuing a decree effective on March 1 which proclaimed a state of national emergency and suspended constitutional rights of individuals.

The heavy-booted and hard-fisted Brown Shirts had been sent out to make more and more secret arrests in the dead of night. Communist members of the Reichstag had been imprisoned; many prominent pacifists, journalists, authors, professors, teachers and lawyers, and later labor leaders, were either arrested or ousted. Many newspapers were closed. The formerly dominant Social Democratic Party and the German trade unions meekly submitted; they did not rise or call a general strike or otherwise fight to retain their independence and protect Hitler's victims.

And all the while this dirty work was being done the Nazis had carried on their election campaign with fury. Their shouting supporters paraded day and night through cities and villages carrying huge Nazi placards, assembled in mass meetings and torchlight processions. These activities and the shrill broadcasts of the Nazi leaders, combined with repression of all capable opponents, were applauded by all but a small minority of the German people. Such was Germany when the Hoover administration, having done little to interfere with these developments, ended.

March 5, the day after Roosevelt became President, was a day of triumph for the National Socialist Party. Together with its coalition partners it had gained a majority in the Reichstag.

President Roosevelt and the group around him, as they read the reports from Germany during their first weeks in office, were confronted with the fact that a ruthless Fascist party with avowed and dictatorial intent had obtained decisive hold upon the German government and over the German people. The Weimar Republic was in its death throes and the Third Reich was a reality. This transformation in the German government was symbolized on March 21 when decrees were passed creating a new national flag. The black, red and gold flag of the Weimar Republic was abolished in favor of the swastika and the army was ordered to remove the small inset of Republican colors on their military standards.

The new German Reichstag with uproarious acclaim passed a

law which gave Hitler virtually unlimited powers and eliminated all constitutional restraints. Hardly had the vote been taken when decrees were issued subjecting all organizations within Germany that might oppose the government to its control and instituting special courts to pass upon accusations of violations of these decrees. These were followed by others which broke up the federal system and centralized all power in Hitler's hands; the former states of the federation were to be governed by individuals recommended by Hitler and appointed by the President of the Reich. As correctly appraised by Messersmith and reported by him to the State Department on April 10, "It is the undisguised intention of the National Socialist Party to get absolute control of all forms of German government, and of intellectual, professional, financial, business and cultural life." [2]

President Roosevelt and most members of the State Department were shocked. But their public comments were restrained by the idea that while these events were having international consequences, and might have even greater ones in the future, the Germans had the right to run their own affairs until or unless they openly threatened or did obvious injury to other nations.

About the future course of Germany foreign policy uncertainty prevailed awhile longer, skillfully sustained by Hitler's deceptive tactics. These were correctly appraised in another report sent by Messersmith on April 28. "There is much reason to believe that the present Government and the leaders of the National Socialist Party are sincere in their desire for peace if one has reference to quiet and undisturbed peace for a limited period; but the sincerity of such declarations with regard to the desire for peace over a long period is inconsistent with the impetus being given in every possible way to extreme militarism among all classes and to the military training of various kinds which is being developed with an extraordinary rapidity, even among small children. . . .

"As an officer of our Government who gets in contact with a good many people in all conditions of life in Berlin I cannot for the present have any confidence with respect to the desire of Germany, either of the Government or the people, for peace. On the other hand, the whole essence of the National Socialist Government is that Germany must reassert its position in the world . . ." [3]

What pains Hitler took at this juncture to give the impression that his foreign policy was not going to be aggressive! How rational and reasonable he tried to make foreign authorities and auditors think he was (most successfully in a major speech he made in May defending Germany's role in the Disarmament Conference, of which we shall shortly be telling)! Such avowals, along with the suave assurances Schacht had given in Washington, and the hope that after their revolutionary fervor cooled the Nazis would act more soberly, all restrained any straightforward American official expessions of antagonism to National Socialist rule.* None of Hitler's affirmations of a wish for peace were in fact as truly meaningful as, for example, the words chiseled into the inscription of the monument which he hastened to erect in West Prussia fronting the Polish Corridor. "Never forget, Germans, of what blind hate too has robbed you. Bide the hour which will expiate the shame of this bleeding frontier."

However, one of the German government's most cruel policies was beginning really to startle and arouse many Americans. That was the cold and ruthless treatment of the Jews, their expulsion from their livelihood, the threats to their lives and fortunes, and the insults and physical maltreatment to which they were being subjected by Nazi troopers, police and hoodlums.

Although the President and most other American officials were revolted as they read the stories of this brutal and sadistic treatment of a minority who had contributed so much to German life, they still remained reluctant to call the Germans to account for-

---

* The President is his talk with Schacht on May 6 had "made it perfectly clear that the United States will insist that Germany remain in status quo in armaments and that we would support every possible effort to have the offensive armament of every other nation brought down to the German level. . . . I intimated as strongly as possible that we regard Germany as the only possible obstacle to a Disarmament Treaty and that I hoped Dr. Schacht would give this point of view as quickly as possible." Memorandum for Secretary of State signed "F.D.R." in Roosevelt Papers.

mally and officially. Roosevelt's formal attitude toward the problem — as summed up in a talk with Ambassador Dodd before he
departed for his post — was this: "The German authorities are
treating the Jews shamefully, and the Jews in this country are
greatly excited. But this is also not a governmental affair. We can
do nothing except for American citizens who happen to be victims.
We must protect them, and whatever we can do to moderate the
general persecution by unofficial and personal influence ought to be
done." [4]

Under instructions from Washington, the American embassy
and the American consuls in Germany did protest injuries and insults to *American* Jews who were in Germany. And during these
months of 1933 the American government also tried, albeit with
prudent formality, to make the Nazi authorities cognizant of the
fact that its treatment of the Jews was repugnant to most Americans and arousing American dislike of Germany. Thus, for example, on March 30, Secretary of State Hull had instructed the American chargé d'affaires in Berlin, George Gordon, to talk over the
situation created by the maltreatment of the Jews with von Neurath. He was told to say that the human element and human tragedy was such that "the friendship of the two countries might not
remain unaffected." Von Neurath, who had almost no influence
over the Nazi leaders, had proposed in his answer that the American government should issue a statement averring that press accounts of what was being done to the Jews were greatly exaggerated and constituted dangerous propaganda which was prejudicing
the friendly relations between the two countries; then the German
government might postpone the boycott it was going to impose
against Jews in Germany. Hull had approved the text of a statement to this effect — moderation to produce moderation — but
before it could be issued, von Neurath told Gordon that he could
not keep his part of the bargain. Gordon had drawn the conclusion
that the moderate elements in Germany were losing out from hour
to hour.[5] Such was the only sort of effort, so timid as to be almost
deferential, that the American government took to bring home to
Hitler and his National Socialist subordinates that what they were

doing to the Jews would in the end make enemies of most decent people and cause Germany to be reviled.

The American government did offer refuge to a few of the more prominent, distinguished or wealthy German Jews who were threatened with death or imprisonment. But even in this it proceeded slowly and stiffly. As far as I could tell at the time, this failure to try to do more was due to a compound of circumstances, feelings and reckonings. The provisions of American immigration laws were rigid, and officials that tried to bend them took a risk. Secretary of Labor Frances Perkins and one or two other cabinet members were ready to take this risk. They urged the President to instruct consular officers to be less routinely exigent and more helpful, and/or to ask Congress to amend the laws. The President, engaged in so many difficult and controversial efforts to bring about improvement and reform in the United States, wavered. Officials of the State Department persuaded the Immigration Committee of the House of Representatives not to report out a measure that had been introduced which would have authorized our consular representatives to issue visas to Jews and others threatened with persecution even though they could not prove that they would not become public charges; they had, by their advice, dissuaded the President from this initiative.[6]

In sum, the reckoning that governed American policy then and for some years longer was that it was inadvisable to hurt our chances of securing the cooperation of the Nazi regime in international economic and political affairs and in disarmament by interfering to protect the Jewish and other minorities in Germany. Not only inadvisable but probably futile, for the Nazi response to American popular criticisms indicated that official protests would be ineffective unless combined with the threat of entering into a military alliance with Great Britain and France. An indication of the probable answer of the Nazi government was its refusal in May to accept the report submitted to the Council of the League of Nations which declared its anti-Semitic legislation to be in conflict with Germany's treaty obligations for Upper Silesia.

These were reasons for the official American restraint, not excuses. But it need not be said that they were based on unjust standards and misguided judgments.

Certainly American restraint did not save the Disarmament Conference or the peace of Europe. A few days after Roosevelt took office, Hugh Gibson, the acting chairman of the American delegation, had sent a despondent report of the prospects of that conference to the Secretary of State. In it he said, "Unquestionably the Conference is in a precarious state . . . A simple adjournment . . . would be equivalent in the present state of feeling to a definite breakdown. It is to be anticipated that the German government would at once declare that states members of the League are not carrying out their obligation to disarm and that, therefore, Germany feels itself free from its obligations contained in Part V of the Treaty of Versailles. No man can foresee what the consequences of such action would be. At least it would aggravate the existing state of tension in Europe; at the worst the possibility of armed conflict in the near future cannot be ignored." * [7]

During the following months the new chairman, Norman Davis, continued valiantly to try to bring about an accord. His irrepressible optimism and energy colored the many very long and reflective communications he sent to the President and to Hull. But the prolonged discussion among the delegations to the Disarmament Conference, and the travels back and forth of foreign ministers between their national capitals and Geneva, defined rather than dissolved the differences that prevented an accord.

The most immediately crucial difference grew out of the demand of Germany for the right to rearm unless the other parties to the Treaty of Versailles proceeded to disarm. The German delegation insisted that Germany should be granted at least a nominal equality arrived at by an increase in the German forces and a reduction of those of other countries. Concurrently, in speech after speech, Goering openly derided both Part V of that treaty and the Disarmament Conference, and affirmed that nothing could stop Germany

---

* Japan, as will be told elsewhere, had on March 6 notified the League that she felt obliged to withdraw from it.

from having a military air fleet. Hitler's denunciations of both were incessant.

It is scarcely to be wondered that the French government could not be prevailed upon to acquiesce to an arrangement acceptable to the Germans. By then it was greatly afraid of the resurgence of the German warlike spirit, and fearful lest the Germans would — as soon as they could — march into the Rhineland, take over Austria and push onward in both the West and the East. The government, therefore, would not agree to reduce French armed strength or acknowledge the German right to have nominal equality. It insisted that it would make concessions only if other members of an arms accord pledged themselves to apply collective sanctions in case the accord was broken or any member of it took aggressive measures in violation of the Kellogg-Briand Pact for the renunciation of war.

President Roosevelt was not willing to pledge the American government to respond to this petition for a defensive alliance. However, after meeting with MacDonald on April 25, the President did say that in the event other governments reached a substantial agreement to disarm, he would make a declaratory statement. "Following a decision by the Conference of the powers in consultation in determining the aggressor, a decision with which, on the basis of our independent judgment we agreed, we would undertake to refrain from any action and to withhold protection from our citizens if engaged in activities which would tend to defeat the collective effort which the States in consultation might have decided upon against the aggressor." [8]

Those few of us in the State Department who deeply regretted the American refusal to join the League of Nations briefly rejoiced at this well-hedged and provisional offer to refrain from asserting what traditionally we had maintained were our "neutral rights." But it very soon became clear that, even should the American government make good on its declaration, this would not suffice to bring about an accord on the limitation of arms.

Along with this basic divergence there were many other clashes of national desires on particular points, each hard to compromise or overcome. The British government was not willing to assent to the re-creation of a German military air force that might be able to bomb Britain — while the German government was seeking equality of air power. Italy wanted greater naval strength in relation to France than France was willing to accord. Japan was insisting on the right to enlarge its army because of the war in which it was engaged in China. It would not consider any ban on aerial bombardment unless other governments agreed not to construct aircraft carriers.

With its members enmeshed in these and other difficulties, the prospects of the conference were admittedly dim. Any day it was feared that the German government, since its claims were being denied, would leave the conference and avow that it was free to rearm; and perhaps, after denouncing the Treaty of Versailles, send its forces into the Rhineland.

So on receipt of the news that Hitler was going to call a special meeting of the Reichstag on May 17, President Roosevelt tried to avert such possibilities by addressing a most serious note to various chiefs of state, including Hitler. In the introductory passages of this appeal Roosevelt connected measures for disarmament with the measures for relief of all peoples which the Monetary and Economic Conference were to consider. Then, after noting that the Disarmament Conference had labored more than a year without being able to reach any satisfactory conclusions, he observed that "Confused purposes still clash dangerously." This was a preface to a series of suggestions, the purport of which was summed up in the paragraph that read, "The ultimate objective of the Disarmament Conference must be the complete elimination of all offensive weapons. The immediate objective is a substantial reduction of some of these weapons and the elimination of many others." [9] He also suggested that in accompaniment to an agreement on disarmament the nations should enter into a definite pact of nonaggression — supplementary to the League of Nations accord and the Kellogg-Briand Pact — in which each agreed to send no armed forces of any kind across its frontier.

Roosevelt's message was read with suspicion by the Japanese

and French governments. The Japanese cabinet thought it might be an attempt to prevent Japan from obtaining a dominant position over China. The view of the French government, as summed up by Alexis Leger, Secretary-General of the French Foreign Office, to the American chargé d'affaires, Theodore Marriner, was distinctly mistrustful. The report received in Washington read: "His [Leger's] first reaction on the President's message was one of fear that it was all an English trick inspired by MacDonald to make France's position more difficult since he said that at the present time, with Germany in its inflamed condition, with the psychology of the whole German people turned toward the cult of force, France and her lesser population could not afford to give up that preponderance in war material which was her only safeguard." [10]

Whether or not influenced by Roosevelt's message, Hitler's utterance the next day was clever and more conciliatory than had been expected. He had begun by saying that Roosevelt's proposal "had earned the warmest thanks of the German government." He averred that "No new European war could improve the unsatisfactory conditions of the present day. On the contrary, the application of violence of any kind in Europe would have an unfavorable effect on the existing political and economic position." Then, after justifying Germany's claim to military equality, he had gone on to say, "Germany is at any time ready to assume further international security obligations if all nations are prepared to and Germany benefits thereby. Germany is also ready without further ado to dissolve her entire military forces and destroy the weapons left to her if neighboring countries would do the same. If, however, they are not willing to carry out the disarmament stipulations of the Treaty of Versailles, then Germany must at least maintain her demand for equality." [11]

As John Wheeler-Bennett has observed, by this speech Hitler had gotten out of the position of being ostensibly responsible for the breakdown of the conference and placed the onus on the allied powers.

Many commentators in the United States, however, took Hitler's speech to be reassuring. The question it posed was clearly stated by

Walter Lippmann in a piece evoked by the speech: "For the address itself, both as to its substance and its manner, there must be a very high degree of general approval. The difficulty, which will cause the world to be reserved in its judgment, will come from trying to reconcile it with the Nazi propaganda, with Herr Hitler's own speeches in the past, with the recent speeches of some of his own ministers, with the ruthless injustice of the treatment meted out to the German Jews, with the violence of the attack, as symbolized by the burning of the books, upon the spirit of peace and international comity. How does one reconcile this genuinely statesmanlike address with official words and official actions that have caused consternation throughout the civilized world?" But still, Lippmann rejected the opinion that the address was "merely a shrewd maneuver" and, after a brief review of other spells of hysteria following great revolutions in other lands, he concluded, as did many equally mistaken others, "the outer world will do well to accept the evidence of German good will and seek by all possible means to meet it and justify it." [12]

By all possible means open to the American government? Lippmann, who had opposed American entry into the League of Nations many years before, did not explain what would be required of the United States. But Hugh Wilson, an American delegate to the Disarmament Conference, in a message to Hull sent the day after Hitler spoke, was more forthright. "We have made," he said, "during these years some generous initiatives but we have never been able to recognize the inescapable fact that it was not our armaments that mattered in Europe, but our political positions." [13] And Davis rushed to urge the heads of the four Western European countries who were fending off one another to enter into a new four-power pact. The President gave Davis discretion to try to bring about a meeting of MacDonald, Mussolini, Hitler and Daladier.

Hull had encouraged the passage by the House of Representatives of an arms embargo resolution which would have enabled the President to make good on the promise held out in his April declaration to withhold protection from Americans who interfered with collective action which other countries might take to deter or stop aggression. But Senator Pittman told the President that in order to be passed by Congress any such measure would have to be made equally applicable to all disputants. Hull, on learning this, sent a cautiously worded letter to Roosevelt. In this he said that if the President had not already agreed to Pittman's proposal, he would suggest that since it "is directly in conflict with our position in Geneva as expressed by Norman Davis, it would be well for our government to deal with this matter in the light of this situation.

"If, in other words," the Secretary continued, "certain extremist Senators desire to take the responsibility of preventing the adoption of the policy of peace that is being pursued by every other enlightened nation, they might be given the privilege of tying up proposed peace legislation in the next few months." This was a typical instance of Hull's floppy prose and methods.

Still, he was genuinely aggrieved when, on May 30, the Senate Committee on Foreign Relations appended to the resolution a provision which would have transformed its original purpose. The provision stipulated that any order prohibiting the export of arms "shall apply impartially to all the parties in the dispute or conflict to which it refers." This was a marked triumph for those who wished the United States to stand aloof and neutral in all and any circumstances. It balked Hull's and Davis's efforts to provide reassurance to countries that were fearful of the rearmament of Germany.

Thus, perforce, when the four European governments did sign a pact affirming their wish to be friends, the statement issued by Roosevelt on June 9 conveyed his general approval without obligating the United States to cooperate in making the pact more than paper-strong. He called it "a good augury," and remarked that "This agreement of the principal European Powers to work closely together for the preservation of peace should give renewed courage to all who are striving for the success of the Geneva and London Conferences." [14]

This semblance of concord in Europe briefly refreshed hopes

that an agreement for reduction of arms might still be reached. It also transiently lessened the fear that political disturbances would make it impossible for the Monetary and Economic Conference, which was about to assemble in London, to achieve anything.

PART III

The Monetary and Economic Conference

CHAPTER 16

Off to the Conference

ON the night of May 30, just before the American delegation to the Monetary and Economic Conference departed for London, the President gave its members their final instructions. These had been roughly stitched together. They were set forth in a general memorandum on policy to be supplemented by six resolutions which the delegation was authorized to introduce into the conference. These had been written by Warburg with his usual purposeful clarity. I (and probably others) suggested various changes, some of which were made. Hull, who was to head the delegation, had gone over the resolutions cursorily. Only one really aroused his interest — that which would have obligated all signatories to reduce their trade restrictions and end their exchange controls as fast as circumstance permitted them to do so. This one Hull had taken close to heart; and it was the first to be abandoned.

The President also signed a covering letter for the general guidance of the delegation. Its last two sentences read: "I need not emphasize the importance to the welfare of the American people of the mission you are about to undertake. You may be sure that in that effort you may rely upon the full cooperation of myself and the whole of the American government." Presumably he thought that the Secretary knew enough about the political and economic flux through which the United States was going to realize that he, as President, would have to maintain a flexible attitude toward the doings of the conference.

As the members of the delegation rose to leave at the end of their final talk with him, the President, with a grin of farewell, said, "Get fast action and cut the speeches short." Hull seemed to lean with confidence on the incubated instructions of the President.

Most of the American delegation to the Monetary and Economic Conference sailed on the S.S. *President Roosevelt* amid excited bustle. The reporters and cameramen who crowded around them on the main deck almost outnumbered the passengers. Streamers of hope had been set blowing for months before the departure, and the confetti of optimism was still falling when New York harbor faded out of sight.

The Secretary had as usual a kindly word for everyone. He did not seem deeply troubled, as a man who was clutching a forlorn cause. His equanimity may have been sustained by his failure to grasp or his unwillingness to acknowledge the impending difficulties — after all, he had not paid close attention to the astringent discussions about the debts or monetary matters. But at bottom it probably came from his habitual adaptation to disappointment — for so often in the past his views and preachments had been disregarded — upheld by a belief that somehow or other the nations would learn that the route which he urged them to follow was the only trail to salvation. As a younger man this conviction had enabled him to persist until he secured a reversal of the original decision against income tax legislation; and to endure the defeat of Woodrow Wilson's policies and the advent of extreme tariff protectionism. His remarks to the press, as he was about to leave for London, were imbued with this faith. "The fact that the entire world is in a state of bitter economic war and all the world is at present functioning on an artificial basis affords the strongest reason for an agreement between countries to lower trade barriers and stabilize the currency exchange, with a corresponding restoration of international finance and trade. . . . The result of this is that . . . there should be an agreement as to the fundamentals of the situation in a few weeks, that should apply equally to currency stabilization as well as to trade barriers."

Of the troubles ahead he had had ample notice; for example, a warning from Davis that most members of the British cabinet thought that if it were not for their debt obligations and the unhinged dollar, Great Britain could face the future with equanimity even if the conference failed, since British commerce would be sufficiently protected by the Ottawa agreements and other preferential trade treaties. "MacDonald," Davis had reported, ". . . told me that some of his associates felt it was rather unreasonable for us, with our present high tariff and fluctuating currency, to ask them to 'stop now' and do nothing to protect themselves." The Prime Minister had implied that the attitude of the British could be converted into one of active cooperation only if the American government yielded on the debts, agreed to stabilize the dollar and refrained from imposing still higher tariffs on imports into the United States.[1]

Nor did Hull show anxiety because Moley, who was staying behind, would be the liaison between the delegation and the President, and one of the main authors of the answers to messages which it would be sending to Washington — although later it became evident that Hull was, even then, nursing black thoughts about a cautionary address which Moley had delivered on May 20 without consulting him. Although Moley's aim may have been the foresighted one of warning the American people not to expect too much of the conference, the effect seemed to Hull to be depreciating. The closing sentence of the address will indicate its trend: "With clear understanding of the nature of the conference and its objectives, the people of the United States can place the advantages that they expect from it in the proper relation to their general view of their own economic recovery. Above all, they must recognize that world trade, after all, is only a small percentage of the trade of the United States. This means that our domestic policy is of paramount importance. We must recognize, all of us, that common sense indicates that we build the basis of our prosperity here and direct all our efforts to the end that our national welfare and prosperity may lead us away from the distress into which the depression plunged us. But wise international cooperation can help distinctly and permanently."

This address set national and international policy in antithesis to each other, instead of viewing them as conjunctive. It diminished the importance of the matters with which the conference could concern itself. It was advance justification for any national measures that might be taken. For these and other reasons, it would make the task of the delegation harder.

Nor was Moley the only one close to the President who visualized the conference in this way. Tugwell shared Moley's attitude of indifferent disbelief. The entry made in his *Notes from a New Deal Diary* for May 31 read: "The argonauts leave this morning. Moley pronounces the word sardonically and I think we feel alike that the results of the Conference are sure to be pretty slim — in the vague, hazy sense that Hull means. His rambling, lisping speeches on the evils of protection, and his extolling of the old laissez-faire liberal internationalism have become harder and harder to bear." [2]

The way in which members of the delegation were chosen reminded me of the game in which the careless gambler looks at a board with a hundred small holes all papered thinly over, and then, having paid his fee, plunges a small wooden pick into a few of them, hoping to find below a tag entitling him to a prize. Three shots for a devalued dollar!

In April it had seemed almost settled that the delegation was to be wholly official. The Secretary of State was to be accompanied by Moley, the Secretary or Under-Secretary of the Treasury, two Senators, Key Pittman (certainly) and Robert La Follette, Jr., of Wisconsin (probably), and some member of the House of Representatives. Warburg was to be secretary-general. Bullitt was to go in some capacity still to be determined.

But by May, Moley was beginning to wobble in his ideas. This possibly was because of the views he aired in two radio addresses; possibly also because of fear that while he was away his position in the White House might be usurped. In any case he was suggesting that Hull and he stay in London for a week only, leaving behind Senators Pittman and Hiram Johnson of California (whom the President had come to prefer over La Follette), former Governor James M. Cox of Ohio, who had been the Democratic nominee for President in 1920 with Roosevelt as his running mate, and Warburg. This group was to be assisted by an advisory committee on which Henry Morgenthau, Sr., Bernard Baruch, Joseph P. Kennedy, and one or two unknown political henchmen were to be asked to serve. Bullitt was to be the executive officer.

But this slate had been changed again in the week or so before departure. Senator Johnson had refused, and Senator James Couzens of Michigan, another Republican, was asked in his place. Several other members were added. For diverse reasons, the advisory committee was never formed.

For his meek acceptance of the delegation chosen by the President to serve under his chairmanship, Hull was to pay. The only earnest believer besides himself in the purposes of the conference was Cox, an energetic worker and a goodnatured coworker. Couzens was a self-made and pernickety millionaire who had no coherent view of the policies to be discussed in London and little liking for international associations.

Then there was Senator Pittman. He was mean. Although chairman of the Committee on Foreign Relations, he cared little or nothing about any other foreign country. His interest in monetary policies was centered on improving the prices and prospects of silver mined in Nevada and neighboring states. The Secretary of State, who had known him for a long time, kept peace with him by never giving way to angry opposition to the Senator's moods or actions. Thus he seemed distressed rather than surprised when, during the ocean voyage, the Senator would go into a drunken rampage from time to time.

Of the two other members of the delegation one was Congressman Samuel D. McReynolds of Tennessee, chairman of the Committee on Foreign Relations of the House of Representatives. Amiable and modest, he was unfortunately out of his depth and not given to making trouble for himself or anyone else. The other was Ralph Morrison, a wealthy Texan. What Morrison was supposed to do in London neither he nor anyone else knew. The general supposition was that he was a generous contributor to the funds of the Democratic Party. Postmaster General James A. Farley and the Vice President, John Nance Garner, are to be credited for his selection.

What a motley group, I thought as I read the roster. But as the saying goes, I had not seen anything yet. No reflection of mine could be more pertinent than the one made by Moley after the fiasco: "It's doubtful whether a collection of the political geniuses of all the ages could have represented us satisfactorily under these circumstances. But the odds were a million to one that the delegation Roosevelt chose could not negotiate satisfactorily on the basis of these confused, confusing, shifting purposes." [3]

On the way over Hull received shattering news. He had clung to the hope that his wishes about commercial policies would prevail in the struggle of opinions. He had done so despite the clear signal of an inclination in Congress, not contested by the White House, to prevent intrusion of imports which might interfere with the attempt to achieve recovery on a national basis.

At the Secretary's request a small interdepartmental committee had written a legislative act authorizing the President (1) to enter into agreements for a simultaneous percentage cut by all countries in tariff duties, and (2) to enter into reciprocity agreements with other countries for such cuts in trade restrictions as each might make. But the President had reserved judgment about asking the current session of Congress to enact it; and Senator Pittman was known to be against it.

Still the President had not questioned the meaning of the pertinent resolution which the delegation was authorized to introduce into the conference. This seemed clearly to urge that an immediate attempt be made to bring about a worldwide lowering of trade restrictions.[4]

Midway across the Atlantic, Hull heard from the President that he had decided not to ask Congress to pass the new law affecting the tariff. Hull realized that unless it did, other governments would be dubious of our intention to reverse the trend to higher and more comprehensive restrictions. So on June 7 Hull appealed to him to reconsider. "I earnestly trust," he said, "reports are unfounded that Congress will not be asked for executive authority to negotiate reciprocal treaties based on mutual tariff concessions. . . . My deliberate judgment is that, in addition to most seriously handicapping the mission of our Delegation . . . it would be a major error to defer until 1934 any authority thus to negotiate this type of commercial treaty. . . . Furthermore it seems to me that such an eventuality would necessitate serious alterations in your instructions to the Delegation, and that the Delegation would be reduced to a passive role at the Conference, rather than the active role contemplated." [5]

The President sent Hull an explanation. "I wholly understand and approve your anxiety for tariff action at this session. The situation in those closing days of the session of Congress is so full of dynamite that immediate adjournment is necessary. Otherwise bonus legislation, paper money inflation, etc., may be forced. The veterans amendment alone may upset the whole situation if I cannot straighten it out in the next three days. Therefore, tariff legislation seems not only highly inadvisable, but impossible of achievement." [6]

The Secretary of State and those technicians who shared his ardor for tariff reduction tried to adjust their plans. But the earlier expectations of what could be done at the conference began to slip overboard. It was with this decision in mind that Hull later wrote in his memoirs: "I left for London with the highest of hopes but arrived with empty hands." However, to the historian, this retrospective lament seems histrionic. Hull's hopes should not have been of the highest before he left the United States — and his hands were not entirely empty when he arrived in London.

Cox and Couzens were not in our company on the way to London, having chosen to leave later on a faster ship. Neither were the three designated to engage in talks with French and British officials about currency stabilization — Sprague, Harrison and Warburg.

Secretary Hull seemed to enjoy slow walks about the deck and long talks with those of us who served with him in the State Department and were sympathetic listeners: Bullitt, Dunn, myself and other members of the group of technical advisers of which I had been named the chief. What a diverse lot! Most of them were well-qualified, hard-working permanent professionals like Harry Hawkins, who later was to be in charge of the Trade Agreements Division in the State Department. But on the list also were some individuals who had pestered the President for the chance to participate in the conference and whom the President had not wished to appoint to the delegation.

Only later did I learn that I might have had one colleague more spectacular than any other. On June 9 six Senators, headed by Senator Thomas, petitioned the President to appoint the Reverend Charles E. Coughlin of Detroit as one of the economic advisers to the delegation. In their letter they said that "if no goverment funds were available . . . Reverend Coughlin is able and willing to meet all expenses connected with the mission suggested." Well he might have out of the profits made or expected from the sales of silver. On the next day fifty-six members of the House of Representatives sent a similar request. Among its signatories was Congressman Everett M. Dirksen of Illinois.

Our ship stopped for a short time at Cobh in Ireland. In a statement to the representatives of the Irish press Cordell Hull made a slip by referring to either the Free State of Ireland or the Republic of Ireland. There I found myself surrounded by a small cluster of reporters who sang a lively Gaelic ballad to me. Their reason for doing so, as I learned from one of them, was that my name — Feis (pronounced Fesh in that language) — means a song and dance festival, usually an uproarious social occasion.

When on June 8 we stepped off the ship in England, officials of the Foreign Office welcomed us warmly. We took our ease in the luxurious railway carriages which sped us on to London, and the troubles and exhaustion that awaited us there.

CHAPTER 17

The Conference Starts and Stalls

IN any meaningful sense the conference never really got under way.

The sessions at the Kensington Museum brought together distraught officials of many countries who failed to find a working rhythm with each other. Their daily assemblies resembled a cafeteria crush rather than a cohesive gathering with determined common purposes and roughly similar ideas about the ways in which they might be achieved. Instead of the needed clear companionship between the American and British governments, the two original sponsors of the conference, there were only jagged consultations.

It had been agreed in advance that the work of the conference would be divided between two main committees, one on economic affairs and the other on monetary and financial affairs. Hull had longed to serve as chairman of the economic committee, which was to deal with the restrictions on international trade. Some members of the American delegation — particularly Senators Pittman and Couzens, who did not share Hull's ardent wish to lower tariffs — had been lackluster about his seeking this assignment. They were spared the need openly to object, since Roosevelt's decision not to ask the current session of Congress for authority to reduce tariffs meant that Hull could not validly take the lead in the economic committee.

Mugginess crept over the delegation meetings even before the conference formally opened. On June 11, the day before it assembled, Hull sat brooding at his desk from nine o'clock in the morning till nightfall. He listened dejectedly while the delegation, in wavering talk, reviewed the reasons why we ought not to seek the chairmanship of the economic committee. At the end of the meeting he remarked bitterly that the United States would apparently have to leave leadership in the economic field to some small country which believed sincerely in its objectives.

But because of pride of place the delegation decided to claim an equivalent position. It was proposed that the conference be asked to name Cox chairman of the monetary committee. Since he himself was hesitant and Hull dubious, the three officials who were discussing a possible accord for stabilization of currencies were summoned for consultation. Sprague and Warburg told of the several preliminary talks which they had had with representatives of the British and French Treasuries. They recounted the fact that they had made it utterly clear that the American government at this time had only *de facto* stabilization in mind with a view of keeping relative monetary values steady enough to enable the conference to proceed with its other business, and that they were not authorized to discuss *permanent* stabilization. The American government would not fix a permanent rate for the dollar until experience indicated what rate was suitable to its total economic needs. It would be for the conference to agree on principles of permanent international monetary standards and systems. They also reported that the French representatives were pleading for immediate action while the British representatives seemed uncertain whether they favored any action. Harrison, who had been concurrently talking with representatives of the English and French central banks, gave a similar account.

Their reports suggested that although a pall of uncertainty still hung over the question of stabilization there was a good chance that an agreement could be reached which the President might approve. This also encouraged the belief that the monetary committee under Cox's impetus could achieve something important. After listening to them the delegation agreed to insist that Cox be appointed chairman of that committee.

The French Foreign Minister, Georges Bonnet, was the rival for this post. Warburg and Bullitt, their combative spirits aroused, contended that Washington would be offended if he were chosen and that the prestige of the United States was involved. Bonnet addressed himself directly to Cox, saying that "France would not look with favor upon the selection of someone to head the monetary committee who comes from a country that has recently gone off the gold standard." Cox rejoined, "Nor will the United States look with favor upon the election of a man presented by a country which has repudiated its debts." This crackling exchange was a sign of the thunderclaps in the atmosphere that hovered over the conference even as it was convening. Bonnet then suggested the place be awarded to a representative of one of the smaller powers. The matter was left in suspense until after the conference assembled.

Cox and Bullitt tried to raise Hull's wilted spirits. They informed the President that "Hull [is] deeply distressed by reports from America that you and administration are no longer supporting his desire and that of Delegation to reduce tariffs and remove obstacles to international trade. Advise urgently that you should send him as soon as possible personal cable telling him that you are behind him." * [1]

Any reassurance he might offer was necessarily frail in view of the domestic legislation that was being enacted. However, the President responded blithely. "Please do not worry," he said, "about situation here in regard to tariff reduction and removal of trade obstacles. The eleventh hour rows in Congress over domestic programs made general tariff debate dangerous to our whole program.

* Warren Delano Robbins, cousin of the President, wrote him a few days later that the delegation had arrived in a rather depressed condition, that Hull had been on the verge of resigning, and that Pittman had been on a "beano" but was functioning again.

"I am squarely behind you and nothing said or done here will hamper your efforts. There is no alteration of your policy or mine." [2]

On the day the conference opened, June 12, the price of wheat was 54 per cent higher than when Roosevelt had taken office on March 4; corn was 34 per cent higher, cotton 52 per cent and copper 60 per cent. But still all were much too low. The average value of listed common stocks had risen by half. The rate of steel mill production had doubled, though it was still less than 40 per cent of capacity. Would the assembled representatives of the nations be able to agree on measures that might bring increasing benefit to them all?

In the address with which Prime Minister MacDonald opened the conference he alluded to the debts. The Americans deemed this a violation of his promise. Hull's speech, made on June 13, was a fervent plea for international cooperation. "If, which God forbid, any nation should obstruct this great Conference with the short-sighted notion that some of its favored interests might temporarily profit while thus indefinitely delaying aid for the distressed in every country, that nation will merit the execration of mankind. . . . All excesses in the structure of trade barriers should be removed, all unfair trade methods and practices should be abandoned. . . . In the monetary field suitable measures must be taken to provide for an immediate policy which will give the greatest possible measure of stability for the period during which the groundwork will be laid for enduring reform. Simultaneously all the nations must stimulate the natural sources of employment, restart the wheels of industry and commerce, and so build up consumer power that a rise of the price level will of necessity follow." [3]

Hull was listening to his own heart, not to the pulse of Washington.

During the next several days the conference set about organizing itself, determining its order of business and discussing the proposals that would come before it.

With or without reason, several members of the American delegation got the idea that MacDonald had promised both Bonnet and Cox the chairmanship of the monetary committee and was trying to wriggle out of his embarrassment. Warburg and Bullitt as well as Cox badgered him about it. The Prime Minister disliked Bullitt's methods. But he finally used his influence in behalf of Cox. Bonnet capitulated when appeased by a promise that he would be named rapporteur for the committee.

There was another welcome development. For the time being disputes about the debts due to the American government ceased to pour their corroding fluid on the relations between the United States and the countries with whom it was essential to cooperate. President Roosevelt refrained from reprimanding the French government when it gave notice that it was not going to pay on June 15; and he accepted without a show of animus the British offer of a token payment of ten million dollars. This response made it possible for the conference to shelve the issue. But it is probable that the default washed away the remnants of Roosevelt's tolerance for the French effort to cause us to return to the international gold standard at a fixed rate to the franc, and made him more determined not to let the British authorities ease him into an agreement about the relative pound-dollar value which might be to Britain's advantage.

While carrying on routine preliminaries, the conference was waiting to be informed of the outcome of the talks about temporary currency stabilization. On June 13, Warburg had reported to the President that the French were pressing for immediate actual stabilization; that the British authorities were vague; that he, Sprague and Harrison could not recommend that the American government meet the French demands unless the British authorities supported it. However, he had ended, "If we arrive at a plan which we can recommend, cannot urge too strongly that you go just as far as you possibly can in agreeing to proposal."

Within the next two days the negotiators verged on accord. Warburg recorded in his journal that at 4 P.M. on June 15 there was a

"Meeting of Neville Chamberlain (Chancellor of the Exchequer), Sir Frederick Leith-Ross, Sir Frederick Phillips — for the British; Bonnet, Bizot and Jacques Léon Rueff for the French; Hull, Cox, Bullitt and Warburg for the Americans.* The draft we had presented was adopted by all three, the Americans agreeing to submit it to Washington with their recommendation of approval.

Concordantly Harrison, with Norman of the Bank of England and Moret of the Bank of France, agreed on arrangements and methods for making the declaration effective.

Through what channels, American or foreign, word sped to the United States that an agreement had been reached is still a matter for conjecture. But it did. The value of the dollar climbed. Stock prices fell. Disturbed by these developments and provoked by the fact that he had not yet received an adequate report on the outcome of the discussions, Roosevelt that evening sent an admonitory message to Hull, Cox and Sprague: "All kinds of wild reports here about stabilization at some fixed rate, some reports saying around four dollars and other reports at other rates. I feel sure these reports are not founded in any fact. Of course any proposal must in any event come here for approval or disapproval by the Treasury Department to me." [4] Woodin asked Sprague to report fully on the negotiations, and he made it known publicly that no proposal for stabilization had yet been received in Washington, that the talks in London were only exploratory and that any agreement would have to be endorsed in Washington.

On the next day, June 16, the decline of prices in the United States of commodities and stocks grew steeper. The gold value of the dollar rose from 80 to 83 cents. Sterling, which the day before

* I believe the inclusion of Hull in the list of those present at this meeting was an error. But he had implied that he approved the effort being made to reach a *de facto* stabilization accord by stating in his opening address on June 14, "In the monetary field suitable measures must be taken to provide for an immediate policy which will give the greatest measure of stability for the period during which the groundwork will be laid for enduring reform." An earlier version of this address had been sent by Hull to Washington and the President had suggested various changes; then on the night of June 13 Hull had transmitted the final text, which included this sentence, and no objection was made to it.

had cost $4.19, now could be bought for $4.02. Stock prices declined to the lowest levels in weeks.

All this came in advance of the receipt of official knowledge of the terms of the proposed accord. These, as sent by Sprague to Woodin that night, were inscribed in two connected documents.[5] One was a draft of a declaration by the French, American and British governments, wherein the French government was to confirm its determination to stay on the gold standard; the American and British governments were also to state their intention of limiting — "as far as may be feasible" — fluctuations in the exchange value of their currencies during the period of the conference and to promise "in the absence of exceptional and unforeseen circumstances [not] to take any measures which will be incompatible with the principle of maintaining or restoring monetary stability." The other document contemplated an agreement between the three Central Banks stipulating that they would cooperate to maintain the existing relative rates of their currencies within a 3 per cent up or down range of fluctuation vis-à-vis the gold franc. The middle rate for the dollar-pound was to be $4.00, which was about the then current ratio. If necessary, each bank was obligated to expend up to three million ounces of gold, equivalent to sixty million gold dollars.

The ambiguity of the language of the declaration may have made it acceptable to the three sets of authors. On quick reading — and even after careful study — no one could be sure how tight or how loose the clamp imposed by it upon the President's program to achieve recovery might be. Sprague candidly acknowledged that it would obligate Roosevelt, at the least, while the conference lasted to use the powers conveyed by the Thomas amendment only "in exceptional and unforseen circumstances arising out of our domestic situation." What would be considered such was not defined.

Warburg, in a message to the President, endorsed Sprague's exposition and recommendation. He thought that the declaration and the central bank arrangement went no further than what the Americans had said before, most recently in Hull's address to the conference. "We have tried," he reported, "to protect your freedom of action to the utmost at the same time giving the assurance that can reasonably be asked of us as lenders in the monetary field to the effect that we are not going to be willfull and unnecessarily violent in our monetary policy."

These expositions rubbed the President the wrong way. Along with other observations in Sprague's and Warburg's messages they exhaled air akin to that which blew through the corridors of the Banque de France, the towers of Wall Street and the grimy roosts of the bankers along Lombard Street. They gave the impression that the stresses within the conference had blurred the American negotiators' memory of the stresses and excitements within the American economy.

Roosevelt asked Woodin, Acheson and Moley to come to the White House. After their talk the President formulated conclusions which Moley undertook to write out for the guidance of the negotiators and the delegation. The message sent to London on June 17 was signed "Phillips, Acting, R.M."; it was addressed to Hull — for the guidance of Cox and the information of Harrison and Sprague.

The recipients were informed that the President was afraid that while the declaration might be construed by us as general and permissive in scope, because of its wording London and Paris might later charge the American government with bad faith if it did not go along with their interpretation. "It is my thought," he said, "that at this time we should avoid even a tentative commitment in regard to any definite program of this government to control fluctuations of the dollar. It seems wiser to content ourselves for the present with an informal statement that if the pound should rise to an excessive point, say, $4.25, that we will then consider unilateral action of some kind." [6] Moreover, the President flatly stated, he could not forego the use of the powers granted under the Thomas amendment if needed to uphold the price level at home.

The final paragraph indicated the presence in Roosevelt's thoughts that conventional and self-serving banking interests were trying to crowd him into a corner because of American involvement in the conference. It read, "It is my personal view that far too much importance is being placed on existing and temporary fluctuations of pound, franc and dollar and that the bigger ultimate objective of balanced budgets and permanent national currencies . . . outweigh these temporary conditions in importance." [7]

Harrison had been tipped off by his colleagues in the Federal Reserve Bank that the proposed agreement was going to meet with strong opposition. So, without waiting for the President's answer, he had rushed off to catch the *Bremen,* which was sailing for the United States at once.

In a joint message Cox, Sprague and Warburg tried to convince the President that he need not fear charges of bad faith. They also took issue with the conclusion that the permissible zone of fluctuation envisaged was too small. But they said if the President thought it essential they might get others to agree to an enlargement. As for allowing that this question might have acquired undue importance, they forecast that a refusal by the American government to cooperate in controlling fluctuations would be interpreted as a change of mind on its part and would cast doubt on the authority of the delegation to present the permanent program.[8]

Before this message was received, Roosevelt had taken off on the schooner *Amberjack,* which was now being borne along on the fair winds of June towards Campobello. He answered the joint message by one in which he denied that he had changed his mind and gave no indication that he was being swayed by the importunities of his representatives in London.

On the morning of June 19, Secretary Woodin met with the executive committee of the Federal Reserve Bank of New York. In answer to those members who feared inflation was on the way and if continued would bring a crash, Woodin said there had been no inflation as yet, only the anticipation of inflation. Stabilization, he was afraid, would reverse the psychological forces that had been set in motion.

Owen Young agreed with him that stabilization at that time "would be something of a wet blanket on what the Administration was trying to accomplish." But because of the effect of a failure to do anything he said a way ought to be found to limit fluctuations in the value of the dollar without restricting our power to raise the domestic price level. Woodin asked him whether it was not unfair of foreign governments to hinge the success or failure of the conference on this matter. Young said he also was inclined to think so. The British government, he thought, would not let the conference be wrecked on that account, but the French government might. "The English would merely like us to play the trump card we held, now, that is all." [9]

Perhaps after hearing from Woodin the opinions voiced at this meeting, the President seemed to fall in with Young's idea. In a message which he sent to Phillips he said that despite his hesitancy he might agree to undertake to prevent the value of the pound from arising above $4.25 during the conference; and perhaps even assent to a medium rate of $4.15. This seemed to signify that for a good bargain he might come round.

But after talking the next day with Moley, who — as I shall soon be telling — had flown from Washington to join him on the *Amberjack,* he scudded about again. Via the destroyer *Ellis* which was hovering near the *Amberjack,* he sent word to tell Hull that after full consideration and discussion of the views stated in the messages from London he thought it best to stand on the principles and suggestions which he had outlined. "You are," he informed the Secretary, "in a position to insist on consideration of the larger and more permanent program, working towards a means of exchange among all nations. Remember that far too much importance is attached to exchange-stability by banker-influenced cabinets. In our case it means only a very small (perhaps 3) percent of our trade as measured by production." [10]

While waiting to learn of the President's decision, the committees of the conference had continued to meet. Pittman, with the assent of Hull and Cox, had submitted to the conference that resolution about permanent monetary policy which the President had approved before our departure from Washington. Its determinative paragraph read:

"Now, therefore, be it Resolved that all nations participating in the Conference agree: (a) That it is in the interests of all concerned that stability in the international monetary field be attained as quickly as possible; (b) That gold should be re-established as the international measure of exchange values."

This was intended as a statement of our *ultimate intention* when and as conditions in the United States favored measures for putting it into effect. But the anxieties and desires of the gold bloc countries were centered on the *immediate present*.

The introduction of this resolution was the only initiative taken by the American delegation during this first spell of waiting. Its morale and the relations between its members had deteriorated. A note which I wrote for myself at the time read, "The news from Washington implies a determination to build along national lines, and at any sign of intrusion by foreign interests which might affect domestic arrangements, to add new bricks to the national wall. This has left the American delegation without clear and dependable purpose and further impaired the confidence of the Secretary and others. The way in which American policy is shaping almost necessarily thwarts his ideas for restoration of trade and finance. With repressed rage and dejection he is fumbling with the affairs of each day, agonizing over every decision, but unwilling to take any step which would force the issue."

My own mood was affected by a disheartening personal experience. In an effort to buoy up the Secretary, a few technicians patched together a list of subjects in the international trade field which might be proposed for the consideration of the conference. In this we included the possibility of a 10 per cent cut in all tariff rates. With Hull's explicit assent I submitted this to the secretariat of the conference. As soon as Pittman heard of it, he issued a statement to the press denying that the American delegation was sponsoring any such action. When the delegation next met — I believe it was on June 18 — he not only repeated his objections but asserted that the paper had been passed to the secretariat without approval by the delegation. His manner and his language hurt and angered me. After waiting for the Secretary to explain, if not defend, what I had done, I answered Pittman in kind. I then stood up and said that I wished to resign and return to Washington. Silence followed. After the meeting Hull asked me to come to see him. He urged me to bear in mind the fearfully hard circumstances under which he was acting and trying to sustain the good reputation of the American government. By this time my self-important rage had simmered down and I agreed to stay on. I even read with composure that evening the explanatory message that Hull sent Phillips in order to appease Pittman and ward off possible protests from Washington. In this he explained that the press reports that the American delegation had proposed a 10 per cent all-around tariff cut were inaccurate. "We have made no such proposal but merely listed various topics on the economic agenda for discussion, which does not in the least constitute a statement of our position." [11]

Remembering this occurrence incites me to recall two other experiences that I had shortly thereafter — one upsetting, one cheerily ironic. The first was an encounter with Pittman as I was walking along the corridor on the way to my room in Claridge's Hotel. He appeared with a hunter's knife in his hand and pursued me. I hastened my pace and walked, or rather ran, past my own door towards the stairs that led to the lobby. Just as I reached there, Ned Bruce, a husky painter from California who was in London as Pittman's friend — or, I should say, guardian — appeared. He threw his arms around the Senator, quieted him, and took away his knife. I realized the Senator was tipsy.

This aggravating incident accentuated my impression of the harsh treatment to which the band of technicians was being subjected. What a bedraggled lot most of us had become! So I remember well how, sometime during the next day, after coming out of a long, tiring and futile session of the delegation, I found myself in the same corridor near the charming young daughter of one of the socially well-placed members of our group. She was in a long and gleaming white satin gown, with the three traditional ostrich plumes in her hair, for she was about to leave for Buckingham Palace to be presented at Court. Around her twittered not only her mother but other ladies of the delegation. The contrast between the grim working session I had just left and this gay display caused me impulsively, as I passed the young lady, whom I knew rather well, to lean and lift the hem of her gown and kiss it. Then with a wave of the hand and feeling very much better, I went to my room. Sometime later I learned that the adoring mother had told her friends that although greatly impressed by the royal reception, the one action that had pleased her most was mine, having been most expressive of heartfelt admiration for her child. I wish to add that the mother and I remained friends as long as she lived — which only goes to prove that a kiss is a kiss, no matter in what spirit it is given.

I must, however, desist from rambling on about my personal experiences and revert to the business of the delegation and the conference during the week of June 21 to June 27, when Moley was on his way from Washington to London.

During these days the English and Continental press in crescendo carried stories which implied that Moley was going to bring word from the President which would enable the mired conference to get under way at last. They created a state of expectation among the foreign delegations.

One day a story appeared in the London newspapers which particularly enraged Hull. It derived from a speculative item printed in the *Baltimore Sun* to the effect that Hull was going to resign and that Roosevelt was going to appoint Baruch Secretary of State. Hull suspected that the rumor was set off by Moley. Then Cox and Couzens had a nasty quarrel over a story in a Detroit newspaper in which Cox was reported to be complacent and not talking to the other delegates; Cox was sure this story had been inspired by Couzens and resented it.

Despite this cacophony, Warburg, encouraged by the reception in the monetary committee of the resolution about a permanent monetary system, sent a buoyant progress report to the President.

However, as foreign officials learned that Roosevelt had turned down the accord on temporary stabilization, all discussions in the conference became disjointed and unreal. The French and Italian members of the monetary committee were very excited. Cox and

Warburg tried to soothe and cajole them. Hendrik Colijn, Premier of the Netherlands, a stolid and healthy-minded Dutchman who was chairman of the economic committee, spoke pessimistically. While the conference must not break up, he said, anything that his committee might do would have to be provisional, based on the supposition that currencies would be stabilized later on. "Perhaps," Colijn explained, "the needed demand for inflation in the United States would fade away soon, thus making it possible to agree on stabilization and for the conference to continue."

Early on the morning of June 21 Warburg was told by Moley's secretary — who had come to London on the same ship as the delegation, and whom Hull subsequently maligned — that just before he sailed Moley had asked her to "Tell him [Warburg] it's dead and bind up the wounds."

Down but not despairing, Warburg got Hull's permission to talk to MacDonald about how the President's decision could be so handled as to be least disturbing to the proceedings and projects of the conference. When he and Cox tried to explain to the Prime Minister that the European press was partly responsible for the denouement — since its premature announcement about stabilization had set off an abrupt drop in commodity and stock prices in the United States — MacDonald answered, "This knocks the whole thing into a cocked hat."

Cox and Warburg urged MacDonald, as president of the conference, to appeal to Roosevelt not to take a wholly negative attitude toward a temporary stabilization accord. He asked for time to consider what to do next. Senior officials of the British Treasury and the Bank of England were not eager to stabilize the value of sterling at the current rates. Quite possibly the Prime Minister himself was not sure it was advisable. However, as head of the British government and president of the conference, he was faced with the probability that unless an accord was reached the conference would fail miserably.

In the afternoon, when Cox and Warburg saw MacDonald again, he showed them a four-page appeal to Roosevelt which he had written out in his own hand. On reading it Warburg and Cox drew back; it was so cordial that they were afraid of the effect on Mac-Donald and his British colleagues if Roosevelt answered negatively, which he well might.

Warburg told Hull of his perplexity. The Secretary refused to become involved and said that if MacDonald should dispatch this message it was better that he know nothing about it. Thereupon Warburg informed Maurice Hankey, the secretary of the conference, that he thought the Prime Minister had better defer sending this message until the President had clarified his position, for he was afraid that it might embarrass both of them. Later that same afternoon, after consulting the delegation, Hull advised the President that, mindful of his rejection of the proposal for temporary stabilization, the delegation "shall promptly and whole-heartedly comply" with the instructions and concern itself only with the principles of permanent and universal stabilization. It, the message continued, "thus far had not considered nor treated temporary stabilization as falling under its function and jurisdiction, but under that of Professor Sprague and Mr. Harrison, acting under separate instructions." [12]

Who can fathom with certainty Hull's calm compliance, even though the prospects of the conference were dimmed? Was it his sense of his duty to respect the President's wishes? Was it influenced by the fact that he was pleasing some members of the delegation? Did he find consolation in the thought that if the conference was disrupted, he could not be held responsible and his relations with the President would survive the event?

Warburg, though believing that the President had misjudged the import and probable impact on the delegation of his position, tried to be helpful. He informed Roosevelt on June 22 that the delegation thought it necessary to give out a statement explaining why the American government believed it best not to join in the declaration. Having written it with Hull's approval, he and Cox showed it to MacDonald, Bonnet and Jung. Bonnet exploded. Jung said he was sure it would cause the French and Italian governments to withdraw from the conference. However, after back and forth talk both calmed down and acquiesced in its issuance to the press. Mac-Donald expressed apprehensions similar to those of the others. Yet neither he nor Chamberlain nor Leith-Ross protested strongly, Warburg noticed, and he surmised that they were hardly more enthusiastic than Roosevelt at the thought of stabilization at this time and at the rates envisaged. However, when Warburg jokingly said that Bonnet was "entirely happy" with the statement, Chamberlain remarked that "like Mr. Pickwick's friend he was easily amused." [13]

The statement as released to the press did not tone down the President's views. It said in part: "Undue emphasis has been placed upon consideration of the plan proposed for temporary *de facto* stabilization of currencies. . . . The fact is that this was never an affair of the Delegation. . . . The American government at Washington finds that measures of temporary stabilization would now be untimely." It then went on to state the reasons why it was thought to be untimely, and reaffirmed that the American government favored the ultimate worldwide stabilization of currencies. The efforts being made to raise prices were, it alleged, the most important contribution which it could make to the conference.[14]

Warburg spent the remainder of the day being diplomatic. With the approval of Hull and Cox he sent off two messages to the President. In the first of these, after transmitting the text of the statement, he informed the President that MacDonald and Chamberlain were gratified at the way the French had been brought around and that Jung was giving the American group "thick and thin" support. He said he thought this emergency had been mastered and much of our lost prestige restored. This judgment was, I think, colored by his sense of personal achievement. But in the second message he warned the President that the situation could flare up again at any time if there were violent fluctuations in the value of the dollar. Therefore, he asked, would the President consider authorizing the Federal Reserve Banks to take such actions to limit fluctuations as might be from time to time desirable and practicable?

Cox on the same day supplemented Warburg's messages with one of his own which read, "I learned that American action hung like a pall over Conference. In our statement we made clear to delegates from other countries just why you had to act as you did. It seemed necessary to restore the prestige of our delegation at home. This is why the separated operation of our delegation unit and financial unit was made clear. We won the French over as we were completely frank with them and permitted them to see the statement before it was issued. MacDonald freely expressed opinion that the worst crisis of the Conference had been passed. If you love us at all don't give us another week like this one." [15]

These proceedings, which had left Cox shaken, did not depress Pittman. For he was still free to ask the conference to restore silver in national and international monetary systems and was making headway in the cause. His display of high spirits that evening would have been unusual for anyone but him. Several members of the American delegation, including Pittman, were dining with the Astors at Cliveden. After the meal was over, when the gentlemen and ladies had separated and the men were sitting in Lord Astor's study drinking brandy and discussing world affairs, the Senator disappeared. All of a sudden sounds of shouting and laughter in the drawing room where the ladies had assembled were heard. On peering in, the surprised gentlemen saw that Pittman had Lady Astor on the floor and was tickling her. Her Ladyship did not seem amazed by this rowdy performance.

Perhaps it was because I had no similar diversions that the memorandum I wrote on June 24 about the situation with the delegation and conference was so downcast.

"The position of the delegation today seems to be at low ebb. The course of events has left the members spinning about in their individual orbits of thought and calculation.

"The Secretary has arrived at a point of virtually giving up hope that any of his ideas or purposes can be carried through the conference. He desires to strive to place on record his own judgments and attitudes and what he wanted to do. He does not know how to contend with the divergent and opposing forces which have been active both within the delegation and at home.

"Senator Pittman is occupying himself in the silver subsection of the monetary committee, and virtually ignoring the rest of the committee's work — up to the point of no longer attending the morning meeting of the delegation. As shown by the statement he issued regarding the 10 per cent tariff cut, he is striving his utmost to disassociate himself from any activity in the field of commercial policy.

"Senator Couzens is convinced that our policy must be worked out on national lines and is indifferent as to whether any arrangement is arrived at in the conference. From the beginning he has looked forward to returning home quickly. . . .

"McReynolds plods along on the economic committee, not however keeping up with its detailed development.

"Morrison, disappointed at not finding a chance to work in the monetary field, takes almost no part in the conference's deliberations.

"This is the condition of stalemate and confusion that has resulted from the events of the past few weeks. The press dispatches which flow in from Washington every day and which are featured throughout the London press more and more emphasize the fact that because our government is committed to a policy of price increase, no tariff reductions may be expected. . . . This turn in the field of commercial policy accompanied by the President's decision in regard to temporary stabilization is producing increasing antagonism between ourselves and the rest of the conference, and generating an atmosphere most unhealthy to the whole future conduct of the foreign relations of the United States.

"From here, I can only surmise what may be going on. We do not know the source of the constant news stories originating in Washington bearing on the question of American tariff and monetary policy. It is probably, my guess would be, Hugh Johnson and Bernard Baruch." *

The thoughts of the President were not beaten down by any such impressions as those which infused this memorandum. To the con-

---

* It was Moley who started the story about Baruch being in charge of the State Department during his absence by saying to reporters, "You'll see a lot of Mr. Baruch around here while I'm away."

trary, they were enlivened by a pleased sense of vindication. The dollar had fallen back again in terms of gold; the exchange value of sterling had risen. The prices of stocks had shot up once more. The prices of wheat and corn had advanced a little. So Roosevelt informed Hull and Cox that he was "Delighted way things are going. . . . The real trouble of first week lay I think with French and British press trying deliberately to discredit us for certain clear objectives." He assured Hull that "Prestige of Delegation is generally excellent at home and most people are saying you were all clever enough to avoid an obvious trap." Yet, probably mindful of the reports that Hull, Cox and Warburg had sent about the state of the conference, he asked Phillips in this same message to discuss with Baruch and Woodin the advisability of having the Federal Reserve Bank take steps to prevent the value of the dollar relative to the pound from fluctuating violently about $4.25, and if they thought well of it, to prepare a draft of a further message to London.[16]

Roosevelt's expression of faith and satisfaction did not convince us in London. For the implications of the journalists' reports from the United States appearing in the English press were a refutation. Most of them were similar, for example, to the dispatch in the *Daily Telegraph* of June 24 from its correspondent in Washington. Its headline was: AMERICA AND HER DELEGATES' COMEDY OF ERRORS RESENTED. This correspondent had gone on to opine that the prevailing view of the Democratic leaders that the domestic recovery program was to have priority was so strong that the importance attached by the administration to the work of the conference was steadily declining. More depressing to the Secretary still was the guess of this reporter that "With Mr. Moley virtually in charge of United States interests in London, and Mr. Baruch at the helm here, it is likely that the Secretary of State's pleas for world service by international action will carry even less weight with his colleagues than appears to be the case at present."

The work of the conference had come to a halt. The American and foreign delegations both were waiting to find out whether Moley was bringing any new instructions from the President that would refresh the prospect of accord and achievement. His trip across the Atlantic was being followed as a harbinger of helpful or hurtful turns of decisive import. It is now in order to glance back at how Moley came to set out on this journey — and to travel with him on the S. S. *Manhattan* to London.

CHAPTER 18

The Conference Champs

WHETHER Moley would go to London at some time or other had been left in limbo. For our knowledge of how it came about that he went — and why — we must rely largely on the only account available, that of Moley himself.[1] He has recalled that on the evening of June 16, when the conferees at the White House decided that the proposed declaration about stabilization should be turned down, the President said to him that no one in London "seemed to get his drift" and that he, Moley, ought to go over. Though foreseeing that it might be a "nasty chore," he agreed to do so in the next few days if it became clear that his intercession was necessary.

Despite Louis Howe's protest and Stephen Early's and Marvin McIntyre's doubts, Moley insisted that Herbert Bayard Swope be invited to accompany him to London. The President agreed to ask Swope to do so, though he too had misgivings. For he regarded Swope as an intimate of Thomas Lamont, of J. P. Morgan and Company; in fact, he told Farley that he thought Lamont had an agent on the boat to contact Moley and Swope.[2] Actually the two individuals who had recommended Swope to Moley were Baruch and Frankfurter. He was an ebullient and congenial companion who had learned how effective it was to flatter everyone in high position — whether it be Roosevelt, Moley, Farley or Mills, or the financially powerful such as Lamont or Baruch. His exuberant praise was natural, for Swope had an omnivorous interest in the activities of them all, and an affection for them all.

Between June 16 and June 20 — while the delegation was rocking over Roosevelt's rebuff — Moley wavered between the temptation to go and the fear that his trip would turn out badly. A disorderly troop of thoughts, hopes, ambitions and fears pranced through his mind and spirit.

In deciding to go his judgment may have been lured astray by the conceited belief that he might achieve a triple triumph: serve the President well; straighten out the delegation; switch the conference from the wrong track laid down by the internationalists and get it going along the one which the President and he thought it should travel. But after the last-minute talks with McIntyre and Senator Byrnes, his misgivings returned. They earnestly advised him not to imperil his career by entering an unmanageable situation. Worried and uncertain, he decided to talk with the President and find out whether he wanted him to go; Roosevelt's assurances would be his insurance.

He asked Roosevelt whether he could see him. The President said he could. Thus, early in the morning of June 20, he flew to Nantucket by navy plane. There he boarded a destroyer which carried him to his rendezvous with the President on the *Amberjack*.

He explained to the President his misgivings about going to London. However, "FDR laughed at my fears. Nothing would do but that I should go." [3] So Moley laid aside his doubts and worry over what might happen while he was away and said he would go.

They then discussed what he was to do and say in London. He reminded the President that no answer had yet been made to the latest pleas from Sprague and Warburg. Thereupon the President wrote out in pencil on a scratch pad the message to Hull stating his wish to stand fast of which note has already been taken.

The next turn in the conversation is puzzling. For right after inscribing this denial of the importance of temporary stabilization of currency, Roosevelt seems, in response to Moley's request for instructions, to have reopened the way toward some sort of arrangement for the purpose. He had in mind the possibility of some kind of accord which might calm the gold countries and steady the dollar, provided it did not result in a loss of gold nor check the advance of prices in the United States. Neither Roosevelt nor Moley had — we may surmise — a definite idea as to how this could be contrived.

Any competent technician would have said that if the American government pursued any course of action that would steady the dollar, it must accept a risk (though probably only a small one) of having to lose some gold, and of experiencing a temporary decline in prices as speculative activity waned. But Moley was not a technician. So without compelling the President to think harder about whether, and on what terms, his fancy could be turned into an operative policy, he fell in with the notion that it could be realized. He quotes himself as saying, "If we were ingenious, there was scope for action that would permit our recovery to proceed, but, at the same time, check speculative excesses," and as asking Roosevelt, "Did that represent his beliefs?"; and Roosevelt as answering, "It did," adding, "You know, if nothing else can be worked out, I'd even consider stabilizing at a middle point of $4.15, with a high and low of $4.25 and $4.05. I'm not crazy about it, but think I'd go that far." [4]

Moley told the President that probably he would be receiving other proposals from London while he, Moley, was on the water; he then took out of his pocket a memo written by Swope. It was, Moley explained to the President, background material on stabilization; he might find it helpful in replying to any propositions for a rigid and arbitrary stabilization. "FDR took the memorandum. The whole transaction was over in a minute. I no more dreamed of its ironic consequences," Moley remarked in his subsequent account of this talk, "then de Maupassant's villager forsaw the consequences of picking up the piece of string." [5] What Moley had in mind was that when, two weeks later, Roosevelt rejected the proposal which Moley sponsored, some of Roosevelt's reasons and phraseology were derived from this Swope memorandum.

This was not the only ironic feature of the situation into which Moley had boxed himself. In the press conference he held before leaving for London, having previously secured the nod from Roosevelt, he said that Bernard Baruch would take over his duties during his absence. Did Moley really know what the views of Baruch were on financial and monetary questions? They were epitomized in letters that Baruch had written to H. V. Hiscoe on December 7, 1932; to Senator Pat Harrison of Mississippi, chairman of the Finance Committee, on March 7, 1933; and to Lewis Douglas, the Director of the Budget, shortly after the President had agreed to accept the Thomas amendment. To Hiscoe he had written, "I think there is a difference as wide as the poles between the policy of reducing the gold content of the dollar and the policy of increasing our currency. I am opposed to both." To Senator Harrison he had written, "There is no necessity to go off the gold standard, as the whole world owes us money." To Douglas he had written, "Let us make no mistakes — controlled inflation is sheer nonsense. It always starts that way with good intentions, which have been used for the pavements of Hell." [6] In short Moley had selected a *locum tenens* whose views were quite the opposite of those which the President was soon to adopt.

The agreement made that Moley was to go to London, Roosevelt told him to be sure to impress on the American and foreign delegations that the primary purpose of the American government was to raise the world price level. He was to explain what our domestic program was doing to raise prices — increasing purchasing power and reducing the burden of debt in the United States — and he was to make clear that if other countries strove for the same ends, the American government could cooperate. But if they would not, there was no basis for cooperation. In sum, the American government was not to be restrained by their timidity.

Before leaving the *Amberjack,* Moley told the President that he would like to have his status and assignment made clear. He asked the President to issue a statement about them. This the President wrote out at once. It read: "Assistant Secretary Moley is sailing tomorrow for London at the request of the President. He will act in a sense as a messenger or liaison officer on his short trip, giving the American Delegation first hand information of the various developments, Congressional, etc., in the country since the Delegates left and conveying the President's views of the effect of these developments on the original instructions given the Delegation before they sailed.

"Assistant Secretary Moley will stay in London only about a week and will then return to give the President full information of the Conference up to that time."

Moley, understandably, construed this to mean that he was not to be a member of the delegation or its staff; and also that he was entitled to regard himself as representing the President and was authorized to communicate directly with him. But the President failed to make clear to Hull personally what he expected Moley to do and what his relation with the Secretary was to be. The statement itself later allowed Hull, also understandably, to entertain the opinion (as he did) that Moley thrust himself into the discussions about stabilization, and that he exceeded his authority by entering into negotiations with foreign officials of higher rank — such as the Prime Minister and the Chancellor of the Exchequer of Great Britain and the Ministers of Finance of the gold bloc countries. With less justice the Secretary could also conclude that by sending messages to the President (of which he was kept in ignorance) Moley, at least nominally his subordinate, was transgressing. The Secretary passed by (or over) the fact that Moley had right along worked closely and confidentially with the President and had often gone around or over Hull's head on matters of concern to the State Department, and that he had neither reproved Moley nor objected to the President. The Secretary, as will be seen, brooded and bided his time.

But these reflections have flown ahead of the tale of Moley's journey to London. His departure from New York took place in a blaze of publicity. One common report was that the American delegation in London was in a state of complete confusion and simply marking time. Another was that Moley was carrying new instructions for the delegation; and that, acting on these, he would while in London induce decisions which would enable the conference to make a fresh start. Stories to this effect appeared each day not only in the English and continental presses but in many American newspapers. The artifact which remains most clearly in my memory is not a news report or printed commentary but a cartoon by Herblock in the *Washington News* on June 29. It was entitled: PROF. MOLEY ARRIVES IN LONDON. The artist pictured a crowd gazing with curiosity at a limousine drawn up before the Houses of Parliament. In the foreground a typical English workman is explaining to his typical East End wife, "Oo is 'e? Wy, that's the bloke wot's come 'ere to save the Conference wot came 'ere to save the world!" *

My wife and Edmund Day sailed on the same ship as Moley, Swope and Arthur Mullen, Moley's assistant and son of a prominent Democratic politician. They told me later that this group kept aloof from the other passengers. Moley seemed to them to swagger, and on the boat train to London to be peremptory toward British railway officials.

Baruch kept in touch with Moley and Swope while they were en route. He sent word to them that because prices had risen and the exchange value of the dollar had declined since their departure, he thought there was a possibility of reopening the question of stabilization. Baruch favored joint stabilization measures over those which the individual countries might take, on the score that the British government would then be obligated to maintain the value of the pound and the French government to maintain the value of the franc. "But," Baruch's message ended, ". . . stripped to the naked fact and truth until we make up our minds at which price dollar is to be stabilized to gold nothing can be done except temporizing with situation."

The message the President sent on June 24 telling Phillips to consult with Baruch and Woodin about the possibility of having the Federal Reserve Bank of its own volition take steps to prevent the

* Under-Secretary Phillips mailed this to Secretary Hull, who did not find it funny.

value of the dollar vis-à-vis the pound fluctuating violently below $4.25 was relayed to Moley on shipboard. This may have confirmed the impression which Moley had formed during his talks on the *Amberjack* that it might be possible to reach some kind of loose understanding with other governments which would reassure them and still observe the provisos which the President mentioned.

On this day Acheson, with Roosevelt's approval, asked Sprague, who had remained in London, to delay his return to the United States so that he could talk over with Moley the relative merits of an international agreement on stabilization and a coordinated attempt by individual countries.

As the *Manhattan* neared the shores of Ireland Moley belatedly became disturbed over the high flare of publicity and exaggerated reports of his errand. He and Swope wrote out a statement to be given to the press on his arrival in London. It was a candid effort to moderate expectations about his mission and to dissipate any resentment that Hull and Cox might have at his dramatic appearance on the scene.

This statement began, "The interest manifested in my arrival prompts me to make clear my purpose in coming. My mission is simple. It can best be described in President Roosevelt's own words to the press last Tuesday when giving me his final instructions." Then followed the presidential statement which I have just quoted. Thereafter the statement branched off into general comments on the importance of the task of the conference — praising the resolution which the delegation had placed before the conference.[7]

Moley submitted the text to the President before releasing it. Roosevelt's comment, sent while he was still on the way to Campobello, was relayed through Phillips. It was enigmatic. He said that the statement seemed "fully lucid," but added that he was inclined to think from now on Moley and Swope should give out no further statements or talk with the press because Moley was under the Secretary and not a member of the delegation. The President told Phillips to inform Hull in London of this cautionary message to Moley.

The excitement and speculation about Moley's visit flared up all the higher when he asked our embassy to send a plane to Cobh to meet him so that he might get to London the sooner. An old and none too reliable plane was hastily chartered. Walter Prendergast, a member of the foreign service and a witty bachelor, was asked by Ambassador Robert Bingham to fly to Cobh to meet Moley and accompany him to London on the plane. Prendergast's flight turned out to be arduous and dangerous. The pilot managed to get the plane to Dublin after moments when it looked very doubtful whether they would land anywhere safely. This was the nearest landing field to Cobh, about 170 miles away. Prendergast, sustained by the tradition of the foreign service that its officers must never give up, managed to procure a dilapidated automobile and rode the night through to Cobh, arriving at half past four in the morning. Then he had to scurry over to the waterfront to find a boat out to the *Manhattan,* which was anchored five miles off shore in the bay. The first two small boats in which he started off broke down. The third chugged on until alongside the steamer, just as its crew were hauling up the ladder. But Prendergast did get aboard and immediately scurried about to find Moley. In his hurry, because he was told that the ship was about to sail, he almost knocked down the Lord Mayor of Cobh.

Ambassador Bingham had asked Prendergast to convey his greetings to the newcomer. Prendergast gave Moley the ambassador's message and then told him that the airplane was waiting at Fermoy to take him to London. Moley's only remark was that he had decided not to fly but to remain on the steamer. Whether or not this was due to the receipt of a message from Hull is not known. In this message Hull told Moley that he ought to know that the press "have constantly heralded your coming personally to interfere with and assume more or less the functions and undertakings of the Delegation, in fact that you are to be virtually in charge of the United States interests in London." This, Hull said, was harming the efforts of the delegation. Therefore he suggested that it was advisable for Moley to indicate in his first press statements "definitely the extent, if any, which you personally, under special authorization from Washington, propose to participate in or supervise the Delegation." [8]

In the memorandum which Prendergast made of his exhausting trip, this good-natured foreign service officer noted: "Not a word of thanks for the trouble the Ambassador had been put to to send the plane, and no intimation it was thoughtful to have someone sent over to greet him. I disliked his face from the start . . . but perhaps I am wrong, for certainly he seems to have a great reputation . . . even if most of it had been acquired since last November and his authority made his hat too small. I was presented to Mr. Swope, whom I had once heard deliver a lecture on Mr. Swope at a dinner party in Washington.

"Then just as the steamer was starting, up rushed a tall young man whom I recognized as one of the two people who had so precipitantly run down the pier . . . cursing the Irish telephone service; but I don't quite see what he could expect at 4:30 in the morning in Queenstown. His name is Mullen and he talks out of the side of his mouth."

What a critical observer was Prendergast! And also what a reflective one, for his memorandum which I have quoted ended with these sentences: "I shall be interested to see Mr. M. in action, for he strikes me as a queer sort of fellow. But then, maybe genius should be allowed a lot more rope than we poor mortals. They should be cleverer about hanging themselves."

The voyagers arrived in London about midnight on June 27. They did not stop at Claridge's, preferring to live apart. Before Ambassador Bingham had left Washington he had asked Hull and Moley to be his guests at the embassy during the conference. Hull had sent his regrets on the score that he wanted to live in the same place with the other members of the delegation. Moley had neither accepted nor declined. But just as he was about to sail from New York he had sent a cable to Bingham asking whether he and Mullen might stay at the embassy. Bingham answered that they could. When a few days later Moley radioed from shipboard asking whether Swope might also stay there, Bingham, though annoyed, expanded his invitation.

But the ambassador and his wife almost at once began to regret the presence of those three in the embassy. The ambassador was not well, and he wanted peace and quiet. Moley was a restless and active guest who had official visitors at any time of day or night, used the transatlantic telephone frequently, slept fitfully and bothered the staff in the code room. Swope was dynamic, rowdy and convivial. Mullen was common and swaggering.

But it was Moley who in the end suffered most from his decision to seek quarters at the embassy rather than live at Claridge's. It was another reason why Hull thought that Moley was trying to disassociate himself in the minds of foreign statesmen, and why he suspected Moley of wanting to keep him in ignorance of his activities. Bingham lent a sympathetic ear to Hull's reproaches and complaints against Moley. The ambassador's antipathy became so strong that when Moley left to return to the United States he wrote long letters to Colonel House and to Louis Howe about Moley's demeanor and alleged activities in London. These may well have caused Roosevelt to have less misgivings about excluding him thereafter from his circle of intimate advisers. Of these reports more will be told.

Just before Moley arrived Hull let the President know that Mac-Donald had told him that the governments of France, Belgium, Switzerland and Holland were saying that unless something was done to stabilize the dollar they would be forced to leave the gold standard in the near future and that this would create complete confusion and make the further work of the conference difficult if not impossible. Among other things it would make the temporary tariff truce that was in effect null and void.

The Secretary then went on to remark, "Naturally we [the American delegation] explained that we could not consider any phases of this matter. They said that the present situation was due largely to the depreciation of the dollar. We did not agree." Then after reporting on his efforts to make other delegations understand the American situation he concluded warily, "I am not offering any suggestions pro or con, but simply detailing the chief facts affecting occurrences today. If you desire any suggestions from Sprague,

Warburg or members of the Delegation, kindly advise. Just now this gold standard situation in the countries just mentioned is in fact very acute if representations are reliable and inevitably the effect is to somewhat slow down and confuse our work in the Economic Conference." [9]

This was the deferential technique of hinting rather than leading. But had Hull decided to take a more positive position he might have had a harsh disagreement with three members of his delegation — Pittman, Couzens and Morrison — for it was my impression that they would have preferred to have the conference founder rather than to have the value of the dollar even temporarily stabilized.

On this same day Roosevelt received the comments of his consultants in the United States about the messages from Warburg and Cox.* The group explained why it seemed to them that any action to control fluctuations in the value of the dollar should be done by international agreement rather than merely by attempting through the Federal Reserve Bank to prevent a rise in the value of the dollar. They ventured the opinion that it had become much safer than it had been two weeks ago to consider some form of tripartite arrangement. The last sentence read, "We all feel that some brake upon speculative developments is necessary to anticipate dangerous reaction."

Concordantly, at Acheson's suggestion, Harrison telephoned Sprague in the afternoon (New York time) to tell him that the President was agreeable to having him stay in London long enough to talk with Moley about the various proposals on stabilization. Acheson and Baruch, Harrison said, wanted Sprague "particularly to emphasize the difference between unilateral action by the Federal Reserve Bank and the tripartite proposal which we made in London two weeks ago. I told him [Sprague] we had got a request from the President to consider the possibility of doing something unilaterally as had been suggested in a cable from Warburg, and

* The message was sent to the President by Under-Secretary of the Treasury Acheson, but he stated that the opinions therein were held by Baruch, Harrison and Douglas as well as himself.

that we did not think unilateral action nearly as satisfactory as tripartite action. . . . Sprague had not heard of Warburg's cable . . . and therefore put Warburg on the telephone. . . . Warburg said 'Yes' he agreed but it might be very important to do something in a great hurry. . . . He merely paraphrased the difficulty by saying that 'Philomena is very sick.' I told him I understood what he meant." [10]

But that this advice was against the grain of Roosevelt's inclination is indicated by the message which he sent from the U.S.S. *Ellis* at seven o'clock that night (June 28) to Phillips, asking him to discuss with Acheson, Baruch and others an answer which he had written to Hull's report, and if there was no serious disagreement to send it on as early as possible to the delegation. This read: "I fully appreciate the importance of staying on gold by France, Holland and Switzerland, but I think this importance is distinctly debatable from the point of view of an ultimate permanent settlement. For example, if France goes off gold it will be very difficult for her to finance a continuing deficit and this will result in realistic efforts to balance her budget. It is also questionable whether under any circumstances they will find it advisable or possible to stay on gold. I do not greatly fear a bad setback to our domestic price level restoration even if all these nations go off gold.

"But the most important fact is that our London Delegation is absolutely right in distinguishing between government action at Conference and private action by central banks. The United States must continue to make this distinction clear and that the Treasury Department cannot participate in the exercise of any form of tripartite action.

"In view of all the circumstances at this time I suggest that special care be taken by Delegation and Moley and those close to it to insure no publicity of any kind except through Secretary Hull. Please read this to all concerned." [11]

Had the President's observations been sent on to London at once they might have alerted Moley in time to stop him from enmeshing himself in the talks about stabilization. But they were not. Two hours after they were radioed from the U.S.S. *Ellis* Phillips sent on to Roosevelt a variant statement of advice by his group as to how to respond to Hull's worried report. It said, in substance, that it seemed to them likely that unless some action were taken promptly the countries now on gold would have to devalue, and if they did the relative value of the dollar might rise abruptly — to our detriment. In view of that possibility and Hull's report on the situation of the conference, they thought it advisable (1) to restrict outflow of capital from the United States and tell the British authorities we expected them to take similar measures to prevent speculation on he exchanges; (2) "to re-open consideration of the temporary and flexible tripartite arrangement recently proposed in London on the basis of the present market level." [12]

Before the President replied to this Acheson sent him word that Sprague and Moley were working on a new proposal, which was expected to arrive the next day, June 30, for submission to the President. "In view of these messages," Acheson concluded, "it seemed best to us to withhold your proposed cable to the Delegation and await messages from Sprague and Moley." [13] The President held his hand and his pencil, thereby greasing the slope of coincidence down which Moley was already skidding.

CHAPTER 19

The Conference Gasps

SEVERAL turns of circumstance combined to impel Moley so hastily to stalk into the situation. During this, his first day in London, the dollar declined to about 77 cents of its former gold value and the value of the pound rose to about $4.40. Moley remembered that on the *Amberjack* the President had said he would be willing to consider stabilization within a range of $4.15 to $4.25 to the pound. That he was still so inclined seemed signalized by the message which had been relayed to Moley on the S.S. *Manhattan,* wherein Roosevelt had asked Woodin and Baruch whether it might not be advisable to have the Federal Reserve System take steps to prevent the pound from fluctuating violently above $4.25. Now it was doing so, and the dollar was getting relatively cheaper.

On the morning of his arrival Moley talked with John Maynard Keynes and Walter Lippmann about the possibility of persuading other countries to adopt an international currency unit — the *dinard* — the value of which would be stabilized in terms of many commodities, not merely gold. None of them knew how this could be done; but Moley learned that Keynes and Lippmann favored general devaluation of currencies, including the dollar.

At noon Hull complained to Moley about the way in which the

press had featured him as the savior of the situation. Moley defended himself, averring that his coming was in accord with their previous understanding and his only purposes were those which he had described publicly before leaving New York and on his arrival at Plymouth. This did not turn out to be strictly so, for he was about to engage in talks about currency fluctuations as presidential representative — possibly feeling freer to do so because in this talk Hull professed to have no authority to deal with this issue which was stalling the conference.[1]

In any case, early the next morning (June 29) Moley learned that the gold countries had drawn up a short declaration and had asked MacDonald to join in signing it; and that MacDonald had indicated he was willing to do so if the American government also would. It had been arranged that Neville Chamberlain and Leith-Ross meet with representatives of the gold countries at eleven o'clock that morning, and Sprague, Cox and Warburg had been asked to be present. Moley, of his own volition, thereupon decided that he should find out what was going on.

Having been delayed at the embassy, Moley asked Bullitt to tell Hull before the delegation met that he thought it advisable that further discussions of foreign exchange should be conducted by himself and Sprague, and that Warburg and Cox should drop out of them. He would be obliged if Hull made a statement to this effect to the delegation. He, Moley, would follow it up.[2]

In his subsequent account, Moley has given diverse reasons for his decision to take the question in his own hands. Cox was without authority to deal with the subject. Messages sent by Cox or Warburg would probably be seen by all members of the delegation and leak out. In this surmise Moley may have been correct; at least one member of the delegation and possibly two were thought to be talking to intermediaries in New York and passing inside information to them; they were speculating in stocks, cotton and silver.* More-

* When we returned to Washington, Moley told me that he knew that one member whom he named had been telephoning across the Atlantic to someone named Jackson, keeping him informed of the discussion about the rate of stabilization under consideration, and that Jackson was passing on this information to a banking or brokerage company.

over, had not he, and he alone, last minute instructions on the subject of stabilization to impart and a way of communicating directly with Roosevelt through the embassy? *

Moley breezed into the torpid meeting of the delegation at Claridge's about ten o'clock. When those of us concerned with trade and tariffs reported that we were not able to make any progress because other countries would not assent to even vague generalities until they knew whether uncertainties in monetary matters were going to be ended, Hull spoke up. He said that from now on, with his approval, Moley would join with Sprague in the conduct of the talks about stabilization. While he expected Cox and Warburg to inform Moley of what had been done and said up to then, they would thereafter have nothing further to do with the talks; Moley remembers him adding — and if he did, it was with sly irony which Moley did not appreciate — "that while he himself, as a member of the Delegation and as Secretary of State, had no authority to touch the negotiations into which I was stepping, he could authorize me to call on anyone in the Delegation or subject to its direction for assistance.³

But seemingly Moley had a last-minute gust of hesitation about engaging personally in the negotiations. He wondered whether it might not be wiser to let Sprague attend the meeting and to himself remain aloof as liaison with the President. However, as soon as the delegation meeting broke up, Warburg went to the Conference Hall. No sooner had he entered the building than the British, French and Dutch representatives told him that the question of issuance of the declaration about stabilization must be settled before the conference could do anything. They seemed to think that Secretary Hull was coming to the conference that morning and were waiting for him to join them. Warburg thereupon rushed back to Claridge's and got Moley, Cox and Sprague into Hull's office. Hull flatly refused to go down to the Conference Hall and thereby allow himself to be dragged into the discussion on stabilization. Warburg said he had no wish to take part in these discussions, but that the

* Moley's wish to exclude Warburg may have been also due to personal animosity and mistrust. They had a nasty row.

American authorities simply could not at this stage merely back out. When the others asked Moley whether or not he would be willing to talk informally with just two or three of the conferees whom he had met in Washington and whom he liked, he said he would be glad to see Leith-Ross, Jung of Italy, and Rist of France. But he would not, he said, go down to the Conference Hall, since that would arouse still more excited speculation. It was agreed that Warburg should telephone these foreign officials and ask them to come to Claridge's to talk with Moley and Sprague.

They were soon on their way, Moley remembers their talk as being brief but pleasant. He explained to his callers, according to his subsequent account, that he was merely acting as a conduit, an intermediary who was willing to transmit for consideration any suggestions their group might have. He quotes Leith-Ross as saying bluntly, "You will accept the declaration *ad referendum*," and himself answering, "Precisely. I will take it for transmission to the President — for *his* consideration. My transmission of it implies neither my advocacy nor my approval of it." [4] Thereupon the emissaries left, and Moley returned to the embassy.

Then, still according to his account, much to his surprise Neville Chamberlain appeared at the embassy along with Leith-Ross. Chamberlain told Moley that he thought that, as further toned down that morning in a meeting between British and gold bloc officials, the declaration could not possibly be construed as imposing even a moral obligation on any steps the President might take to raise prices by monetary action. While he thought it completely harmless, Chamberlain said, the authorities of the gold bloc countries believed it would end the fears which were causing their people to hoard gold and to send it out of the country. So he had come to plead for the cooperation of Roosevelt, the one person in the world who could quiet the panic in the gold countries and enable the conference to progress; to plead not for the sake of Great Britain but for France, Holland, Switzerland, Italy and others.

Moley, in his published explanation of what he did, recalled that he took the revised declaration Chamberlain gave him and then read it carefully. "Chamberlain was quite right. The declaration would commit Roosevelt to absolutely nothing except to ask the Federal Reserve to cooperate in limiting fluctuating due to speculation. . . . *It did not mean stabilization.*" [5] Still Moley suggested some minor changes of phraseology further devitalizing the document. That afternoon Warburg resumed work with Leith-Ross over the text of the declaration.

When, after Moley had left London, Hull reproached MacDonald for having discussed this proposed agreement about currencies with Moley, the Prime Minister denied that he ever had. He asked Maurice Hankey to show Hull the daily record of his activities in verification of this denial.*

The Prime Minister may have been quibbling. He may have felt the denial to be literally correct since the text of the declaration had been completed by others before he saw it and talked to Moley about it.

Moley, in his account of his talks with the Prime Minister, has definitely averred that MacDonald took the initiative. Chamberlain had told him that MacDonald would like to have him call at five o'clock that afternoon (June 29) at 10 Downing Street. This unusual invitation, extended by the Prime Minister without first consulting Hull, may (here I am resorting to conjecture) have been due to one or both of two reasons: that Hull had refused to discuss stabilization; that Sir Ronald Lindsay's reports to London caused MacDonald and Chamberlain to conclude that only Moley had direct authority to speak for the President on this subject. Moreover, Moley states that he took pains to observe the proprieties: before accepting the invitation he told Hull of all that had happened since that morning and asked Hull if he had any objection to his going to see MacDonald; Hull said he had none.[6]

Thus it came about that at five o'clock Moley was in the Prime

* Stimson in his diary for July 14 tells of meeting with MacDonald in the Geological Museum and that "the Prime Minister had told him that Hull had suspected him, MacDonald, of entering into these gold bloc negotiations with Moley and on this morning, July 14th, the Prime Minister had been having it out with Hull on the subject and had made up a record showing that the Prime Minister had had no connection with the negotiations."

Minister's study in the official residence. Moley thought MacDonald was much more emotional and vivid in his description of the situation in the gold countries than was Chamberlain. The Prime Minister recalled that their people had undergone the ordeal of rampant inflation after the end of the First World War and were exceedingly frightened that it might happen again as a result of American monetary policy. If it did, MacDonald feared, it might even produce revolution in these countries. In sum he thought it essential, politically and socially, that some "simulacrum of general agreement on immediate currency objectives" be reached. Would Moley not therefore tell Roosevelt, "in God's name, that acceptance of the declaration would not only save the Conference from possible wreck but repel the panic that held Europe in grip?" Moley answered that he would gladly transmit the declaration to the President.[7]

He then returned to the embassy, where Sprague and Swope were waiting for him. Sprague hurried off a message to Woodin; and Moley hurried one off to Woodin and Baruch. He also notified Acheson who was in Washington and asked the group to meet the next morning at Woodin's house in New York. He would telephone them there at eleven o'clock (New York time) so they might discuss the declaration.* That night Moley and Swope were in good spirits.

Sprague, in his message, said once again that those countries still on the gold standard were becoming more clamorous because the rumors regarding possible general devaluation of all currencies were endangering their situation. Then after describing the nature

---

* Sprague's message was sent at 2 A.M. (London time), June 30, and received in Washington about 11 P.M., June 29. Moley's message was sent and received an hour later. Both messages were relayed to the President in the morning of June 30 (Washington time). They are in *Foreign Relations of the United States* — 1933, Vol. I — General, pp. 664-666.

In the afternoon of that day Acheson informed Roosevelt of several changes in the text of the statement which Moley had conveyed over the telephone. These made explicit that countries *not* on the gold standard would remain free to determine gold values for their currencies and decide for themselves what measures they deemed most appropriate to limit exchange speculation.

of the statement — the one directed toward checking speculation that had been drawn up by British officials in consultation with those of countries on the gold standard — he ventured the opinion that it would be wise for the American government to endorse it as a helpful gesture. The government might discharge its obligation by having the Federal Reserve Bank of New York begin making any small sales of gold that might be necessary in order to maintain roughly the current dollar-sterling rate.

In the separate message which Moley sent off about an hour later, he said that he favored the proposals which Sprague was presenting. And he reported that he and Sprague had tentatively agreed with British representatives upon a statement to be approved by the President and to be made by Great Britain and the United States on the one hand and the gold standard countries on the other. He then went on to quote the statement.

In the concluding passage of his message, however, Moley seemed to qualify his recommendation by saying, "You are the best judge of whether the American situation will be favorably or adversely affected, thereby taking into consideration the always [present] danger that even such a temporary project if known might be regarded as the beginning of permanent stabilization."

On one other count this message was destined later on to become part of the bill of recrimination against Moley. He sent it through the embassy code room and asked Woodin and Baruch to reply directly to him in care of the American embassy, not through the delegation.

After the meeting of the delegation Warburg and Moley went to Cox's room. They asked Rist and Jung to join them. After an hour's discussion they ironed out two passages in the text of the declaration with mutual satisfaction. Then Warburg, again active as an intermediary, went down to the Conference Hall. There he asked Leith-Ross to step out of the meeting in the Prime Minister's room and told him what had been done. He thought everyone was delighted — including MacDonald. When he talked to the Prime Minister alone a little later, MacDonald expressed his appreciation and remarked that he hoped that Moley would secure the necessary authorization from Washington to approve the declaration quickly, since at 3:30 that afternoon Chamberlain, Bonnet and Jung were going to see Moley to learn the answer.

The foreign officials and the trio of American negotiators were all in for a longer wait than they expected.

The morning of the same day — June 30 — in New York, Baruch, Acheson and Harrison met with Woodin at his house. Acheson remembers it as the most scary conference he ever attended. The Secretary of the Treasury was lying abed, very ill. The other three perched on the edge of the bed or sat in chairs drawn close up. Hardly had their discussion begun when the first of two telephone calls Moley made from London that day came in. Sprague talked first. While he was explaining the declaration to Baruch, who although hard of hearing was in turn trying to explain it to Woodin, the Secretary fainted. His face, pallid even when he was well, turned as white as a shroud; his eyes shut and his head slipped off his pillows. All jumped up from their seats, alarmed, fearing that he had died.

The telephone conversation with Sprague and Moley was briefly interrupted and the doctor summoned. As soon as Woodin came to, it was resumed. Harrison took over the phone because his voice carried best. Moley then learned to his dismay that the group in New York had not yet received the text of the declaration which had been sent from London hours and hours before. So Moley read it to them. They said that just as soon as they had a chance to form an opinion of it, they would send it to the President and would let Moley know when they heard from him.

The President by then had sailed into Campobello on the *Amberjack*. There shortly after his arrival Henry Morgenthau, Jr., had joined him. Sensing that the foreign officials with whom Moley had been collaborating were on pins and needles, Acheson tried to get in touch with the President by telephone. Failing to do so (there was no phone connection to Campobello), he talked with Steve Early, who went over to the mainland to take the call; but before he could give Early the views of the group about the declaration, a violent thunder and lightning storm broke and the line went dead. Acheson therefore hurried off a telegram to the President in the name of Woodin and Baruch as well as himself.

"After talking with Moley and Sprague and discussing the proposed joint declaration among ourselves," began the message, "we feel that the situation in Europe is so delicate and the further continuation of the Conference so precarious that we should take a sympathetic attitude toward the proposed declaration." Moreover, they thought the declaration to be in accord with the resolution that had been introduced to the conference by our delegation and with the President's letter to chiefs of state of May 16. However, they added — and this was probably a blunder — if its issuance should cause the value of the dollar to rise they did not think that would be harmful as of the moment, and it would be easy for the government to check such an upward movement if it became too pronounced. Thus they recommended that "you give your approval to the declaration and suggest that you advise the American representatives to add that, should the declaration have an unintended effect and produce any undue movement in any exchange, it may be necessary to ask the central banks to cooperate, not only in the measures referred to [in one paragraph of the declaration] but to take other cooperative steps, possibly including permitting export of limited amounts of gold." [8]

Early also got word to McIntyre for the President, telling him that Moley had telephoned again and said that every moment was vital, that the fate of the conference hung in the balance.

The messages were received by the President in the late afternoon. By then he also had on his desk copies of those Sprague and Moley had sent and of the text of the proposed declaration.*

* The text of the declaration which Roosevelt had before him when he wrote his reply began by recording that the signatory governments agreed that "stability in the international monetary field be attained as quickly as possible" and that "Gold exchange be re-established as the international measure of exchange value, it being recognized that the parity and time at which each of the countries now off gold undertake to stabilize must be decided by the respective governments concerned."
The governments whose currencies were on the gold standard reasserted

That evening the President and Mrs. Roosevelt, Morgenthau and Howe sat around and talked for several hours about foreign exchange, gold and world exports. Morgenthau brought out charts based on relationships between the three which Professor George Warren of Cornell had developed. He also summarized for the President an article in the *Saturday Evening Post* by Garet Garrett, a talented but tricky journalist.[9] Its oversimplified contentions may be indicated by two brief excerpts. "Does foreign trade promote prosperity, or is it the prosperity of individual nations that produce foreign trade? If it is the latter way — if it is the prosperity of individual nations that produces foreign trade — then obviously the first problem in a state of world-wide depression is not how to reinflate foreign trade; the first problem is that of mending the internal economy of nations, each one to find out how it shall balance its own budget, re-employ its own people, restore its own solvency." And, "the war of currencies . . . is not a competitive debasement of money in the world of foreign trade; it is a money war among nations, carried on by governments." Roosevelt listened attentively.

Either before or after this seance — the records do not make

---

their determination to maintain that standard at the parities which existed at that time.

The governments not on the gold standard reaffirmed that their ultimate objective was to restore, under proper conditions, their international monetary standard based on gold.

The two concluding paragraphs contained obligations against which Roosevelt rebelled:

"(4) Each of the governments whose currencies are not on the gold standard undertake to adopt the measures which they deem most appropriate to limit exchange speculation, and each of the other signatory governments undertakes to co-operate to the same end.

"(5) Each of the undersigned governments agrees to ask its central bank to co-operate with the central banks of the other signatory governments in remedying speculation in the exchanges and, when the time comes, in establishing a general international gold standard."

In the final text, which the President did not receive until after he had sent his answer, the phrase "in limiting speculation" was substituted for "in remedying speculation" in paragraph 5.

The texts are in *Foreign Relations of the United States* — 1933, Vol. I — General, pp. 665 and 667.

clear — the President sent a telephone message to Acting Secretary of State Phillips, instructing him to inform Hull that he would send an answer to the two messages from Moley and Sprague "just as soon as possible." Meanwhile he asked that the delegation be told to refrain from any action or comment. That this terse notice was addressed to Hull, not Moley, was significant. Might the President have been influenced by the fact that his wife had said to him earnestly that it seemed to her to have been a mistake to send Moley to London, since it was belittling to Hull, and Moley's presence must weaken Hull's position? [10]

In London noon had come and gone by. Still the awaited reply from the President could not be conjured out of the code machine. Moley called MacDonald and asked him to tell the various negotiators not to meet at the embassy that afternoon, as arranged, since he had not yet heard anything. But they came anyway, and were joined by Senators Pittman and Couzens, who had lingered after lunch. The occasion was used to compare the English and French versions, since Moley thought some phrases in the French version had been twisted slightly, enough possibly to justify an interpretation of the declaration as a firm pledge to stabilization. Despite Jung's laments Moley insisted on changes of language that would make such an interpretation untenable. Moley hastened to send this final revised text to the President.

Still without word, but still confident that when word came it would be favorable, the meeting was set forward until ten o'clock that night. In Moley's later account he avers that he urged Hull to meet these high-ranking officers and inform them of the President's decision — out of deference and to enable Hull to get the acclaim. The Secretary, Moley wrote, agreed to attend. [11] But this, in his own memoirs, Hull flatly contradicts. He states that Moley urged him very strongly to go, on the score that his presence would make it manifest that the American government attached genuine importance to the declaration, and that this would improve the prospects of the conference. "I," he relates, "quickly and bluntly declined to go and stated that as a Delegate to the Conference I had nothing to do with the stabilization question. He pleaded with me, but I choked off further attempts at conversation." [12]

What historian could or should refrain from surmises about these two conflicting stories? One that attracts me is that Hull may have intimated earlier that he might attend this meeting and changed his mind on thinking it over.

Fretting even more anxiously, Moley and Swope at eight o'clock in the evening telephoned to New York again. Moley relates that he explained once more to the group that he had only accepted the declaration subject to approval by the President and without expressing any personal opinion on it. However, in response to queries put to him, he said that he did not think the declaration could be by any stretch of the imagination construed "as even a remote approach to stabilization." At most it could check only the ultraspeculative element in the revival of prices and business. However, it would suffice, he thought, to avert the threatening breakup of the conference.

The consultants told Moley that they had urged the President to accept the declaration. Baruch said that he, Woodin, Acheson and Harrison all heartily agreed with him. They were greatly impressed because Pittman and Couzens favored it. Moley remembered that "the conversation ended with the congratulations of Woodin, Acheson and Baruch on what they called our 'victory.' " [13]

But still Moley was without word from the President. So the scheduled ten o'clock meeting had to be called off. When Moley so informed Bonnet he shrugged his thin shoulders, ran his fingers over his damp forelock, put on his hat and coat and rushed to catch the night train to Paris. On being told of the postponement, the Secretary was noncommittal.

Moley and Swope, at the embassy, gradually succumbed to apprehension as they sat smoking cigarette after cigarette almost until dawn. Their fears of an adverse answer were quickened not only by the delay but also by the fact that Hull, in the several telephone talks which Moley had had with him, showed signs of a wish to disassociate himself from Moley's action by reminders that he had no real responsibility for what Moley had been doing. The anxiety of these presidential emissaries turned out to be well grounded.

Before he went to bed late that night the President wrote his reply, addressing it to Hull.[14] He flatly rejected the joint declaration. After some dubious and jumbled comments on some of its details — indicating haste in composition — Roosevelt said that he could not assent to any accord that might morally obligate our government now or later to approve the export of gold from the United States.

In the main paragraphs concluding the message the President in effect dismissed the whole effort to reach even a quickly terminable accord about the relative value of the dollar and other currencies — an effort which he had allowed to proceed so far. "At this time," he averred, "any fixed formula of stabilization by agreement must necessarily be artificial and speculative. It would be particularly unwise from political and psychological standpoints to permit limitation of our action to be imposed by any other nation than our own. A sufficient interval should be allowed the United States to permit in addition to the plan [play] of economic forces a demonstration of the value of price lifting efforts which we have well in hand. These successful forces will be beneficial to other nations if they join with us toward the same end.

"It would be well to reiterate the fact that England left the gold standard nearly two years ago and only now is seeking stabilization. Also that France did not stabilize for three years or more. If France seeks to break up the Conference just because we decline to accept her dictum we should take the sound position that the Economic Conference was initiated and called to discuss and agree on permanent solutions of world economics and not to discuss the domestic economic policy of one nation out of the 66 present. When the Conference was called, its necessity was obvious although the problem of stabilization of the American dollar was not even in existence." [15]

Apropos of this exposition of the President's reasons for rejecting the proposal, it may be remembered that Roosevelt had — until the dollar went off gold — favored the conference because it would afford an opportunity to persuade or induce the British government to stabilize the value of sterling vis-à-vis the dollar.

But the fact that Roosevelt's aim had changed in the interval should not blur the essential questions posed by the message to the historian in his self-appointed role as judge. These are: (1) Was Roosevelt's interpretation of the meaning of the declaration correct? (2) Would acceptance of the declaration seriously have impeded or menaced the program of domestic action to raise prices and incomes which Roosevelt was determined to carry out? (3) If he had accepted it, would the outflow of gold from the United States have been so great as to compel him to choose between abandoning his program and denouncing the agreement?

Roosevelt's interpretation of the declaration was a guarded and anticipatory one. Its provisions would not have obligated him to refrain from taking any measures he decided upon in order to raise prices, except one of those authorized by the Thomas amendment — deliberate reduction of the gold content of the dollar — which could have been properly regarded as an incitement to speculation. He could have gone forward with all other elements of his domestic program, including the contemplated expansion of the currency and credit, without exposing himself to just accusations that he was acting contrary to the engagements accepted.* But should he engage in the deliberate policy of lowering the exchange value of the dollar, foreign governments would certainly have protested and accused as of bad faith. Since by this time the President's mind had probably been smitten by the idea of resorting to this means of increasing prices, in whatever measure might be deemed necessary or serviceable, he was right in concluding that if he

---

* But of course the declaration did not, and could not, have prevented the French and other governments that were still on the gold standard from averring, if these measures were taken, that the American government was breaking its pledge. There probably would have been ample leeway within the current parities for as large a rise in prices and money income in the United States as occurred during the next few years. The pinch would have come only after World War II; then a second devaluation of the dollar might have been necessary.

joined in the declaration he either would have to renounce this intention or brave a storm of reproach.

The third question is hardest to answer. The United States still had large amounts of gold, far more than it needed as reserve for its currency obligations. It could have spared a half-billion dollars or more without fear of defaulting on them. But it is doubtful whether by doing so it would have restored confidence in the value of the dollar and reassured investors and industrialists sufficiently to revive the economy. It is more likely that the drain upon our gold reserves would have caused the alarm about the future of our currency to flare higher, and that speculation against the dollar would have fed upon itself. For irrationally, most people (including many financiers and businessmen) continued to identify gold with security, with national wealth and stability. Perhaps the President did not, but he regarded our gold supply as one of the chief means of protecting the United States against the accidents of fortune and the wiles of other nations.

But these conjectures are an indulgent foray into the hard-to-predict consequences of a decision contrary to the one Roosevelt made. They may be left for all eternity in the interesting company of other speculations about what never happened.

Moley, at the embassy, was called to the telephone, soon after it was light. A clerk in the code room of the delegation told him of the short message which had been relayed through Phillips in Washington the evening before; this was the one in which the President said that he would answer the messages from Moley and Sprague "just as soon as possible," and gave orders that until his reply was received the delegation was not to say or do anything.

Moley correctly sensed this to be ominous as well as puzzling. Why, the question must have occurred to him, was the President communicating with him through Phillips and Hull rather than through Woodin or Baruch? On edge, Moley decided to try to get in direct touch with the President. In the message he sent this morning, Moley, after referring to his phone talk with Woodin, Baruch and Acheson, reiterated the reasons why he thought the declaration conformed with Roosevelt's instructions and would not interfere with his objectives. "[I] really believe," he said in conclusion, "success, even continuation of the Conference depends upon United States agreement." [16] Swope hurried off a message of similar import to Woodin and Baruch.

This urgent recommendation from Moley was received in Washington about seven o'clock in the morning on July 1 and relayed at once to the President on the U.S.S. *Indianapolis*. In all likelihood it would not have affected the President's response in any case, but Roosevelt had dispatched his negative answer before he read it.

After breakfast Moley went over to Claridge's. There he met Hull on the staircase, designed to enable earls and their ladies to make impressive descents. He too must have been on edge. For no sooner had Moley greeted him than the Secretary said he understood that the belief that Moley was going to supplant him in office — an office for which he had given up a life-long seat in the Senate — was still alive. Then, in effect, he accused Moley of subjecting him to constant humiliation. What must have been in his mind was the fact that Moley had engaged himself to meet with the Prime Minister of Britain and other high foreign dignitaries without seeking his explicit permission or consent. The crow had flown over the hawk's nest in his sensitized sight. Moley tried to soothe him and convince Hull that he had done his utmost to defer to the dignity of his office.

Was the Secretary's outburst, after his former acquiescence in Moley's activities, a sign of his prescience that Moley was about to be put down? That it might have been is suggested by the fact that at the meeting of the delegation that morning Charles Michaelson, the chief officer for press relations, complained that he knew nothing of the talks about currency matters and that the newspapermen had been going to Swope for information. Hull joined in, saying that he himself had known nothing of them until about five o'clock the previous day — a statement which Moley has disputed. Then, in the course of this same afternoon of strain and waiting, the assistant press officer of the delegation, Elliott Thurston, repeated

Hull's disavowal to the press. The Secretary was evidently beginning to conclude that Governor Cox's soothing advice to him was about to prove good: ". . . merely be patient and await Moley's disappointment sure to come. We knew what Moley was about and as I put it to the Secretary, 'He will have the trap door sprung on him just as it was on you.' " [17]

Moley returned to the embassy, hoping to find there the President's answer, which was still en route. Finding none, he chased back to Claridge's and resumed his patrol in the code room of the delegation.

Meanwhile, the Secretary of State and Mrs. Hull were getting ready to leave for a weekend with the Astors at Cliveden. So were Warburg and Bullitt. So was Pittman — but when Hull saw the Senator staggering about he sent word that he had better not go. The Senator went anyhow.

The several versions in print of what happened just as the Hulls were about to leave for Cliveden differ in their precision and intensity. Moley, in his subsequent account, wrote merely: "The message from the President was coming through. I rushed out to find Hull. He was on his way out of the hotel. He received the news coldly. He would go to Cliveden anyhow, and I could have his secretary bring him the message when it was ready." [18]

Hull's memory of the brusque encounter was: "At that moment I was starting for Cliveden. As I walked to the head of the stairs leading out of the hotel, Moley rushed down to meet me and said, 'There's a cable coming in from Washington and it is unfavorable to stabilization. We have just got to do something about it.' I then turned on him. I saw that he had reached the end of his rope and was through. I proceeded to talk to him. I started in by saying, 'You had better get back home. You had no business over here in the first place.' I elaborated along these lines. I then walked to my car to spend the week end in the country. . . ." [19]

Whatever the Secretary's exact words were, his meaning was unmistakable. For after Hull drove off, Moley told Hugh Cumming, Hull's secretary, that he had just had a most upsetting conversation. The Secretary, he claimed, misunderstood his motives. The idea that he, Moley, wanted to be Secretary of State was nonsense. Had he not urged Roosevelt to appoint Hull? The criticisms of his actions were unfair! Had it not been understood by everyone, from the beginning, that the title of Assistant Secretary of State was simply "a peg to hang his hat on?" The notion that he, Moley, had sought publicity for his mission to London was wrong. Was he not actually still unused to the sight of his name in print and did he not shrink from it? * [20]

At Cliveden, Lady Astor by her vivacity drew together the eminent British guests and the American visitors. But during a pause in the jovial talk Secretary Hull told Robert Brand, a distinguished banker who was married to Lady Astor's charming sister Phyllis, that the President had rejected the declaration, and after dinner Brand passed the news on to Warburg.

If Hull was deeply disturbed at the threat of the conference, he did not show it that night. Having tried so sorely already he may well have slipped into a mood of resignation — relieved possibly by the thought that in any event he could not be blamed for the failure. Warburg and Bullitt, those two sardonic observers who had been through the same turnstile as Moley, retired that night to the cottage assigned to them in the grounds of Cliveden and there "laughed a great deal at the predicament we are now in. Why on earth the President should turn down this innocuous Declaration completely baffles both of us, and the funniest part of it is that Moley, who is supposed to have been the anti-stabilization man, is now put in the same position as the rest of us." [21]

Despite Hull's harsh reproofs, Moley followed his advice not to broadcast in haste or anger the actual text of Roosevelt's message. The press was tersely informed by Michaelson that the President had rejected the declaration as written and that the Secretary of State would give out a statement of American policy on Monday,

---

* Apropos of Hull's suspicion that Moley wanted his job, among Hull's papers in the Library of Congress is an anonymous note lettered in pencil on a piece of brown wrapping paper which reads, "Look out for Moley. He wants your job!" It is signed, "A Columbia Professor."

July 3. While the Secretary was dining at Cliveden, Moley hurried off a message to the President in which he said, "I bow to your superior judgment with no inconsiderable relief."

Moley and Swope enlisted Walter Lippmann's aid in composing the statement. They strove to expound the President's ideas convincingly without exposing what they thought to be the faults of interpretation or judgment. That they found this hard to do will not be surprising to any reader of the message, for as I have remarked sections of it were incoherent and tangential to the actual proposal presented by Moley. Partly in the hope of obtaining clarification, partly for consolation, Moley telephoned Baruch, who said that he and Woodin and Acheson were also taken aback. But Baruch gave Moley and Swope a bit of information which they found illuminating. It was that Louis Howe and Henry Morgenthau, Jr., were with the President on the *Indianapolis*. Morgenthau, whose interest at this time centered first of all on the prices of farm products and the plight of the overmortgaged farmers, had obtained his rudimentary knowledge of monetary affairs from Professor Warren.* Howe disliked Moley and resented his constant association with Roosevelt, and Moley thought he would be concerned first and foremost about any transient adverse speculative reaction to the declaration. "It was," Moley later wrote, "all that we needed to know. Now the picture began to make sense." [22]

Had Moley and Swope known that Henry Morgenthau, Sr., was writing his son from London that the situation was hopeless, they would have been even more sure that this combined influence swayed Roosevelt at this juncture.[23]

Before Moley, Swope and Lippmann completed the statement

* Years later Mrs. Morgenthau was reviewing their experience in office with an inquiring publicist who remembers her relating that both Roosevelt and Morgenthau, the neighbors on the Hudson, were interested in tree planting. For help they turned to the staff of the School of Agriculture of Cornell University. In the course of their consultations Morgenthau had been introduced to two economists who were especially concerned with the welfare of the farmers, Warren and Pearson, and Morgenthau had introduced Warren to Roosevelt. Mrs. Morgenthau reflectively commented, "How different life would have been had Franklin and Henry not met those arboreal experts."

much of that Saturday night was spent. It was a competent attempt to explain, defend and tame Roosevelt's decision — but destined to wind up in the files, not the press.

Warburg, who had hustled back from Cliveden, was also trying to rationalize Roosevelt's decision. The next morning, while he was working at his task, Moley went to 10 Downing Street; he has related that MacDonald had telephoned him from Chequers and said that, as presiding officer of the conference, he must talk to him as soon as possible and would start for London at once. Moley found MacDonald greatly agitated. He said that he despaired of the fate of the conference. He asked Moley whether he thought there was any chance that the President might accept some other form of declaration that would satisfy the gold countries. All that Moley could answer was that the President did not want the conference to end dismally and that there was no reason why he, Moley, could not transmit to the President any new proposals. Before leaving Moley asked MacDonald to make it clear to Hull that their meeting had been at the Prime Minister's initiative. MacDonald promised to do so — and Moley recalls that the Prime Minister went on to explain that he had sought him out since he found it so hard to understand the wishes of the delegation.[24]

From 10 Downing Street Moley returned to the embassy. There he was told by Thurston that the Secretary was becoming more and more upset at the prospective impact on the conference of the President's rejection of the declaration, and that his anxiety was "expressing itself in a dirge of accusations against me." [25]

Moley called on Hull — who had returned from Cliveden right after luncheon on Sunday — and again tried to clear away Hull's suspicions and ill feeling. Apparently he thought he had; Pittman, who was present, reassured him that he had.

At the meeting of the delegation later that afternoon (July 2) the Moley-Swope-Lippmann explanation of the President's decision was approved. Hull transmitted it to Roosevelt, stating that he proposed to issue it the next afternoon in his capacity of Secretary of State rather than as chairman of the American delegation to the conference. Before midnight (in London) word was received that the President thought the statement excellent and that it would *supplement* one he had dispatched to Hull some hours before. He sent his congratulations to Hull "on the clear and dignified position you are taking . . . and my warm regards." [26] In the outcome Hull's statement was never issued because it was superseded by Roosevelt's own. This was more dismissive and challenging than the earlier one in which he had rejected the declaration.

Howe, either on his own initiative or at the President's request, had written a draft explaining why the American government felt impelled to reject the declaration. Roosevelt had not thought it satisfactory, so he had written out one by hand. This he had read to Morgenthau and Howe, who praised it. It had been sent to the radio room on shipboard for immediate dispatch. Morgenthau asked him for the original draft, but Franklin Roosevelt, Jr., got it.[27]

This message to Hull was received in London at eight o'clock that night. "Herewith," the President began, "is a statement which I think you can use Monday morning (July 3) as a message from me to you. If you think it best not to give it out in London let me know at once and in that event I will release it as a White House statement."

Because of its detonating effect it became known as the "bombshell." With scathing words it dismissed the whole idea that it was necessary or advisable to stabilize the relative value of currencies even for the duration of the conference. Its opening sentence (which was taken over from Howe's draft) read, "I would regard it as a catastrophe, amounting to a world tragedy, if the great Conference of Nations called to bring about a more real and permanent financial stability and a greater prosperity to the masses of all nations should, in advance of any serious effort to consider these broader problems, allow itself to be diverted by the proposal of a purely artificial and temporary experiment affecting the monetary exchange of a few nations only."

Other excerpts indicate its tenor:

"The sound internal economic situation of a nation is a greater factor in its well-being than the price of its currency in changing terms of the currencies of other nations." (Lesson by Garet Garrett!)

"It is for this reason that reduced cost of government, adequate government income, and ability to service government debts are all so important to ultimate stability. So, too, old fetishes of so-called international bankers are being replaced by efforts to plan national currencies with the objective of giving those currencies a continuing purchasing power which does not greatly vary in terms of the commodities and need of modern civilization." (Lesson by Professor Warren!)

Our aim, it was explained, was to seek "the kind of dollar which a generation hence will have the sum purchasing power and debt paying power as the dollar value we hope to attain in the near future."

That Roosevelt did not think that aim was exclusively national, or incompatible with some sort of international monetary arrangement, is suggested by his supplementary avowal that "our broad purpose is the permanent stabilization of every nation's currency." But only "when the world works out concerted policies in the majority of nations to produce balanced budgets and living within their means, then can we properly discuss a better distribution of the world's gold and silver supply to act as a reserve base of national currencies." [28]

What inflow of thought and feeling, what incident, impelled Roosevelt to conclude that he must convey his ideas to the conference more incisively and brusquely? I am inclined to believe it was a sense that the governments of the countries on the gold standard, working in close concert with international banking houses (who wanted to preserve their advantage as creditors), were trying to force his hand. Or, to state the thought in another way, that they were trying to use the currents of opinion that swirled through the conference to subdue his will to resort to whatever national measures, no matter how drastic, might bring about a quicker and greater economic revival in the United States. He thought any obligation that might be regarded as a promise to keep the dollar stable would slow it up even more, or perhaps even set it back. He was being more and more beguiled by quite a different monetary policy, which might achieve what he wanted in time. And, more than that, according to its sponsors, this policy could make the United States immune from the erratic effects of the international gold standard and enable it to have a dollar that would retain substantially the same purchasing power year after year.

CHAPTER 20

The Conference Expires

THE Roosevelt statement was for release at ten o'clock in the morning on July 3. Moley was baffled; Hull benumbed. Cox and Warburg tried to buffer the impact on the conference. They hurried to the Geological Museum and read the statement to Prime Minister MacDonald before he could learn of it through others. The Prime Minister seemed to rally. He did not repeat his laments or reproaches, but he said to them, "If the worst comes to the worst today — then our job would be to see that the Conference dies like an airplane making a good landing, but not in a nose-dive. . . ." Cox and Warburg, good troupers, then went on to inform the French and other delegations.

On their return to the embassy, Moley urged Warburg to try to formulate for submission to Roosevelt some plan for an international commodity dollar which could be put in the form of a resolution to be submitted to the conference. Warburg flared up. He said that he did not think the President had a clear notion of what he wanted; and moreover, even if he did, he, Warburg, would refuse to have anything to do with it. He thought it would be bad enough to be insane at home without trying to impose our insanity on all other nations.

The monetary committee of the conference met in haste. The French representatives wailed that it had become futile to continue their discussions, whereupon MacDonald sent word to Cox and Warburg that he would like to talk to them again. Since, he said to them, he was at the end of his resources as presiding officer of the conference, he would like to make one more effort to see if the President could not be made to realize that if nothing were done to stabilize currencies, the conference would adjourn. Together they drove to 10 Downing Street. The entry which Warburg made in his journal recorded his impression: "For the first time since I have known him [MacDonald] he was in a complete state of depression and could see no hope for reviving the Conference. I asked him if there was anything we could do. He said, 'When a man says something with which you disagree, even if he says it unpleasantly, you can argue with him, but if he says nothing in a hurtful way, there is nothing you can say.' We tried to bring the matter to a question of substance but it was quite impossible. He went on to say that the results of the failure would be universal disappointment, possibly social disorder, and almost certainly, the resignation of his government." [1]

That evening the American delegation met again. It agreed to urge the President to clarify the meaning of his statement and ask for further guidance. This message, signed by Hull, was adroitly composed to win the President by a show of respectful loyalty rather than criticism. But at the time I was displeased by its deviousness.

The first two sentences read: "Your very able and courageous statement given wide publicity. Its entire subject matter highly praised by those to whom I have talked except there is a serious difference of opinion as to meaning of reference to the dollar and also the language as to ultimate gold standard."

Hull then went on to say that he had heard many expressions of hope that when the President clarified the language it would mean, ultimately, a managed gold standard. And then he softly added, "The only general criticism against which I and all Americans and others are strongly defending you, charges harshness and untimeliness to the language. The five gold countries profess to be very angry and MacDonald for the moment seems much displeased. . . . the American Delegation is busy taking every step possible in resistance of any movements to adjourn." [2]

After this meeting of the delegation I wearily returned to my own room and wrote a short account of my impressions of the effect of the President's statement. Although it contains no novel thoughts, it records the situation more truly, I think:

"The French have, of course, the sense of a diplomatic fiasco. But they also have someone in criticism of who they can rally the country. The French feeling of surprise is not without justice. When Herriot was in Washington the President went so far as to sanction a stabilization proposal supported by a tripartite fund. . . . I believe that the French will stubbornly maintain that without stabilization nothing can be done with the conference. The Dutch, whose currency is weaker than any of the other gold standard currencies, are greatly agitated and in the event that the florin weakens badly during the next few days they may very well move the adjournment of the conference. . . . The episode brings into question not only the future of the conference but the whole closely connected question of the future of the MacDonald government. If adjournment *sine die* is resorted to, MacDonald's prestige may be so greatly injured that he will have to resign, and a general election will be held — which according to all signs would bring in a straight Tory government. . . .

". . . The American delegation is now without guidance. No one knows clearly what type of monetary system the President envisages, and whether it would be made consonant with an international gold standard. . . . Obviously it would not jibe with the principles of permanent monetary policy outlined in the monetary resolution that Senator Pittman has presented to the conference. . . .

"Under all this, the Secretary has stood up relatively well. He made a plea again that everything possible be done to save the conference and assure its continuance. Moley was subdued and noncontributive. Cox was grim; Pittman, grave and reasonable; Couzens, anxious to have the cable [the President's] taken as a sign that we were going to have nothing to do with the rest of the world and had therefore better go home. As of tonight, that seems to me to be indicated. It might be well to leave behind some technical committees to strive for a new definition of what might be attempted sometime hence at another meeting."

Moley tried to reach the President by telephone. He wished to describe the desperate state of the conference and to warn the President that the blame for adjournment would be placed on him. But two other positive purposes were also surging in his mind. One was to suggest that the President assent to a short adjournment of the conference, during which his novel monetary plans could be put in precise and complete form. The other was to advise the President that the personnel of the delegation were not qualified to give effect to the ideas contained in his statement and should be reconstituted.

The President was still afloat on the *Indianapolis* and could not yet be reached. So Moley sent him a telegram to provide guidance for the phone talk which he wanted to have as soon as possible. This message, which turned out to be his undoing, he sent through the embassy code room. It was relayed through the State Department and was headed by an instruction to the decoding officer: "From Moley to the President alone and exclusively, with no distribution to the Department." It briefly described eight numbered topics which he wished to discuss with the President (in order to baffle anyone who might be listening in when they talked).

Moley, after stating that he thought the best immediate course would be a recess of from two to ten weeks — to enable the President to define his ideas in the form of a resolution which could be presented to the conference when it reconvened — went on to evaluate the fitness of the delegation and its staff. He thought that "on personal side, Pittman is only member of Delegation able intellectually and aggressively to present your ideas to Conference." Pittman, that unprincipled man without any genuine concern for the general welfare! Moley was also of the opinion that "expert group

needs strengthening on progressive program." That large and het-
erogeneous group of which I was presumably in charge had been
selected by the President and Moley. It included experienced and
interested officials who were capable of giving effective form to any
coherent program; but Moley, while in London, scarcely troubled
to nod to them.

The need to reconstitute the delegation, Moley said, was another
reason for favoring a recess on the conference.

In the last of the eight topics Moley outdid Hull in his attempt to
show he was a faithful follower:

"I consider your message splendid. It was the only way to bring
people to their senses, and do not be disturbed by severity of language. It was true, frank and fair." [3]

It does not seem to have occurred to Moley that Ambassador
Bingham would see this message, which as a matter of routine bore
his signature, and feel it was his duty as head of a diplomatic mission linked to the State Department to acquaint Hull with it. Nor
did Moley perceive that if Hull saw it, he would resent the fact that
Moley had sent it without consulting with him; that his pride would
be hurt; and that he would think it deceitful in view of Moley's
avowals of admiration and friendship with him. Or if all this did
occur to Moley, he thought that his essential duty — irrespective of
personalities — was to advise the President that he must replace the
group in London by one which would adapt to the President's
newly formulated views as smoothly as he himself was adapting. If,
for that purpose, individuals were hurt, it was too bad but just one
of the hazards and vicissitudes of public life.

A few eminent figures spoke in praise and defense of the President's decision. Keynes was first among them in an article he
dashed off for the *Daily Mail* which was published under the headline: PRESIDENT ROOSEVELT IS MAGNIFICENTLY RIGHT.[4] He interpreted the crisis in the conference as the result of a European attempt to drive a wedge between Great Britain and the United States
and to compel the British Commonwealth to link its fortunes to

those of the European gold standard countries by threats to break up the conference. He upheld the President's challenge to all conference members to explore new paths — new to statesmen and bankers but not to thought — toward the managed currency of the future rather than to tread old unfortunate ways. "On the broad political issue — on the things which it should be the business of Presidents and Prime Ministers to understand," he wrote, "he is magnificently right in forcing a decision between the two divergent policies. . . . On the one side we have a group of European countries of great political and military importance . . . which cling frantically to their gold perches. They see no virtue in a rising price level, putting their faith in a revival of confidence which is to come somehow by itself through business men gradually deciding that the world is safe for them. On the other side, the United States of America invites us to see whether, without uprooting the order of society which we have inherited, we cannot, by the employment of common sense in alliance with scientific thought, achieve something better than the miserable confusion and unutterable waste of opportunity in which an obstinate adherence to ancient rules of thumb had engulfed us."

I wondered as I read this article whether Keynes's enthusiasm may have been due partly to his memory of the depression that ensued after Winston Churchill, then Chancellor of the Exchequer, had (in 1925) returned the pound sterling to gold at too high a valuation. It may be presumed that Churchill himself had this experience in mind when, addressing the House of Commons on July 10, he said: "If any one had told us a year ago that the United States were to join Great Britain in abandoning the gold standard we should have thought him far too sanguine. . . . But the great event of the United States going off gold has happened, and I for one greatly rejoice." He then went on to reprove the gold bloc countries as openly as had Roosevelt, saying; "I'm tired of hearing that superior virtue and integrity attaches to the Gold Standard countries which already, like France, devalued to the extent of four fifths of its indebtedness . . ." and he asked rhetorically, "what harm has been done to the Conference?" And then he added sententiously, "conferences exist for men and not men for conferences."[5]

As I write this the vision returns to me of the appearance of Churchill as I saw him one evening during the conference when he was at the lowest swing of his career. I was quite ignorant of his achievement and the depth of his talent. As I watched him make his way out of Claridge's after dinner, his mien was impressive but heavy — moon-faced and flushed — as he ambled along. How was I to know that these were signs of his indomitable love for life and his determination never to be downed?

At eight o'clock the next morning, July 4, the Prime Minister telephoned and asked Moley to hurry over to 10 Downing Street once again. He was distraught, remarking that the President's message did not sound like the utterance of the man he had known in Washington, but like Lloyd George. The President's action, he bemoaned, had both wrecked the conference and shattered his own personal position.[6]

When the American delegation met at ten o'cock Moley described the Prime Minister's sentiments and Cox and Warburg reported on the angry reaction of the gold bloc representatives and their intention to advocate immediate termination of the conference. The dismal silence that fell on the group was broken by Swope. He said they should not accept that necessity until one more effort was made to find out more precisely what the President meant and whether the other delegations might be brought to agree to consider it. Moley was asked to try to obtain some helpful guidance by telephone. Cox and Warburg were asked to let MacDonald know that an effort was being made to communicate with the President and request him to prevent the adjournment of the conference.

The President had still not come ashore. So in lieu of personal talk, Hull at three o'clock in the afternoon hurried off a flash review of the situation. He informed the President that "Conditions calculated to disrupt further regular sessions of the Conference developed considerably overnight." The five gold countries, he reported, were united in their views that the conference could not possibly progress and should adjourn, and the British were only feebly and haltingly resisting this course. "Is there anything more," he asked, "that you care to say or do in support of our position . . . first preventing adjournment, then standing for recess. The situation is thoroughly alarming." [7]

The President had sent off some hours before from the U.S.S. *Indianapolis* his answer to the earlier request of the delegation for an explanation of his statement which would be helpful. Their lingering hope rested on the belief that he still favored the *ultimate* restoration of the international gold standard, actual or potential. But instead of leaning that way, the President now compounded the confusion by throwing out an even more novel idea. "I wish," he said, "that the Delegation would also confidentially explore the possibility of establishing a unit of measure in which international trade transactions would be conducted. While this would not effect national currency values, it would simplify mental processes of trade by giving a unit which at all times would mean the same thing in grains of gold." * [8]

On reading this the delegation would have been justified in throwing in its chips and leaving for home.

Nevertheless, Hull, Cox, Bullitt and Moley each in his own way were striving to keep the conference going and protect the President against the accusation of having wrecked it. Hull, on learning that MacDonald had agreed with the gold countries that the conference should be adjourned and a resolution to this effect was to be brought before the meeting of the steering committee of the conference at six o'clock that night, allowed Bullitt to go down and talk with the Prime Minister. MacDonald was hardly in a mood to listen to any emissary of the delegation. Of all the American group Bullitt was probably the least welcome conciliator. MacDonald thought him to be bumptious and bullying; he had been angered by

---

* At this writing a similar proposal is being favored by the American government, and discussed by its representatives in international financial institutions.

a report from members of the British delegation that in the course of a difference of opinion Bullitt had threatened to tear up the Naval Treaty and build the largest navy in the world, and also to denounce the Kellogg-Brand Pact.[9] The Prime Minister's position inside and outside the government had been hurt, and he felt personally duped. He felt, as did the King when he talked with Stimson at a garden party at Buckingham Palace, "Ramsay MacDonald had been made a fool of . . ." Furthermore, he resented what he regarded as President Roosevelt's censure of his conduct of the conference.

So it is not surprising that Bullitt found he could not budge the Prime Minister. Thereupon Hull decided that he had to attend an emergency meeting of the steering committee of fourteen. In a speech MacDonald, fired by indignation, said that he thought that Roosevelt's message made it useless for the conference to continue and he proposed that it adjourn at once. Hull, resorting to the technique of quiet but cutting questioning, caused the Prime Minister to falter in his contentions. On the ground that the action under discussion was so important that it ought not be decided upon in haste, Hull urged that the decision be postponed. If it was, a mutually beneficial solution might still be found. Richard Bennett, the Prime Minister of Canada, sided with Hull at once, and he spoke for other British dominions as well.

Possibly for this reason Chamberlain, to Hull's surprise, swung round. He said that he agreed that it was advisable to have a short recess to review the situation rather than to adjourn in wrath. The representatives of the Scandinavian countries then spoke to the same effect. Whereupon Bonnet, Jung and Colijn capitulated. It was agreed to defer the decision until the morning of July 6, two days away. This was a triumph for Hull. It also revealed that Roosevelt's views about the relative unimportance of immediate stabilization had supporters in other countries and among other delegations.

While Hull was at the Conference Hall, Moley was working with Keynes and Lippmann on another statement of reasons why the

President had departed from the monetary policies implict in our resolution. Keynes's enthusiasm for a more expansionary monetary policy caused him to overlook the fact that one of the reasons Roosevelt had given for not attempting to stabilize currencies was that many national budgets were out of balance. In his books, which so greatly influenced world opinion, Keynes had advocated that governments should stimulate lagging economic activity by public investment, whether or not the expenditure was covered by income.

Lippmann's talents were those of a fluent journalist who can quickly sponge up impressions and ideas. That very morning the *New York Herald Tribune* carried a dispatch which Lippmann had sent over from London in which he confirmed what Moley was telling the President — that the delegation did not know what was in his mind and that it lacked technical competence and unity. "Mr. Roosevelt's purposes," he wrote, "may be excellent. But he has completely failed to organize a diplomatic instrument to express them. If Mr. Roosevelt means what he says he must send a new Delegation to London which knows what he means and has power to act for him."

The persuasive exposition which these authors produced had for its purpose not only the protection of the President against criticism but also the recruiting of as many members of the conference as could be persuaded to stand out against the gold bloc. They did not finish the job until three o'clock on the morning of Wednesday, July 5. Herbert Swope typed it out and a copy was sent off quickly to the President.

Roosevelt was adjuring the delegation to oppose any recess since the conference had not yet considered most of its agenda. An adjournment of even sixty days, he thought, would be defeatist. "We cannot," he said, "in any way admit or agree that no progress can be made on economic problems until temporary exchange fluctuations are settled." In conclusion he said, "The people and the press here are united in praise of our stand and regard the French position as highly selfish and ignoring utterly the objectives of the Conference." [10] Obviously he had not talked with or heard from many persons whose souls were in their deposit boxes.

By then the President was back in the White House. He telephoned (at 5 A.M. London time, July 5) and spoke to both the Secretary and to Moley. In answer to Hull's inquiry he said, "Everything is fine." The Secretary described what had happened at the meeting of the steering committee the day before and the situation that he faced. Roosevelt repeated his dislike not only of an adjournment but even of a recess, subject to the call of the chairman, MacDonald. "That might be," he said, "six months. That was intended to nail us to the cross." But since the Secretary stated that he did not think it would be possible to prevent the members of the conference from voting to recess, the President told him to try to have it as short as possible.

In further explanation of why he thought the conference should not adjourn the President observed that "we are not blocking London, Paris or Rome from making some agreement. I heard over here — we have pretty good information — that if the plan had gone through originally and we had approved it, they would have earmarked a half a million [billion] of gold in this country and if they had done that there would have been a flight from the dollar and we would have been morally compelled to stop gold exports again."

Moley took over the receiver. He thought the President's greeting "breezy, warm, affectionate." In his subsequent account of this talk Moley relates that "with the light-heartedness of a boy he [Roosevelt] had received my confidential cable of the preceding morning and appreciated my general size-up." [11]

In this interval MacDonald sent Hull a letter in which he defended himself against the President's censure and vindicated his position in regard to an adjournment of the conference. He wrote that the President seemed to be under the impression that the conference was called to do one thing and one thing only — to take measures that would raise prices. In fact, however, it had been summoned to try to reach agreements of great scope about the numerous questions dealt with in the report of the Preparatory Commission of Experts; and progress was being made on many of these questions until the President made his unjust accusations.

Moreover, MacDonald wrote, "When the message reflecting upon the Conference was not sent to your Delegation to communicate to the Conference, or to guide yourself, but was broadcast to the world in the first instance, the most bitter resentment could not be avoided and the prospects of agreement were for the time shattered." Consequently, contrary to what he understood the President as well as he had wished to avoid, adjournment of the conference was necessary. "Had I," he concluded, "been asked before the publication of the President's censure what actually was happening, I think it would have never seen the light of day, because . . . it proceeds upon a complete misapprehension of how an international Conference, representative as this is of sixty-six different nations who are here in the persons of Prime Ministers, Foreign Secretaries, Finance Ministers, has to be conducted if any good results are to be had from it." [12]

In the afternoon of July 5 the President telephoned again. Hull asked him what he thought of the statement which Moley, Keynes and Lippmann had written and was told that it was "All right." He went over it sentence by sentence, suggesting several changes and omissions. (And incidentally, he remarked again that the main reason for rejecting Moley's proposal was that if he had approved it ". . . the Federal Reserve Bank would have obligated the Treasury to export gold and we can't allow that." And he added, "I got word — and pretty good word, too — that there might have been an earmarking of gold to the tune of half a billion dollars." [13]

Hull, Pittman and Moley hurried to show the statement to MacDonald. Though it is hard to believe, the Prime Minister, according to Moley, blurted out, "Oh, Moley, tell me why this kind of message couldn't have been sent on Saturday. It would have saved the Conference. Maybe it will save it still. Will you give it to me now so that I can present it to the others?" [14]

The statement was released publicly at nine o'clock that evening. I will not rehearse its familiar and well-expressed arguments. It ended with the assertion that it was hard to believe that our position in "the minor issue of temporary stabilization" lessened the advisability of going on with discussions of more permanent and fundamental matters.

When the bureau met on July 6, Hull won a reprieve. He maintained that it was the responsibility of all to continue the effort and not "in a spirit of pique suddenly to pick up their hats and go home." Kikujiro Ishii, privy councillor and head of the Japanese delegation, spoke up in Hull's support, then after him Chamberlain, Bennett, the Swedish Minister of Finance and the Chinese representative. The spokesmen for the gold bloc countries and Spain insisted it was futile to continue. Bonnet was particularly critical — as "cooperative as a rattlesnake," in Bullitt's phrase. But in the end all agreed to continue in session awhile longer.

What could the American delegation say or do to secure enough support for a continuation of the conference with the acquiescence of the gold bloc or over its opposition? When Hull recounted to the President his success in gaining time, he stressed that it was vital that the delegation should receive just as soon as possible definite instructions not only about monetary matters but also about economic ones. Up to then, the many questions that had been posed in Washington, in an attempt to find out what proposals our delegation might sponsor (in line with the program of domestic legislation being enacted), had brought unhelpful answers.

The President was unperturbed. He acknowledged Hull's report of the wrangle in the meeting of the steering committee in a short message which begain: "Splendid work. We are all proud of you." He promised that an effort would be made to transmit further instructions soon. His mood and thought are recorded in an entry which Pierrepont Moffat, after talking with Norman Davis, made in his diary that night: The President, although wondering whether his message to the conference might have been too strong, did not regret it, "the more so since he believes it will counteract an impression which he feels is widespread throughout the country that at every Conference we come out the losers. For better or worse he has tried to prove to the public that Europe cannot force us to accept what he does not want, and the psychological effect, at least here, should be very valuable."

During the course of the day (July 6), Warburg wrote a letter of resignation as financial adviser to the delegation and gave it to Hull. He explained that he was resigning because he thought that while ideas forming in the President's mind might lead to a more effective currency system than the world had ever known, he did not think he could interpret them so far away — since "we are entering upon waters for which I have no charts and in which I therefore feel myself an utterly incompetent pilot." This courteous disclaimer of unfitness overlay a disturbed sense, on Warburg's part, that the President had lost his bearings; that he was hearkening to the soothsayers and, for the time being, was deaf to his advice.

That night Moley and Swope hurried to catch the first boat home. By Moley's account, he asked the Secretary, on bidding him goodbye, whether it was now clear that he had lived up to the avowals of good faith he had made shortly after his arrival. The Secretary said that he was completely satisfied.[15] No mention of this farewell talk is to be found in Hull's memoirs. Hull had not yet seen a copy of the secret message which Moley had sent to the President two days before — that message in which Moley denigrated him and said that he thought Pittman was the only member of the delegation quick enough of mind and vigorous enough to present the President had lost his bearings; that he was hearkening to the constituted. Whenever Hull later referred to the message, and he did so often in after years, he spoke with scorn of Moley as a double-faced trickster. With a touch of malice he used to recount how he had called the members of the delegation together and read Moley's cable to them, and the effect produced upon them.

At this juncture I may be privileged to comment myself on this message, the main features of which I have reviewed. Before reading it, I too had been led by Hull's account to think that it contemptuously criticized each and every member of the delegation by name. On reading it much later, however, I found it unjust but I did not find it as harsh as I had conceived it to be or its purpose as unworthy.[16]

The Secretary's resentment at the way in which Moley had allowed himself to be regarded as the prime representative of the President was justified. Moley had violated the traditional rules of good conduct in public office by not informing the Secretary of this and all messages he sent to the President and not discussing their substance with him. But for all of that there is ground for the impression that the depth and durability of Hull's hatred was extreme; that it was the type of antagonism that lasted for decades among the men that grew up, as Hull had, in the hills of Tennessee.

Moley went out the same door through which he had come in, but far more quickly. On his return journey he was anxious and despondent even though he did not realize how greatly his position was impaired. He had expected to be kept informed while at sea of what was taking place in London. He sent a cable congratulating Hull on his victory and saying it would be very helpful to him if Bullitt was told to send him daily reports, including summaries of all messages from the United States. Hearing nothing, he sent an inquiry. Since this was not acknowledged, he sent another. By then Hull had seen Moley's critical report to the President and the only answer Moley received was signed by Hugh Cumming, Hull's assistant. It read, "Your cable has been on the Secretary's desk but no instructions issued."

Moley at this time was unaware of the stories and rumors that were being circulated about his personal conduct and financial looseness while in London. These were being passed along by Hull and Bingham to correspondents in the United States, including the President.

To Howe, Hull wrote, "I constantly ruled at each session of my Delegation that the Treasury, through Dr. Sprague and other agencies other than the Delegation, were handling it [stabilization]. My cablegrams show this fact and that I constantly turned down urgent pleas of the gold countries and of MacDonald to suggest to the President or join with them in suggesting something to him relative to temporary stabilization. This was the situation before he rejected the first proposal, and afterwards until others here without my knowledge or participation until late in the afternoon, when I was called on the telephone and informed 'we have all agreed,' referring to the agreement that was forwarded to the President putting up to him for the second time the temporary stabilization question for decision." [17] This, as noted, is a very different story than Moley's account.

In a cable to Roosevelt on July 11, just before Moley landed, Hull vented all his grievances. He said that he regretted to have to report that Moley's attitude and conduct had been "utterly dumbfounding." He attributed the inability of the American delegation to function to the fact that during the eight days when Moley was on his way over to London the British and French press most unfairly assailed the delegation and dramatized Moley's errand; they had also given their readers to believe that he was coming to speak and act for the President and to take charge of American interests in London. He complained that after Moley arrived the high officials of other countries riveted all their attention upon him. He charged that Moley had asked him to inform the delegation that he, in company with Sprague, would be in exclusive charge of the stabilization question — Hull's assumption being that the President had authorized or directed him to do so; and he accused Moley of alleging after his failure that he, Hull, had on his own initiative directed him to assume the task. He denied having any knowledge of Moley's June 29 negotiations with MacDonald and the Treasury officials until Moley asked him on the telephone at about five o'clock that afternoon to join in the meeting which was to ratify the accord — which he had refused to do.

These complaints culminated in an account of his shocked surprise when he learned that Moley was informing the President that the Secretary of State was incapable of functioning in London "[while] at the same time pretending absolute loyalty of friendship and of official attitude toward me. . . . My regret only equaled my amazement to discover the deliberate attempt of one I have implicitly trusted thus secretly to undermine and destroy me in my situation, while openly professing both friendship and loyalty." [18]

Two days later Hull, with unassuaged bitterness, gave to former Secretary of State Stimson, who was in London, an even more complaining version of what had happened. As Stimson later noted in his diary: "He [Hull] several times used the expression to me, 'You can properly call him a son of anything you please.' " [19]

Hull's was not the only adverse report about Moley's actions in London which preceded or followed his arrival in Washington. Ambassador Bingham had called Howe several times on the telephone, even before Moley left London, and given him his version of what was going on. Then, at Howe's request, he sent a letter marked "Personal" and "Confidential" which he wanted to have in the President's hands before Moley turned up to tell his story.[20]

Bingham wrote at even greater length to Colonel House. The first part of his letter was an encomium of Hull's representation of the United States and steadfastness under adversity. All the rest was devoted to a denigrating account of Moley and his behavior. He deplored the way in which Moley was playing up to the press as a messiah, a miracle man, the only person in the President's confidence. He hinted that Moley had failed to pay for the airplane which he had asked to have sent to Cobh to transport him to London and then had not used. He explained the permission that he had given Moley to send code messages to the President though the embassy as due to the fact that he had not known of Moley's folly and treachery.[21]

Even though the President may have thought these reports and stories unduly hard on Moley, and maybe tinted by malice, they hit home. Hull's letter to the President made it impossible for him to retain Moley in the State Department. In fact Bingham, in his letters to Howe and House, had written that he thought Hull would resign unless Moley got out. Roosevelt, without ever acknowledging a share of responsibility for the situation that had developed, decided it was essential to get Moley out of Washington before Hull returned, since the Secretary "would kick up such a terrible fuss." In confiding this to Morgenthau he seems to have come to believe that Moley had exceeded his instructions by dealing directly with representatives of foreign governments in London.[22]

After his return to Washington Moley was bitter at what had happened to him in London. He thought that he had been the object of a conspiracy between Howe and Davis in the United States and Hull and Bingham in London. As already remarked, he believed that Hull had understood the nature of the triangular relation between the two of them and the President when he accepted the office; and that he, Moley, had made more than a reasonable effort to bolster Hull in London and to show respect for him and his office. Was he to be blamed because the press sensationalized his flight to see Roosevelt on the *Amberjack* and his attempt to save the conference by stepping in to negotiate an accord on temporary stabilization? Could he help it if MacDonald sought him out because he found Hull so vague and unable to talk for the President?

But the personal hurt that lasted longest came from the harmful and wrongful rumors about his conduct and expense account which were spread about him. Bingham, he thought, was swayed by his wife, an austere woman, and annoyed because his presence and Swope's exuberance disturbed the social-climbing routine of the embassy.

However, in telling of the way Hull and Moley felt about each other at the time of Moley's departure and subsequently, I have strayed far — and perhaps too long — from the scene of the conference. To return to London: I, to whom the Secretary of State had assigned the task of defining American policies on trade and tariff matters, was as much at sea as Warburg was about monetary matters. My uncertainty was soon to turn into certainty that it was nonsense to continue to try to formulate proposals which the delegation might sponsor. For the answers received from Washington to diverse appeals for instructions were unclear, unhelpful and confused.

An entry in Pierrepont Moffat's diary records that Davis was asked by the President to aid Phillips, Baruch, Acheson and my assistant Frederick Livesey in drafting the answers to the delegation's appeals: "[I] reread the telegrams he [Roosevelt] had written from his yacht and found them so clear as to need little, if any, elaborations." What a group of sagacious men not to have tried to elaborate, and to have allowed instead the American technicians in London to stumble amidst obscurities!

In an airmail letter which Livesey hurried off to me, he wrote in part, "The White House bloc did not go very deep into technical difficulties. There was a very non-technical discussion of the desirability of each country accepting a regime of short hours and higher wages for everybody seemed to be for it, the President, rather unfortunately, I thought, mentioning Austria as an illustrative case . . . it seems to me that the advocacy of a 30 hour week civilization by the United States before all countries of the world, plus the President's managed currency program, would justify our suggestion of a year ago that the Conference might accomplish something if it were entering a Wellsian world."

One or two of the suggestions contained in one answer from Washington could only have been acted on in such a world. I will not go into its entangled strands.[23] I gave up the task of trying to explain American trade policies and so told the Secretary of State.

As Hull wrote in his memoirs, after telling of his triumph in preventing immediate adjournment, "the three weeks that followed were a kind of paper chase during which we sought to find odds and ends of topics that could be discussed." The group of technicians did its bedraggled best, more and more wishful of being released from their impossible chore.

The committees of the conference halfheartedly had resumed their sessions. For almost all of the participants thought, as noted in the July 8 issue of the *Economist,* that "Like King Charles the Second, the Economic Conference is taking an unconscionable time to die. . . ."

Rather than giving a day-by-day narrative of what occurred during the bleak days the conference remained in session, I will merely recall a few impressions and events.

One — and one only — occurrence refreshed my spirit, though its tenor was gloomy. The Stimsons spent a few days in London en route to Scotland. At dinner, looking over Hyde Park, he told me that Hull had poured out his woes to him, and I confirmed Hull's report that there was no chance left that the conference would end well. Despite all the ardor which Stimson and I and our colleagues had shared while planning for the conference, it had brought about only greater confusion in international affairs and had marred the friendship between the United States and its former allies. The only beneficiaries were Germany and Japan, who were losing all fear of concerted opposition to their plans for expansion. Though at the end of the talk Stimson grimly remarked, "This cannot go on," he spoke no word of belittlement of Roosevelt and only words of sympathy for Hull. As we walked back to our hotel my wife found the adjective that suited him best — sterling.

On July 11 the President instructed the delegation not to agree to a very general statement of principles which could be deemed to endorse the gold standard. Pittman, in peremptory and enigmatic fashion, informed the other members of the monetary committee which was considering this statement that it did not fit into American policy and was premature. Shoulders were again shrugged. The episode was regarded by other delegations as another and conclusive proof that American monetary and economic policies were in flux and that it was useless to continue in conference.

On the same day, Hull answered the reproving message which MacDonald had addressed to him the week before, when his indignation had been high. The Secretary denied that the President's message — published on July 3 — was censorious. He contradicted MacDonald's allegation that the President seemed to think the sole purpose of calling the conference was to take measures to raise prices. He condoned the emphatic tone of the message by the fact that an overeager small group had tried three times within a few days to force the President's hand about stabilization. He explained that the reason Roosevelt had not addressed his message to the conference was because it had no jurisdiction over the question, it being rather "a political decision which governmental treasuries in conference would have to make." As an epilogue, he assured MacDonald that Roosevelt was a friend of international cooperation; that he, like Hull, appreciated MacDonald's fine service as president of the conference; and that they both wanted to cooperate with the Prime Minister to the greatest extent possible.

MacDonald by then had in some measure reconciled himself to what had happened and was about to happen. But not entirely. On July 15, after luncheon at Chequers, he asked Stimson, "How on earth did Roosevelt send such a Delegation to the Conference? It had no cohesion or initiative. It could act only on daily reports and instructions from Washington. We could not talk to them freely because they immediately gave out to the press the subject of our talks and this they did in erroneous form, for in their inexperience with the matters in hand they could not remember accurately what was said." For Warburg he had some kind words; for Moley, some words of sympathy for what he was in for when he got back to Washington; for Bullitt, critical dislike. When Pittman's name came up the Prime Minister merely asked whether the Senator had not been a patron of a bootlegger.[24] Obviously he had familiar knowledge of all members of the delegation.

Up to the last days of the conference the President stood firm against any and all proposals and steps to prevent the dollar from listing where it would. But soon thereafter it became evident that a flight from the dollar was taking place, stimulated by signs of official desire that its value should decline. American exporters were leaving the proceeds of their sales in foreign banks. Industrial interests and speculators were importing into the United States unusually large stocks of raw materials, such as rubber, tin and wool, in expectation that the decline in the value of the dollar would cause the prices of these products to rise. Foreigners were beginning to withdraw their deposits from American banks.

By the middle of July, the dollar had fallen so low that its value relative to sterling was verging on what it had been before the pound was devalued in 1931. Although prices of commodities and securities had still not risen nearly as far as he wished them to rise, the President began to fear that the decline in the value of the dollar might become too precipitate and provoke retaliation. So he ordered the Federal Reserve Bank of New York to permit the export of some gold. As explained by Harrison to Norman, "I told him that I did not mean anything by way of stabilization. . . . But I went on to say that we might be in a position to use some gold, say up to $30,000,000, for a short period of time, say two weeks, with a view to seeing that no violent fluctuation of the dollar rate would put the pound above $4.86, the ratio before Britain devalued as against the dollar . . . and that these transactions would in no way be construed as a commitment to do anything more than I have said for a limited period." [25]

The word of this spread; the prices of commodities and stocks fell so fast and so far that the grain exchanges and the stock exchange shortened their hours. But the price movement soon began to reverse itself and turn upward. These maneuvers made no impression on the conference.

In a memorandum which I wrote on July 17, I jotted down first that during a talk with Sir Walter Layton and myself, Stimson put into words the core of my anxiety about the situation in Washington — that there was no unity or steadiness in the relationships between President Roosevelt and his individual advisers; that they were changeable, willful and sometimes accidental; and that this was reflected in the resultant policies.

The work of the delegation, I then noted, was becoming "increasingly negligible. The delegates put in a momentary appearance in the Secretary's office now and again, then vanish. . . . Cox follows the meetings of the bureau, Pittman the meetings of the committee on silver. The rest absent themselves from the conference sessions. Couzens, after abruptly snubbing off discussions in the monetary committee on indebtedness (the evaluation of methods and machinery of debt adjustment), has ceased to attend them, leaving this assignment — to which a great American interest attaches — to a junior staff officer who has no authority to express the views of the American government. From the start the delegates have shown themselves to be unused to steady work; they do not read the conference documents that are circulated; they will not patiently follow the discussions in the committees or talk out any subject with each other.

"The Secretary has practically ceased his effort to direct the delegation. His hands have lost all guiding forces against the difficulty of managing this collection of difficult personalities. Resentful impatience closes in on him. . . . The Secretary is so shaken and shocked by his experiences that he is unwilling to express an American position on any point without explicit authorization. Only the calculating silver man from Nevada [Pittman] does anything. He moves on, apparently sure that he can secure approval in Washington for anything that he might do in London. By his abrupt handling of the resolution endorsing central bank cooperation, he has created some opposition to his own resolution about silver. But he remains assured that he can carry it through and his arrogant assertiveness seems to be effective in that committee. He and the Secretary have ceased using each other's first names and now they address each other with the strictest formality. He and Governor Cox avoid each other coldly."

The best remembered scene in which Pittman figured was at the large dinner party which the Astors gave for the Prince of Wales (Edward VIII) on July 18. While the assembled company were awaiting the arrival of the Prince, Stimson asked former Senator George Moses of New Hampshire whether his wife was also in London. Moses said she was, but he had been invited at the last minute to fill in for Pittman, who was not in shape to come. Just then Pittman was shown into the room. Moses exclaimed, "Holy smoke, I lose my dinner." Pittman's unexpected appearance threw

Lady Astor's careful protocol in seating arrangements into disarray, and for once she showed consternation.[26]

The usually dejected expressions on the faces of the staff gave way to a smile one day when someone read aloud an editorial in *The Times* of London. This started with a show of indignation at the misuse in an American newspaper headline of a metaphor — a statement which had been given out by the American delegation was called its "swan song." *The Times* appealed to the World Society for the Prevention of Cruelty to Animals and the Geological Society to arouse themselves out of their deep sleep in order to preserve the good name of that most beautiful of English waterfowls, the silver swan. Here was the American press turning that bird into a songbird. The lines ran on: "as all good singers in this country who know their madrigals are well aware, the swan, contented with her outward beauty, during life utters but one song.

> *The silver swan who living had no note*
> *When death approached unlocked her silent throat."*

Moreover, the editorial observed, the circumstances of the day were imparting to this metaphor an unintended irony. For the swan,

> *Leaning her breast against the reedy shore*
> *Thus sang her first and last and sang no more.*

At this point the writer of the editorial made the mistake of improvising a quatrain of his own which he thought the American press might more appropriately use. I quote it only because it is so dreadful:

> *The dollar swan has sat upon her gold*
> *When death approached unlocked her hoard and gold*
> *Raising her price to meet her need full sore*
> *But sank th' exchange 'til it could sink no more.*

Roosevelt was soon to prove that in reality it could sink quite a lot more.

By July 23 the conference was twitching toward its end. Hull could not keep it going any longer. It resolved to adjourn a few days hence.

Before the conference closed shop on July 27, each delegate received a morocco-bound copy of the New Testament, sent to them as a gift by Bishop John Taylor Smith of the Scripture Gift Mission. In each was the inscription, "We trust . . . that this portion of Sacred Scripture . . . may assume a place among your personal possessions as a memento of your visit to the London Economic Conference." Most of the departing members did indeed feel the need for spiritual as well as spirituous support.

The President sent Hull a message which began, "Before you sail I want you to know once more of my affectionate regard for and confidence in you." He then invited the Secretary and Mrs. Hull to spend a night at Hyde Park immediately upon their arrival. Hull answered that he was deeply grateful for this personal message and accepted the President's invitation with pleasure. The President had been persuaded by Warburg, who was back in Washington, to send a personal message of goodwill to Prime Minister MacDonald. Hull reported that this message had delighted the Prime Minister and that he, Hull, had read it to the full gathering of the conference that morning to general applause. It arrived, Hull remarked, "at a most opportune time, and will accomplish much good. It was as forceful and sound as it was timely." Both Hull and MacDonald were ready for a reconciliation with the President.

PART IV

As the Year Wore On

CHAPTER 21

After the Conference

AFTER the adjournment of the conference the heavens did not fall, but neither did the sun shine brightly.

In Washington, most government officials and the American people were as little regretful as the President about what had happened in London. The President summarily refuted all allegations that his "bombshell" message had been unfortunate in substance and tone; he was pretending to take the currency problem lightly, and the excitement about it for the time being was put out of mind. Thoughts centered on the domestic program. The American economy had picked up enough to bring back hope and lessen distress. Yet production remained far below capacity; unemployment was very large; and prices were still very low.

The administration had many and overdue initiatives under way. To animate and regulate private economic activity it was going to rely on four main ones: the National Recovery Administration (NRA) — with booming General Hugh Johnson in the saddle, riding his horse through the conference rooms with expletives to the rather abashed plaudits of the businessmen who thronged to Washington to work out codes; the Agricultural Adjustment Administration (AAA), which was being caustically criticized for its recommendations to take land out of cultivation and reduce the pig population; and still more public works to provide employment and expand relief measures. Concurrently, the resort to monetary and banking stimulants became bolder.

These were all envisaged as national efforts to which our foreign economic relations were left to adjust themselves. The Secretary of State did not openly contend for authority, nor try to curb the President's inclinations. Roosevelt thought that the State Department was too conservative and too disposed to consider the wishes of other countries.

Thus, as the year wore on, it was subordinated even in some foreign economic affairs which formerly had been in its jurisdiction. Still, it was not inactive in segments of this area, such as American trade policies, governmental debts and the effort to assist private American owners of defaulted foreign bonds.

Under both the NRA and the AAA the President had authority to impose controls or restrictions on imports into the United States. But he used this charily — only when he thought it imperative to prevent a code from being toppled over.

What was harder to bear was the continued chaos and conflict within the government about the nature and direction of our commercial policy. All under the White House — the NRA, the AAA, the State, Commerce and Treasury Departments and the Tariff Commission — had a measure of independent authority in this field. Driven to distraction, we in the State Department strove to inaugurate some plan of unified control. Four times between August and October 1933 Secretary Hull took our recommendations — of which a typical one was headed: "The Urgent Necessity of Working Out an Adequate and Coordinated Method for Dealing with Commercial Policy Questions" — to cabinet meetings. Once there, however, he merely mumbled off his views and proposals and did nothing more when they were ignored.

By early November, the need for coordination became so imperative that Phillips, Acting Secretary of State while Hull was on his way to the International Conference of American States at Monte-video, did warn the President that unless authority to decide commercial policy was coordinated in a single organization there was going to be complete chaos, controversy and confusion. He managed to secure Roosevelt's approval for the establishment of an executive committee on commercial policy. The chairman, it was stipulated, would be a State Department official. Over the first few preliminary sessions Phillips himself presided; then the task was turned over to a new Assistant Secretary of State, Francis Sayre, a Harvard Law School professor and son-in-law of Woodrow Wilson.

But hardly had this committee taken up its assignment than the President created still another rival for control over trade policy. Secretary of Agriculture Wallace and Assistant Secretary Tugwell were finding intolerable the contentions and activities of one of the chief officials of the AAA, George Peek, a former manufacturer of farm implements with many acquaintances among farm organizations and producers of agricultural machinery. Intellectually naïve, he knew little of the complexities of international economic affairs; his solution for the farm problem was to have the American government control all our foreign trade, make deals with each foreign country equalizing what we bought and sold to each, and with the aid of subsidies sell our surplus farm products abroad cheaply. All these methods traversed the principles dear to Hull. Nevertheless the President, in order to get Peek out of the AAA, asked him to make a special report on commercial policies, and soon thereafter gave him a title and assignment which allowed him to think he had a genuine mandate to determine them.

The battle was joined. I shall not here follow its campaigns. Peek lost out.

The actual trade situation as the year came to a close was more, rather than less, troubled. Country after country, following Great Britain, had denounced the short-term tariff truce which we had managed to arrange before the Monetary and Economic Conference assembled. Hearings under both the National Recovery Act and the Agricultural Administration Act on pleas for increased protection were getting under way. But the President was still resisting excessive demands and showing a renewed interest in the enactment of legislation which would authorize him to cut tariff rates in reciprocity for cuts made by foreign governments in the rates they imposed on imports from the United States.

After a meeting on December 28 in his office, I wrote a note somewhat less lugubrious than its predecessors: "The President clearly recognized the fact that if we are to sustain or develop foreign trade we must find a way of deciding that industries should *not* be protected. It was agreed that the type of commercial policy envisaged in the memorandum [of the executive committee] could only be carried out if the President were given certain tariff-making powers. I was told to go ahead and revise an existing draft of a law conveying such powers which we had prepared."

The prospect was improving, because by then the value of the dollar in terms of gold and other foreign currencies had so markedly declined that the competitive position of American producers was much improved. Thereby Roosevelt's monetary policy — which will be examined again in a later chapter — was clearing the way for the step he would take in 1934 which initiated the gradual and cumulative reduction of restrictions on international trade in which, ever since, the United States has been the leader.

During this period the intergovernmental debts became defunct. The question had been temporarily deferred while the conference was on. In the autumn the British Treasury decided to send to Washington Sir Frederick Leith-Ross, an amiable and reasonable permanent civil servant who knew how to defend British interests, to try again to reach a settlement.

In two memos that I wrote on September 20 and 25, I made an effort to define the terms of a permanently equitable settlement. These expressed the expectation that it would not be sufficient to reduce or even cancel the interest; that the principal would also have to be written down under some guise or other. However, in reality I thought there was little chance that Great Britain and the other debtors would, no matter how much we urged them, offer to pay more than they had in June — that is, token payments of 10 per cent on the sum due, the same fraction of their reparations claims against Germany that they had retained.

Whether because of the tenor of these memos or for some other reason, the Secretary of State and the President decided that I should not figure in the negotiations with Leith-Ross. I was informed that they would be carried on by Under-Secretary of the Treasury Acheson with the aid and advice of my assistant, Frederick Livesey. When first told of this my feelings were ruffled. Moreover, I had the probably vain notion that I might win greater considerations from Leith-Ross than either of the other two, since we had formed a pleasant friendship in London. When I took my grievance to the Secretary of State he said at first that he understood why I should feel bad because I was excluded since he had so often suffered similarly. But when I persisted he explained that he would rather not have the State Department play a significant part in the negotiations. He wanted their possible impact on our political relations with the debtors — which were unsatisfactory enough — to be cushioned as far as possible. Moreover, he thought it advisable that the State Department should not be the object of the outcry in the United States which he thought almost certainly would follow the best possible settlement that could be reached. As an outcome of this talk he gave out a statement at his press conference on September 29 explaining my exclusion on the basis of absorption in other vital questions. This I appreciated.

After the discussions between Acheson and Leith-Ross had gone on for a few days, I reported to the Secretary that so far no progress had been made. With a glint of satisfaction in his eyes he said, "Of course. I knew nothing could be done. I needed no report to be sure of that."

By November the President was deeply engaged in his monetary maneuvers. The press release he issued on November 7 was by far the most tranquilizing of any utterance he had ever made about the debts. He attributed the failure to reach agreement to "the un-precedented state of world economic and financial conditions." Most notably he said that since the British government continued to acknowledge the debt and would give sign of that acknowledgment by paying seven and a half million dollars on the December installment, he had "no personal hesitation in saying that I shall not regard the British government as in default."

Neville Chamberlain's comment in the House of Commons, to which he read the President's statement, was similarly friendly. MacDonald informed Ray Atherton, our chargé d'affaires in London, that the cabinet had been divided about making even this token payment and that it was resented by some of its members.

These discussions and the statements issued after their conclusion turned out to be, in fact, a requiem for the debts. Thereafter, no serious attempt was ever made to collect them. However, remembrance of them later warped American foreign policy. The American government, thinking that it had once been singed, refused financial support to our former allies during the nineteen-thirties, when it might have enabled and encouraged them to stand against Hitler and Mussolini. It also nurtured sentiment for neutrality laws which included a ban on loans to belligerents.

Therefore, in 1940 and 1941, after the fall of France, when the United States became alarmed lest Great Britain and the Soviet Union go down before the German assault, Roosevelt had to devise the lend-lease system in order to support their war effort. This ingenious arrangement avoided a repetition of the quarrels over wartime financial obligations which marred our relations with former associates for two decades after the First World War.

While relenting in our efforts to collect on foreign debts due the American government, we took steps to salvage the defaulted private loans of American investors.

In striving to do so — and in this I was the leading and most persistent advocate — I was badly scarred. In the course of organizing a disinterested and independent organization to represent these investors, I had bruising encounters with mistrustful or rival officials, self-serving financial forces and stubborn members of Congress.

Roosevelt at first thought the project suspect, and Henry Morgenthau, Jr., was graspingly eager to get the assignment in his own hands. When ultimately the job was done and the organization was created, I found myself, as a State Department official most directly concerned with foreign debt situations, seriously at odds with the officers of the organization I had worked so hard to create. For during the first two or three hard years of its operation they seemed to me too exigent in their demands on the foreign debtors. Hardly ever did the succession of dignitaries who earned substantial fees as officers of the corporation give me a nod of recognition or thanks. Among those whose zeal to collect I found myself forced to restrain was an old friend, Francis White, former Assistant Secretary of State for Latin American Affairs (who had once called Secretary Stimson's attention to a book I had written and thereby opened the way for my entry into the State Department). But the most stubborn and acquisitive of all was J. Reuben Clark, Jr., who had been Under-Secretary of State under Hoover, a really hard-fisted Mormon.

The tale, I believe, retains enough interest to be briefly recalled.

When hard times came almost all the foreign loans and investments that had been made by Americans became vulnerable. Some of the loans — especially those to Latin American governments — had been extended or used for purposes which did not strengthen the national economy of the borrower. Excessive amounts had been loaned to financial, industrial and governmental institutions in Germany, Austria and Hungary, even though they were subordinate to other obligations. The interest rate on many loans, especially those made to governments whose credit rating was poor, was high; hence the amount of dollars required by the debtors to maintain payment was hard to secure. Affecting all the loans was the fact to which too little advance thought was given — that while the sum of interest and principal due to American investors was mounting, the worldwide restrictions on imports were growing more constricting. The suppression of trade reduced the ability of any and all debtors to pay.

As the depression dragged on during 1932, several billion dollars of foreign bonds owned by Americans fell into default or were on the verge of default. Their holders were aggrieved at their losses. When they learned that the banking houses that had sold these securities could do nothing to help, they besought the American government to assist them in collecting. If it had done so, it would have been involved in quarrels with a score of countries and appeared as Shylock before the whole debtor world.

Shortly before coming to the State Department, I had published a study of the connections between foreign investment and diplomacy during the one other previous great era of foreign financing. This was in the years between 1870 and 1914, when the British, French, and Germans loaned or invested abroad a larger part of their income than any nations had ever done before or have ever done since. Occasional defaults had occurred. Rather than itself haggling with the debtors, the British government had sponsored the formation of a Foreign Bondholders' Protective Association. Though not subject to government control, it was accorded broad powers under an act of Parliament. It was non-profit-making. I had studied the operations of this organization with care and had discussed them with its chief officers. Moreover, my studies had acquainted me with the arts which had induced debtors to pay what they fairly could without creating animosity.

Thus when the requests for help of the American owners of defaulted bonds became insistent, and Secretary of State Stimson grew troubled at the extent to which their appeals were absorbing his attention, the British example recurred to me. He commented encouragingly on the memo that I sent him about it and on my suggestion that the State and Treasury Departments might foster the creation of a similar organization. In April 1932, he instructed Harvey Bundy and me to go ahead and try to bring it into existence. An additional reason for doing so quickly emerged. Individuals who were unqualified, or without enough influence, or dishonest, were soliciting the right to represent distressed bondholders.

Trust which they did not deserve was being reposed in them. There was reason to fear that the investors would be defrauded and American official relations with the debtor governments would be abused.

Many problems had to be resolved before the organization could be formed. It was necessary to find an organizing group on whose disinterestedness the State Department could rely and whom the bondholders, many of whom felt they had been sold down the river by the firms that had sold them their securities, would trust. It would also have to be able to secure the desired cooperation of the financial community; and there was the problem of how the organization was to be financed without recourse to the public treasury or dependence on the banks.

A small group of distinguished persons was invited to come to Washington to discuss the project. Of these the two who did the most valuable work were Charles P. Howland, an elevated scholar connected with Yale University and the Council on Foreign Relations, and George Rublee, a distinguished lawyer who had served the government well in various troubled situations, among them as adviser to Ambassador Dwight Morrow at a time when our relationship with Mexico had been most strained.

This group went about the task conscientiously. By the end of May they had reported back that they and the various informed persons they had interviewed thought it desirable to form a central organization which could coordinate efforts for the protection of holders of foreign bonds. However, they thought it would not be advisable to confer upon it powers equivalent to those possessed by the British organization. Among their reasons was the belief that the American banking community was not as homogeneous and closely knit as the British, nor were its members as trustful. They also were somewhat fearful lest an ambitious start arouse the opposition of the banking houses that had issued the securities.

The plans which they submitted for consideration were based on these ideas. On June 2, when they met with Secretary Stimson, he told them that he thought their report was very temperate and in good sense, and he asked them to proceed to determine methods of finance and to select personnel. In their report, however, there was one statement which disturbed me, as I privately confided to the Secretary: "That in normal cases the bankers, supported by the investors, will continue to organize committees. In such cases the Council would exercise its good offices in the formation of strong and proper committees, recognizing the responsibility of the bankers who had issued the bonds in question." In the analytical memo which I sent to the Secretary about the proposal, I ventured the opinion that the bankers might not always put the interest of the bondholders above their own. I questioned whether they had retained the confidence of many of those who had bought the bonds, or the good will of some of the defaulters. Moreover, I pointed out that some of the chief banking houses were rival creditors with the bondholders in some situations, and in these there might be a definite conflict of interest.

Whether or not these considerations would have prevailed had not the defaults compounded during the following months, I do not know. But security-issuing houses were staggering and most American commercial banks were being compelled to close the doors. Thus they did prevail. Subsequent recommendation conformed to the view that the council should play a primary and independent part in representing the bondholders and not merely serve as a co-ordinating agency for committees sponsored by the bankers. By the time the presidential election took place in November definite plans had been approved. The State and Treasury Departments had asked the original group, as a public service, to proceed to enlist individuals to act as trustees and directors of the council, and then bring it into existence.

There was reason to wonder whether the project would be carried forward or dropped by the Democratic victors in the 1932 election. Roosevelt had spoken sardonically of foreign lending. He had implied that the favor shown by the Hoover administration to foreign lending was the cause of the plight of the bondholders. Thus on October 21, in St. Louis, he had said, "This is an unsavory chapter in foreign finance. These bonds in large part are the fruit of distressing policies pursued by the present administration in Washington." In Baltimore four days later he had said, "The Horsemen of Destruction came likewise from lending money to backward and crippled countries. The Administration encouraged the policy that sought to open markets in foreign lands through the lending of American money to these countries. . . . it was utterly and entirely unsound."

Moreover, he had intimated that many who purchased foreign bonds had done so in a well-grounded belief that the American government had passed upon their financial soundness. This charge he based on the fact that early in the 1920's the government had asked the issuing houses to notify it before entering into a foreign-loan engagement, in order to enable it to consider whether such an engagement might traverse our foreign policy. It had tried to safeguard this procedure against misunderstanding by writing in every answer made to the issuing houses and in its public statements about the procedure that "the Department of State does not pass on the merits of foreign loans as business propositions nor assume any responsibility in connection with such transactions. Also no reference to the attitude of this government should be made in any prospectus or otherwise." But in the caustic denunciations, the candidate for office had ignored the fact that such cautions had been issued, and had blamed the administration rather than the banking houses. Could it be that he thought that there was political gold in doing so, even if there was no longer real gold value in many of these foreign loans?

True, the Coolidge and Hoover administrations had definitely encouraged Americans to purchase several of the large bond issues of the German government, loans that were arranged in connection with revisions of the reparations imposed on Germany. But they had done so in order to make possible settlements which they thought would end the animosities that had kept Europe in a state of turmoil since the end of the First World War and which were having an injurious economic effect. I thought that Roosevelt in his discourses should have acknowledged the estimable purpose behind even such instances in which the government could be rightly accused of responsibility for the purchase of foreign bonds which were going bad.

No wonder, then, that those of us who had been trying to bring this organization into existence feared that the new President might instruct us to desist from our efforts. I was uncertain of the response I would get when I submitted, on March 15, 1933, a rather full report to the new Secretary of State to inform him of the status of the organization. The last four paragraphs read:

"As for finance, some foundation has promised to meet part of the burden and it was hoped that certain institutions, such as the Stock Exchange, would meet the rest.

"Mr. Rublee and Mr. [Allen] Dulles are coming to the Department today to report the makeup of the committee, and to try to assure themselves that these plans and personalities are agreeable to the government. . . .

"I intend to tell them that the government does not feel that it has any veto power over either plans or personalities, and that the new council must consider itself as a private organization. However, informally, it may be said that the plans and personalities seem to us excellent and that we trust the council will come into actual existence very shortly.

"Because of the importance of the amounts involved (the council may well have to handle default situations amounting up to several billions of dollars), and because of the fact that in many situations this government will desire to work intimately with the council, it may be that this matter should be called to the attention of the President." [1]

Later, Under-Secretary Phillips sent me a note which read, "I discussed this matter with the President this afternoon. He agrees entirely that it would be wise to have the personnel appointed by outside associations and so avoid giving the impression in foreign countries that they represented the Government of the United States. He did say, however, that their salaries and fees should be approved by the Federal Trade Commission. I told him that word

had got about that he was beginning to favor Senator Hiram Johnson's Amendment,* which allegation he denied explicitly."

This amendment suggested that an agency of the government
might handle default situations. Whether the President might have
been letting Johnson believe he saw merit in his measure, I do not
know; but that members of his administration were, I know.
Among them were Henry Morgenthau and Louis Howe (who
thought thereby to gain credit for the President with Senator Johnson and Congressman Sam Rayburn of Texas).[2]

Nor was this the only influential group that continued to regard
our initiative with doubt and mistrust. While some of the powerful
banking and investment houses in New York City were sympathetic to it, not all were. Some thought that they themselves could
do better for the holders of the bonds which they had sold. Others
feared that the new organization would come under the dominance
of the Rooseveltian officials who would not allow due regard to the
interests of investment houses, or would subordinate efforts of collecting the debts to other purposes.

Against these threatening obstacles I launched another memo to
the Secretary of State on March 28, hoping it would find its way to
the White House. In this I attempted to illustrate the reasons for
favoring the creation of this nonprofit and almost independent organization. I wrote in part:

"It seems plain that there is a great need for an adequate organization of the bondholders to protect their own interests. The issuing and banking houses have proven to be, in many cases, either
unwilling to take the responsibility and cost of dealing with the
situations, or are unwelcome either in the eyes of the bondholders
or of the governments concerned. In some important instances they
are the object of such severe criticism in foreign lands (especially
where the loans were made to some regime which was subsequently
overthrown) that their actions are ineffective. In other instances
the issuing houses have gone out of existence (such as the Lee

---

* This was in the form of an amendment to the Security Act of 1923,
called Title II.

Higginson Company) or are about to go out of existence (such as the securities companies organized by the Chase and National City Banks). A great number of profit-seeking groups are trying to persuade owners of defaulted bonds to entrust them with the task of collection. . . . Some of these are reputable; some verge on being disreputable. All must sustain themselves from the beginning by seeking deposits of bonds and putting charges upon the bondholders who have already suffered loss. None have achieved any substantial degree of public repute or influence. In some situations rival protective committees have sprung up to contest each other's efforts. . . .

"The growing number of defaults, the agitation among the bondholders, the development of inadequate protective associations, the complicating effects on the foreign relations of this country of these default situations — all bring home the desirability of having an adequate and disinterested organization among the bondholders themselves, for their own protection. *This has been visualized by the State Department as a step away from dollar diplomacy, and not toward it.* In the absence of such an organization it is almost inevitable that the government will be dragged into various situations in an effort to protect the American investors against unfair or discriminatory treatment. If an adequate and disinterested body were formed, the Department could keep aloof."

This was written not long before the German government and many of the German states and municipalities announced that they were going to suspend transfer of dollar payments on the bonds held by Americans. When, at our behest, Schacht did enter into consultation about this action, the way in which the banks seemed to be aiming to put their own interests ahead of all others caused some informed observers to urge the President anew to resort to the Johnson amendment rather than to rely on a private organization. Thus, for example, Richard Washburn Child, former ambassador to Italy, wrote to Roosevelt: "The Johnson Amendment is passed and subject to your proclamation and need. The need is great. It is absurd to have the Germans invite our holders of private indebtedness to Berlin and to have John Foster Dulles, with no other background except that of a law firm for issuing houses, go to represent the long-term holders among the rooked citizens. It is unfortunate also that the appearance of the State Department to protect their interest has been so snarled up with what is called 'Secret Six Lobby.' " [3]

During the summer, work continued on the formation of the organization. A board of trustees was selected — although the State Department did not pass upon the individuals selected. But several times I had to remind the small organizing group which did select them that if the organization were closely identified with the issuing banks, or the small group of corporation lawyers who drew up the original contracts for the defaulted bonds, its usefulness would be impaired.

By October the board of trustees had solved its immediate problems and was ready to proceed to the inauguration of the organization. Raymond Stevens, who had just done an excellent job for the State Department in Siam, had been chosen as the first director. On October 7 he told me that he had arranged an appointment at the White House for Under-Secretary of the Treasury Acheson, the Secretary of State and himself, and that he desired me to be there also to assist in explaining the plan. He said that he would ask the Secretary to bring me along, and then later telephoned to tell me that the Secretary had agreed to do so. But when I went to Hull's office on other business shortly before he was due at the White House, he did not suggest that I come with him. Probably guessing that I was about to remind him of what he had told Stevens, he rushed for his hat and carefully avoided my gaze. When Stevens asked me in the afternoon why I had not been at the meeting — which had gone well — I said I did not understand why I had not been asked to be present. Perhaps the Secretary feared that I had antagonized the President by my opposition to the Johnson amendment; perhaps the President had said he would rather not have me there.

Later that afternoon the Secretary asked me to come to his office to discuss several other matters. After we had finished talking about them I said, according to the handwritten memo I made of the talk, "Mr. Secretary, Ray Stevens came to see me this after-noon to tell about the plans for the bondholders' association. May I get it clear? Is it your wish that I drop out of that effort? He squirmed, shuffled and blinked and said, 'Oh! I forgot about that. Why didn't you come before? I didn't know whether you or I was to go. I forgot. Of course you are to go on.' " I tell this story be-cause it was just one chapter of an experience which to this day leaves me smarting.

Not long afterward, former Secretary of State Stimson told Roo-sevelt how happy he was that the President had decided to leave the way open for the creation of the bondholders' association; that it was a courageous and wise decision. Roosevelt seemed pleased and said he had to turn down Senator Johnson, who had grumbled but given in.[4]

By December the organization — called the Foreign Bondhold-ers' Protective Council, Inc. — was legally organized under the laws of the State of Maryland; it held its first meeting in Washing-ton on December 18.[5] But I was not asked to the inaugural meet-ing of its executive committee, possibly because my admonitions had given offense to some downtown bankers, or their lawyers or other associates.

Before many months had passed I was listening to the aggrieved protests of the diplomatic representatives of several Latin Ameri-can countries — Brazil and Colombia among them — against the refusal of the officers of the council to accept offers of payment which they thought were the utmost their governments should be called upon to make at the time. I formed the opinion — and I was rather well informed about the capacity of these debtors to pay — that the representatives of the council were being too demanding. My intervention, authorized by Secretary Hull, to persuade the offi-cers of the organization to accept terms proffered by the debtors, led to acrimonious talks. Gradually these officers sought to consult, whenever they could, other branches of the State Department rather than the Economic Adviser.

But for two years — to the best of my memory — I could not be ignored. For in the agreement on the establishment of the council it was provided that two government officials should keep a light watch over its operations and its finances. William O. Douglas, then on the Securities and Exchange Commission and now on the Supreme Court, and myself were given the job of visitors. As I remember it, we went up to New York a few times to lunch and talk with the officers of the council. Their administration of the organization was admirable and their finances modest, though the officers were well-enough paid. However, rightly or wrongly, I got the sense that the less often we visited their shop the more welcome we would be.

In time their able handling of default situations became rather standard procedure and the State Department was called on to intervene less and less often — and less and less critically. Thus, those who had helped to create the organization could have a sense of satisfaction. But my own feelings were soured by a notion that the desire to secure payment from German authorities on loans which American banks had made to them was causing the financial community and certain elements of the business community to be too conciliatory toward the Hitler regime. It is the one area in which, I think, private American financial interest swayed — if only in a minor measure — American policy during the decade of the thirties.

Many years later, when the council put out a long press release — probably on the occasion of some anniversary — relating its history and accomplishments, my name was not even mentioned among the many. Sometime later, when I encountered one of the officers (a former State Department colleague), I let him know that I was aggrieved by the omission. In some subsequent release a feeble attempt was made to make up for this ill-treatment; but in my answer to the letter with which the article was forwarded, I did not suppress my opinion that the acknowledgment was too little and too late.

Thus ends the sad story of the only personal grudge of mine that remains against those with whom I worked during the year 1933. It may seem — and perhaps it is — a diversion from the main stream of this narrative, to which I will now return by telling of the renewal of the contest within the government over our monetary policy.

CHAPTER 22

The Dollar Is Thrust Down

AFTER the adjournment of the Monetary and Economic Conference, the gold bloc countries continued to be agitated lest the fluctuations of the dollar and sterling compel them to go off the gold standard. They made their controls over imports and capital movements more stringent. The governments of the British Commonwealth, by contrast, became more inclined to adopt Roosevelt's views. For example, in the Empire Declaration on Currency issued on July 27 they expressed the opinion that while the re-establishment of an international monetary standard was the ultimate aim, the attainment of a satisfactory price level was a primary condition precedent to such a step.

In the United States there ensued a short period of watchful waiting upon the effects of the diverse domestic measures being put into effect. The economy was advancing too slowly and irregularly. Prices rose but little and uncertainly. Many millions were still unemployed, and most industries were operating far below capacity. Our foreign trade remained much less than it had been and than it had to be for a balanced economy. Under these circumstances the pleas for monetary stimulants became more urgent.

Two sets of prescriptions warred with each other. One rested on the supposition that if merchants and producers were assisted by generous credit policies and assured about the future of the dollar the revival would gain momentum; the growth in demand and trade — national and international — would bring about the desired rise in prices and incomes. The other was based on the supposition that because of the surpluses, the depth of the depression and the extent of the distress, these measures would not give a sufficient or quick up-thrust to our economy. Monetary inflation (or rather *re*flation) of some sort, the proponents of this course contended, was urgently required to increase values and lead businessmen to take chances.

The President became more attentive to the reasons advanced in behalf of this particular tactic of reducing the purchasing power of the dollar. He asked Henry Morgenthau, Jr., to bring to Washington Professor Warren and two other like-minded economists. On August 7, Warren, in a report turned over to the Treasury, stated his conclusions succinctly. "I believe," he wrote, "there is only one way to end the depression, and that is an adequate devaluation of the dollar. Other things may help, but they cannot succeed without a reduction in the gold value of the dollar." He thought the only way in which commodity prices might be raised and held up was by "controlling the gold value of the dollar and forcing it downward." To him, the time for prompt and effective action had arrived. But his theories and aims stretched beyond the immediate crisis; the fourth point in the summary of his memo read: "Provide some form of a more stable measure of value for the future. If an all commodity rather than a one commodity money is established, it will be an outstanding achievement in history." [1]

Professor Irving Fisher, of Yale, called on Roosevelt in Hyde Park on August 9. He was best known as the exponent of what was generally called the quantity theory of money — which condensed certain contingent connections between the quantity of money and the price level into an oversimplified equation. He was a classmate of Secretary Stimson, whom he used to seek out on his visits to Washington. While the Secretary was fond of him he would soon conclude that I had more time than he to listen to Fisher's theories. It was hard to resist his evangelical fervor as he propounded remedies for so many of the ills to which nations and men are subject. Monetary ills were only one of them. Another was insomnia. To lick that he had invented a bed located within a structure of vibrating electrical wires. Another was the evil of drink; to lick that he wrote books advocating prohibition of the manufacture and sale of liquor.

The presence of these zealots near the President made the officials of the Treasury and the Federal Reserve System nervous. They had reason to be. For Roosevelt was again pondering whether or not to resort to the powers given him under the Thomas amendment. Repeatedly, in talks with Woodin, Warburg and others, he made remarks that indicated he might be on the verge of doing so. For example, having said that he saw no serious objection to the issuance of thirty-year non-interest-bearing Treasury notes in currency denominations in order to pay off debts, he told Morgenthau that he would like to buy gold for the Treasury on the open market at a price higher than the current one. He said, "I think this would do the trick but I do not know how it could be done." [2]

Warburg, hoping to encircle the proponents of such inflationary measures, urged the President to assign the task of formulating American monetary policy to a group that would be centered in the Treasury. One excerpt from two conversations with the President about this proposal, recorded in Warburg's journal, is illuminating as well as informative. "He [Roosevelt] said no commission could answer the two questions as to what kind of a dollar and how big a dollar we should have. I asked him why not, and he said, 'because I myself can't answer that.' I asked him whether he had any objection to a commission trying to answer the questions . . . to which he replied 'it was foolish to try to answer them at the present time because conditions were so uncertain.' I asked him what sort of conditions he had in mind. He said 'There is a town in Pennsylvania of 5000 inhabitants, 1000 of whom are coal miners and 4000 dependent on the coal miners. All of them are out of work and in misery. . . . These people have no faith in [Governor Gifford]

Pinchot or the coal miners of the Mellon interests, but they have faith in me, and until that sort of problem is solved, how can I tell what sort of dollar I want?'

"Finally he said he could see no harm whatever in accepting the suggestions of a commission to study the agenda as outlined, and authorized me to tell Woodin to go ahead. I asked him whom he would have on the commission. . . . He put down on a piece of paper Woodin, Acheson, [Lewis] Douglas, Sprague, Black, Harrison, Rogers [Professor James Harvey Rogers of Yale University], Stewart [Walter Stewart, former adviser to the Bank of England] and me." [3] Warren was not included, presumably because he was in Europe. Henry Morgenthau, Jr., was not included, presumably because he was officially concerned with farm credit operations, not monetary policy.

The President asked this group to consider what should be done about newly mined gold. Warburg proposed that it might be purchased by the Federal Reserve Banks at a price range to be fixed by the President each week; but others thought this was dangerous because it gave the President too much power. An authorization for gold purchase by the Federal Reserve System was, however, drawn up. The President approved it on the following day. But he did not sign and issue it until some days later.

The group was also asked to consider whether the Federal Reserve System should buy fifty million more dollars of government bonds during the coming week. Perhaps to make sure of the answer he would get to that question, he also asked them whether the government should issue non-interest-bearing securities in currency denominations to pay off maturing government debts.

The Federal Reserve officials warned against the issuance of greenbacks in any guise. Their report rehearsed all the objections once again.[4] At one point in the discussion one of the group suggested that if greenbacks were issued the motto on the United States money should be changed from IN GOD WE TRUST to I HOPE THAT MY REDEEMER LIVETH. In the upshot, the President sent word to the committee that he would drop the greenback proposal but that he wanted the Federal Reserve System to buy large amounts of government securities. "As the lesser to two evils," it proceeded to do so.

A little later the group tried again to lead the President back onto what they regarded as a more stable course. It recommended that an effort be made to have the American and British governments and central banking authorities start to cooperate at once in several ways, in order to control exaggerated fluctuations in the value of their currencies. During this trial period, experiences would indicate the proper relative values of the pound and dollar and lead toward the time when the dollar should be devalued in terms of gold (at a rate slightly lower than the one then current, which was about 70 per cent of its former value). It suggested some novel elements of an international gold standard which would permit greater leeway in national policies. The group was convinced that this monetary program would bring about the price increase Roosevelt wanted. But it felt dubious about its reception.

During the first half of September the prices of commodities and securities shot up and the exchange value of the dollar fell steeply. The dollar dropped from 70 per cent to 65 per cent of its former value. Sterling fell to almost the same ratio to the dollar that had prevailed before Britain went off gold in 1931.

At the end of September the Treasury group, led on by Warburg and Douglas, again recommended to the President that discussions looking toward stabilization on a devalued basis be begun. If agreed on, the Federal Reserve was to be instructed to see to it that the value of the dollar did not rise above its former parity with the pound sterling.

But the President's ideas were slanting the other way. He informed the group that he now was inclined to have the value of the dollar decline still further before starting to discuss devaluation with the British. He told Warburg that now he wanted the dollar to fall until the pound became worth $5.00. Warburg reminded him that in March he would have been satisfied with the equivalent of $3.75 for a pound. When in May it had fallen to $3.85, he had said he would be content with $4.00; then on June 17, when Warburg and Sprague had recommended stabilization at $4.00, Roosevelt had said he wanted it $4.30, then $4.50; and when it had fallen to $4.50 in August, he had said $4.85 (the former parity) would do. But now he wished to have the dollar fall until $5.00 was required to buy a pound sterling. Was there to be no limit to it? What would happen to the wage earner and small property owner? Had he reckoned with the consequences if countries still on gold left it and also manipulated their currencies? The President said Warburg did not appreciate the importance of having prices push further forward.

Tension in Treasury and Federal Reserve circles was accentuated by the need to sell new government securities to procure the funds to redeem those falling due. When I talked with Acheson on September 30, I noticed that although he had been looking husky and tranquil on his return only a few days before from a short vacation in Canada, he was already showing strain and fatigue. The problem of monetary policy, I remarked, seemed to me the central problem which the Treasury faced at the time; Acheson agreed. But he said that he ought to be giving all his time now to the question of the conversion of the government debt. When I asked whether Secretary Woodin couldn't handle this staple type of Treasury operation, he answered sadly that he no longer could. Woodin was too ill, discouraged and perplexed. The pressures upon him were too diverse. Lewis Douglas, as Director of the Budget, was infringing on his prerogatives; Jesse Jones, head of the Reconstruction Finance Corporation, was stubborn and inactive. The President had to be consulted about every detail and was interfering in every decision; and this whole situation was proving to be too much for Woodin.

Still, during the next several weeks, the Treasury did carry through several bond conversions on favorable terms, creating an expectation that the government was not going to engage in any further quick devaluation of the currency. Thus the value of the dollar began to rise again. Prices of wheat and cotton fell steeply.

Grumbling throughout the farm regions became loud again, and discontent in some debt-ridden countries seemed to be verging on rebellion.

By the sixteenth of October, the economic scene was set for Warren. He prodded both the President and Morgenthau to raise the price of gold. The longer this action was postponed the more drastic it would have to be, he argued. All the other efforts to support prices of farm products were evidently failing, he averred; government purchases of wheat, cotton and corn, loans to farmers, attempts to reduce future supply were proving altogether ineffective. The Agricultural Adjustment Administration he described in a letter to Morgenthau as "about 10 per cent useful, 15 per cent political expediency, 25 per cent hot air and 50 per cent a measure that will result in violent reaction unless prices are raised. . . ." [5]

The President was becoming very restive. He was bent on having the government purchase newly mined gold. The lawyers were quarreling about the legalities of such an action. Herman Oliphant, counsel to the Farm Credit Administration, had suggested a procedure for doing so through the RFC. Acheson maintained that the government did not have legal power; he told Morgenthau he did not see how we could do this just as the Treasury was completing its sales of new securities. The government, he said, would be accused of bad faith. Morgenthau's answer was, "Well, why didn't you cross that bridge and think it out a couple of weeks ago?" When Acheson asked whether this action could not be put off awhile, Morgenthau said he did not think so; there were two or three important things to be accomplished. [6]

The question was settled at a special meeting of the directors of the RFC, about which Morgenthau has also left an account. He took Oliphant and Warren along to this affray. "Dean Acheson arrived a little late, but scarlet and looking like a thunder cloud. He said, 'Gentlemen, I have just come from the President. You know I am opposed to your buying gold. The President had ordered me to do it. I will carry out his order.' They read him the resolution and he said, 'I will vote for it.' . . . Then Acheson said, 'Of course we shall have to get the Attorney General to rule on this' and Acheson wanted to stall and I said, 'No, let us go over and see the Attorney General now and try to get him to give us a ruling now.' " [7]

So over to see the Attorney General, Homer Cummings, went Morgenthau, Acheson and Oliphant and explained the problem to him. He ruled verbally that the Treasury possessed the necessary legal power. Then together they all went over to the White House. There, Morgenthau recorded in his diary, "The President and Acheson almost came to blows."

The President thereupon moved further toward management of the dollar. He decided to explain his ideas and intentions to the American people in a fireside chat. His assistants spent the day discussing what should be said and how to say it — among them Moley, Morgenthau, Warren, Oliphant, Harry Hopkins and Rogers. Moley threw their ideas together in rough form. The President re-dictated. Soon after teatime the address was completed. That night, October 22, he read it over the air with dramatic intonations. After saying that it was still imperative to raise prices, he added, "If we cannot do this one way, we will do it in another. Do it we will." He was going to try to do it by controlling the gold value of the dollar at home. The Reconstruction Finance Corporation was to be authorized to buy gold newly mined in the United States and also, if necessary, on the world market. The purchase price was to be reset from time to time after consultation with the Secretary of the Treasury and the President. Again the President affirmed that "this is a policy, not an expedient. . . . We are thus continuing to move toward a managed currency."

For Professor Warren and the economic nationalists, this was their greatest night.

The ensuing commotion in American and foreign financial circles bemused rather than perturbed the President. For the prices of commodities and stocks began to go up as the gold value of the dollar went down. Hoping that this move would bring about the wanted improvement in our national situation, he shrugged off the reminders of bankers and economists that up to then no government of a capitalist country had succeeded in so managing its currency that its purchasing power stayed substantially the same over long periods; that all attempts to do so had gone awry; and that at some stage the fears aroused caused the economy to falter.

Nor was the President surprised or upset by the skepticism of the British press and the angry uproar in the press of the gold bloc countries. He rather enjoyed the shock his policy gave to the international banker. Montagu Norman "wailed across the ocean, 'This is the most terrible thing that has happened. The whole world will be put in bankruptcy.' Harrison's instinct was to reassure Norman, but Roosevelt and Morgenthau looked at each other, picturing the international bankers with every one of their hairs standing on end with horror, and began to roar with laughter." [8]

I may be permitted to remark that Norman did have vanity of person and professional pomp. But this behavior of Morgenthau, as a responsible official engaged in business serious enough to affect the fate of nations, was one of his displays of response to Roosevelt's moods and of juvenile humor (*Schadenfreude*).

One reason why Roosevelt had been attracted to the monetary theory with which he was experimenting was that he wished to immunize the course of prices in the United States against foreign influences. "Our dollar," he remarked in his fireside chat, "is now altogether too greatly influenced by the accidents of international trade, by the international policies of other nations, and by poltical disturbances in other continents."

With memories of the Monetary and Economic Conference still in mind, this passage in his anouncement worried me. Unless the United States isolated its economy almost completely, these international influences were certain to affect the purchasing power of the dollar. The President's apparent indifference to the impact of his action on the commercial and financial situation of other countries was bothersome at a time when — as will shortly be told — the Disarmament Conference was breaking down, a militant Nazi

Germany was getting out of the League of Nations and uneasy political divisions were appearing in France. But it did not alarm me unduly. For, if my professional training counted for anything, I was sure that the new measure would turn out to be only a transient expedient — and as such probably advantageous.

On the day after he made this utterance, the President, in high good humor, told Morgenthau, "I had had shackles on my hands and now I feel for the first time as though I have thrown them off." Every weekday morning now, Jones, Morgenthau and Warren met in the President's bedroom to set the dollar price that would be offered for gold that day — while the President ate his breakfast of soft-boiled eggs, toast and coffee. As John Blum has since written, "The price that the morning conference fixed on any given day made little difference. The object was simply to keep the trend moving gradually upward a little above the world price in the expectation that commodity prices would follow." [9]

The RFC first offered to pay $31.36 for an ounce of gold (the price was $20.00 before we left the gold standard in April), then raised the offer little by little. The price each day was set at hazard to keep the speculators guessing, but the pace and rate at which it was increased was affected by the movement of prices of farm products. The objective was to boost the price of a bushel of wheat to 90 cents, a pound of cotton to 10 cents, a bushel of corn to 50 cents before January.

On the day (October 25) when Morgenthau went over to the Treasury and gave Acheson a note from the President suggesting gold purchases, Acheson asked him, "Why don't you move into Woodin's office?" [10] Morgenthau was affronted by the insinuation. But on November 14 the President appointed him Acting Secretary of the Treasury. Woodin was compelled by illness to leave office. Acheson was being asked to resign as Under-Secretary. Roosevelt was incensed at him. According to Morgenthau, this was because Acheson, during the previous few days, "had tried to avoid signing the gold agreement for fear of personal liability to himself." [11]

There was another dropout among the advisers of the Treasury — Oliver Sprague had resigned. After his return from London, he had not disguised the fact that he was smarting over the experience. He did not openly criticize the President's course but tended rather to place the blame upon the American and foreign press for incorrectly construing the two agreements submitted while he was in London as "stabilization"; he deemed the first to have been merely an arrangement whereby central banks might iron out sudden fluctuations of foreign currencies during the conference, and the second to have been just a flimsy obligation on the part of each government to check speculation in the currencies of others. He also deplored the way in which the discussions in London about these temporary agreements had become so enmeshed with the fate of the conference. They might not have been, he thought, if Cox had not accepted the chairmanship of the monetary committee (this having been interpreted as a signal that the dollar would be stabilized).

The President concluded that Sprague had no suggestions as to how the price level might be raised except "the same old ones"; he thought of him as a nuisance "who carried no real weight except with the Bank of England crowd and some of our New York bankers." Moreover, reports reached him that Sprague was trying to line up prominent conservative Democrats — such as former Secretary of War Newton Baker and Senator Carter Glass — to attend a mass meeting in Carnegie Hall to protest the President's financial policies. This suggestion Roosevelt thought "absolutely disloyal." [12] So Sprague's resignation was accepted with relief.

Since commodity prices remained sluggishly low despite the purchases of newly mined gold, the President on October 29 decided to extend the purchases into the world market. To a gathering which included Harrison and Eugene R. Black, the chairman of the Federal Reserve Board, he explained why. He was convinced "that it was imperative to get the prices up and get some inflation. . . . that this program required prompt action, that the country would not wait for results over a period of years, that even now it was absolutely necessary to put up agricultural prices within the next few months above the present lines, say 95 cents a bushel of wheat, in order to avoid a march of the farmers on Washington. . . . he did not know anything about economics but he knew something about politics and from that standpoint action was required." Then, taking note of objections, he added that "he did not like to hear so much complaining and felt that everyone connected with the Administration should pull together. . . . and if anyone was not willing to pull a willing oar he should get out." [13]

Thus remaining opposition to his policy was squelched. None of the officials of the Federal Reserve System resigned — most of them complying because of fear that if they did not, Roosevelt would resort to other inflationary measures they deemed still more objectionable. In appreciation of their concern for their relations with the Bank of England and the Bank of France, the President agreed that the foreign officials might be told what we were doing and what we were trying to achieve. When Harrison told the French officials, they "jumped out of their skins." Norman (of the Bank of England) deplored our intention and predicted that France would be forced off gold.

The first purchases in the world market were made at the elevated price of $31.96 per ounce of gold, and each day the bid was raised a little. The value of the dollar vis-à-vis the pound fell correspondingly. Two weeks after we began to buy gold in the world market, the President reviewed the situation with his monetary consultants. He told them that this program was working, and that consequently the situation in the agricultural sections of the country was less acute than it had been. His immediate aim — to lift the price of wheat to about one dollar a bushel and cotton to 10 cents a pound — had almost been attained. Harrison, Black and others urged that the gold-buying program be slowed up. The damaging effect on the market for government bonds was becoming serious, they averred. The chance that we would compel France to leave the gold standard was becoming frightening. But the President said the time to hold the dollar steady was not yet opportune. He wished to continue to force the dollar down a little further and watch what happened; then perhaps he might consider provisional stabilization — the British went along with us. He anticipated a drive in Congress for $1.25 for wheat and 15 cents for cotton; that would put him in a hole and he might not be able to control the situation. But if he could keep the prices of wheat and cotton going up during the next few months, he thought he could control it without using the other powers under the Thomas amendment. He did not envisage legal stabilization until Congress adjourned, which would probably not be before the following June.[14] Charts and indices and reports of political sentiment in rural areas and factory hours would remain our guide awhile longer — not the standing of the dollar in world markets.

The fears aroused by this new monetary policy began to wane. My impressions of the situation a few weeks after the policy was initiated were recorded in a letter to a friend in which I wrote, "All of this will probably leave in your mind the impression, and it is a correct one, that the master paradox still exists — a government harried above all by surplus either of stocks or of productive capacity. To some extent continuation of the upward movement will take care of the situation, but enough of it will remain to force us either (1) to restore international trade or (2) to go much further in the government control of our whole industrial system. Didn't the five state governors who came to Washington last week suggest that each farmer be given a little punch card on which would be indicated how much he could send to market? And once he had used up his punches he would not be allowed to ship anything outside the barnyard gates?

"I probably give you too strong a sense of confusion and difficulty. For I believe that despite it, affairs continue to move in an upward direction. . . . Blood is rising in the fight, but every sign shows that the great majority of the people still believe that the President is on the right line."

And further in the same letter, "The personal scene has not changed much. Henry Morgenthau has taken Moley's place at the bedside. The President is being his own Treasury Department; the Secretary of State leaves for Montevideo this coming Saturday — to turn recrimination into gentle trust; Tugwell and Jerome Frank continue to propose the impractical, and they say they are doing it because failure will prove we have to change the system.

"The President's performance seems to me to continue to be remarkable, and at the bottom not wavering. He clings to his general objectives with determination."

Roosevelt's sense of having acted wisely was sustained by the improvement in the national situation which was taking place. Toward the end of November he could, for example, write Colonel House from Warm Springs: "This Southland has a smile on its face. Ten cent cotton has stopped foreclosures, saved banks and started people definitely on the upgrade. That means all the way from Virginia to Texas. Sears Roebuck sales in Georgia are 110 per cent above 1932. . . . Hugh Johnson says every section of the country is showing definite gain."

His historical interpretation of what was happening was definite. "The real truth of the matter is . . . that a financial element in the larger centers has owned the Government since the days of Andrew Jackson — and I am not wholly excepting the administration of W.W. The country is going through a repetition of Jackson's fight with the bank of the United States — only on a bigger and broader basis." [15]

At this time Roosevelt was aroused again by tales that a very definite effort was being made by New York bankers, by political groups led by Ogden Mills and by British interests to create a sentiment in the United States in favor of fixing the gold content of the dollar and returning to the gold standard. Reports spread that if the American government would do so, the British government would follow. So, on November 27, Roosevelt asked George Harrison to inquire of Norman of the Bank of England whether he thought the

British government would join with us in stabilizing its currency in terms of gold either at once or after a short trial period. Harrison telephoned Norman. After consulting the British Treasury Norman answered that the British government would not agree to obligate itself to stabilize sterling, but would be glad to consider an arrangement for a trial period involving willingness on the part of both countries to allow the export of a certain amount of gold, if necessary. Would Washington, Norman asked, be interested in such an arrangement? This was about what Roosevelt thought the answer would be.[16]

Yet the decision to return to gold and stabilize was not as far off as he had thought. I was not included in the circle of those who were determining monetary policy. Busily engaged in other matters, I had been free to watch the course of their experiment with reserved assent. Events, I kept assuring myself, would compel a re-examination of the international implications of our gold-buying policy and an eventual agreement. Observation of the many facts and forces influencing the course of the American economy confirmed the judgment that the power of monetary measures to cure the depression had been overestimated. But it seemed to me unlikely that the President was placing all his bets on the Warren theory any more than he had placed them on any other particular theory for long or for keeps. All were trials, some of which offset the effects of others. I believed those who knew the President well and assured me that he always had a trick up his sleeve to gain time in which to mature his main plans.

By the end of December I was writing to a correspondent: "During the last few days a type of concord seems to have settled on Washington in regard to monetary questions. Within its limitations the panacea of the gold-buying plan has been realized. That does not mean that it will necessarily be given up . . . but I think it is realized that this still leaves the government with major problems of internal adjustment and of fiscal policy, and of banking policy."

This realization was quickened by several emergent tendencies:

it was becoming more probable that if the dollar was not stabilized other governments would emulate us and depreciate their currencies competitively; the speculative element in American markets was growing bolder; the market for government bonds was being disrupted. All the impending consequences of continuing the policy of currency manipulation brought it to a speedier end than had seemed likely.

On January 31, 1934, the President announced that the dollar was to be devalued in terms of gold to about 59 per cent of its former content and that this country was thereupon to return to the international gold standard. The profits of devaluation were to be turned over to the Treasury and used as needed as a fund to stabilize the dollar. The very large residual sum — several billions of dollars — could, in a jesting mood, be thought of as "stale money" (a term used by the natives of the West Indies to describe what was left in their pockets after a spree). But in subsequent years it served many good purposes.

The members of the gold bloc seem to have been relieved by the end of uncertainty rather than upset by the depth of our devaluation. They, who had been so nervous six months before, had become more confident of their ability to stay on gold and maintain the value of their currencies. Therefore they decided not to prevent the export of gold. It was correctly anticipated that our action would dispose the British government also to stabilize the pound, but after the rise in prices had gone somewhat further.

Money ceased to be the storm center of our foreign relations. Certainly it was less crucial to the rest of the world than the political deterioration in Europe and the final fracture of the Disarmament Conference, which had been taking place during this period of raging contest over monetary policies. Of this our narrative must now tell, broadening the scene of struggling nations and men in the wash of events.

The Further Ebb of the International Situation

THE pressure that was pulling Europe apart surged out of National Socialist Germany. It was the more disruptive because the other Western countries were vulnerable to the penetrating thrust of Communism. Moreover, three of the stronger and sturdier ones — Great Britain, France and Holland — were hesitant to concentrate their energies and strength against Germany because Japan was threatening their imperial domains in the Far East.

On June 23, 1933, George Gordon, the American chargé d'affaires in Berlin, had reported that it was becoming evident that a new wave of the revolution was definitely under way. The new "wild men" were the secondary leaders who represented the storm detachments and rabble elements of the party. He had predicted that if the Monetary and Economic Conference did not produce tangible results the trend of the Nazi movement toward national Bolshevism would be stimulated. Those of us who were then in London had shared his fear and forecast.

In fact, Nazi activities were in full sweep before the conference was finally stricken. By the end of June all independent opponents of the Nazis — except the Reichswehr — had been absorbed or crushed with startling rapidity. President von Hindenburg's will to assert himself was broken and he could no longer be aroused to try to check acts of lawlessness.

The tenor of the reports about Hitler that crossed my desk after our return to Washington from London is exemplified by the impressions of two Americans who had long talks with him. One report was from a professor who thought the Nazis considered him friendly and who had believed he could influence Hitler to be more reasonable. He had been flown to see Hitler by Rudolf Hess. On his return he recounted the course of his two-hour talk with the Chancellor. As Ambassador William Dodd reported it and recorded it in his diary for August 16: "Hilter talked wildly about destroying all Jews, insisting that no other nation had any right to protest and that Germany was showing the world how to rid itself of its greatest curse. He considered himself a sort of Messiah. He would rearm Germany, absorb Austria and finally move the capital to Munich."

Another American, who is not named in the memorandum I saw, told American officials after several talks with Hitler that he became so emotional at times as to appear abnormal; and that he worked himself into such a passion as he talked that his eyes would lose their ordinary focus and a film appear upon them, his voice growing more and more shrill until he almost choked. The Fuehrer was soon to give the world proof that such alarming impressions of his nature and intentions were correct.

In the middle of October, Hitler, having just announced that Germany was withdrawing from the Disarmament Conference, declared that Germany also was going to leave the League of Nations. This was rightly construed to mean that he was going to challenge every element of the Treaty of Versailles when he felt strong enough to disregard its terms and restraints. Wheeler-Bennett wrote of this occurrence: "On that day the second, or Locarno, period in the years between the wars came to an end and the world entered an uneasy progress toward a new conflict; a period which finally terminated in September 1939." [1]

How well and how sadly I remembered the heartfelt rejoicing on that earlier day, in 1926, when Germany was admitted into the League of Nations! How vividly I can still visualize the exalted look on the faces of those in the Assembly chamber when Aristide Briand, the French Foreign Minister, so eloquently welcomed this new member into the society of nations sworn to keep the peace! And I recall the emotional sincerity with which the German Foreign Minister, Gustav Stresemann, hailed the event as assurance of a new and better era.

That Hitler might have Germany withdraw from the League, the British, French, Polish and others had been well aware. Yet the event was a severe shock to all of them. For it was conclusive proof that Germany would rearm as fast as it could. Since at the same time Hitler dissolved the Reichstag and called for new elections, it was feared that soon thereafter he might order his troops to march into Austria, Poland or the Ruhr. Besides its secretly trained and re-equipped army, Germany had two million ruffians and youths in uniform who were spoiling for a fight, eager for promotion and hungry for loot.

But still none of the alarmed governments bestirred themselves. Hitler therefore concluded that there was nothing to be feared from them; he could crowd them as far and as daringly as Germany's might impressed itself upon them.

The President and Hull had been amply forewarned by our representatives in Geneva. But Dodd was nonplussed. He was convinced, he wrote the Secretary, that the Chancellor, after the event, had come to think that he had acted too precipitously. The trouble was due, Dodd thought, to the avowals which Hitler had made in the spring and the wild demands of the Nazis and other young Germans who "were not in the least doubtful of their ability to smash France and were pressing for more big guns, big airplanes and tanks." [2]

The President did not comment on this momentous event. The statement which Hull issued was anemic. He merely expressed regret at the occurrence and said that anything that marked a check in the disarmament movement was a source of great disappointment.

Time was to reveal that Germany's defiance and Hitler's recklessness affected predominant American opinion in a way that made the ultimate coming of a great war and our involvement in it more likely. But in the autumn of 1933, when Germany took these decisive measures and headed down its destructive course, Roosevelt was cautious and almost quiescent. He did not renew his earlier offer to see to it that Americans should not interfere with any actions which other nations might take collectively to resist aggression. He appeared to be less willing to brook opposition in the United States by cooperating in political affairs with our former allies than he had been in the late spring. Any disposition he might have had to do so was reduced by the still ruffled relationships caused by foreign criticisms of his monetary policies and lingering resentment over foreign debt defaults. His aloofness from Europe was also influenced by a sharpened sense that the progressive aggression of Japan might lead to a dangerous crisis between the United States and that country. The only important measure that the American government took to affect the balance among the nations was to grant recognition to the Soviet Union.

As the end of the year came round, Dodd purveyed to Washington a still gloomier estimate of the Nazi regime and its trio of chieftains, Hitler, Goebbels and Goering. Its last summarizing paragraph, written by a professor of history with Jeffersonian ideals, read: "You have, therefore, a unique triumvirate. Hitler, less educated, more romantic with a semi-criminal record; Goebbels and Goering, both Doctors of Philosophy, all animated by intense class and foreign hatreds and willing to resort to most ruthless arbitrary methods. Each of these has a body of support necessary for the maintenance of the present regime. . . . I do not think there has ever been in recent history such a unique group. There was such a group in ancient Rome, and you probably recall what happened. You may see, therefore, something of the problem which you have to deal with, and also why a man of my background might be doubtful of any early success." [3]

As addendum and postmortem (in two senses) to this very summary sketch of the deterioration in the European political outlook, I am impelled to recall the contemporary American official response to Nazi persecution of the Jews and other minorities and their opponents, which was becoming ever more cruel and comprehensive. Neither the President nor the State Department ventured to ease the visa requirements for German Jews and other refugees or to get the law changed. Appeals and recommendations that consuls be instructed to relax formalities for persons in great distress or danger were allowed to remain in the offices of Under-Secretary Phillips and members of the Western European Division of the State Department who insisted that the law neither allowed discretion nor provided for special procedure or urgent consideration of special cases. Thus only a very small number of the many that could have been rescued, had the State Department acted in time, were admitted into the United States. Luckily some of the distinguished refugees who could not wait for American entry permits found temporary, or permanent, haven in Portugal, France, Britain, Holland and the Scandinavian countries.

In the Far East also the situation had become more ominous. A swift glance backward at its course and our response to it will serve as a reminder. By the time Roosevelt took office the Japanese had occupied not only the whole of Manchuria but the Chinese province of Jehol, north of the Great Wall, as well. On March 4, Inauguration Day, Japanese troops almost unopposed had entered Chengteh, the chief city of that province, not far from the Great Wall. After a short pause they began to thrust farther south along the Great Wall and beyond it.

Roosevelt did not openly rebuke them. But he took the first steps to prepare the United States for a possible eventual war against Japan. He announced that the United States would build up its navy to treaty strength, and allocated the funds needed to make a substantial start to that end. But he refrained from following through Stimson's attempts to organize cooperative action which might cause Japan to desist or punish it for not desisting. He even refused a request of the Chinese government early in May to take the lead in trying to mediate a settlement of the conflict. After a talk with T. V. Soong, the Chinese Finance Minister, who had stopped off in Washington on his way to the Monetary and Economic Conference in London, he did join in a general statement which implied that he would welcome an end to hostilities. Issued on May 19, it read in part, "We agree that economic stability cannot be achieved without political tranquility and that economic disarmament can be attained only in a world in which military disarmament is possible. It is our ardent hope that peace may be assured, and to this end practical measures of disarmament may soon be adopted. In this connection our thoughts naturally have turned to the serious developments in the Far East, which have disturbed the peace of the world during the past two years. There the military forces of the two great nations have been engaged in destructive hostilities. We trust that these hostilities may soon cease in order that the present effort of all the nations of the world re-establish political and economic peace may succeed." [4]

About two weeks later, while the American delegation to the Monetary and Economic Conference was on the high seas, and while the Disarmament Conference in Geneva was engaged in a critical attempt to reach an accord, the Chinese and Japanese governments signed a truce at Tongku, a little town near the Great Wall. Its terms not only left the Japanese in control of the whole of Manchuria but also, as remarked by Dorothy Borg, "gave the Japanese a hold on most of the province of Hopei above the Peiping-Tiensin area, which enabled them to exercise military, political and economic pressure against both the local administration of

North China and the Nanking government, in an attempt to secure ever greater control over the entire Chinese nation." [5]

That this might be so was perceived by the American officials well informed about Far Eastern affairs. But still their fears that the Japanese army might move on to Peiping were allayed. For the time being the views of those foreign service officers who carried most weight with the Secretary of State and the President — such as Ambassador Joseph Grew in Japan, Ambassador Nelson Johnson in China, and Stanley Hornbeck, head of the Far Eastern Division of the State Department — began to incline more toward the conclusion that the American government should accept the situation rather than continue to reprimand Japan. For none of them saw any way of forcing that country to retreat without serious risk of war. And none of them thought we could count on the cooperation of England and France, worried as those countries were by the growing combativeness of Germany and Italy.

The President in general conformed to this advice and to the dominant American wish to stay clear of foreign troubles. Though regretful that the United States had not been able to protect China, Roosevelt seemed to be relieved at the temporary lessening of tension between the United States and Japan. He probably hoped against hope that the Sino-Japanese truce was more than a temporary diminution of mutual distrust and suspicion. Even if it was only that, it would at least avert an immediate crisis which might interfere with his efforts to end economic and social distress in the United States (this was before the time when Americans accepted with resignation or equanimity the fact that greatly increased expenditures for defense and war were indefinitely buoying up their economy, and before they had ceased to quail and quiver at huge budget deficits).

Another factor which led the White House and the State Department to remain inactive during the remaining months of 1933 was fear that any outright constraint against Japan might hurry it into an alliance with Germany and Italy. This possibility was deemed the more ominous since before the close of 1933 any chance of an accord limiting armaments had gone by.

Hitler's re-enactment of Japan's refusal to continue discussion about the limitation of arms brought about the demise of the Disarmament Conference. First the Monetary and Economic Conference, then the Disarmament Conference, then there was none! Gone were the visionary hopes of the early thirties!

The tale of its last months need only be briefly sketched because it has been so often and amply described and analyzed in many specialized histories — and because I had, and have, little novel or special knowledge of it.

The general commission of the conference at Geneva had adjourned on June 8. The unflagging attempts all through the summer to resolve the difficulties by direct negotiation failed. The Nazis were hurling every sort of accusation and insult against the Austrian government, and the Nazis within Austria were boasting that they would soon control the country. The French government was becoming more and more fearful as Hitler's denunciations of the Treaty of Versailles became blunter and the German claim of equality of armed strength more insistent.

In a short note Roosevelt sent Norman Davis, the chairman of the American delegation, on August 30 (as cover for a letter addressed to Davis to be shown to Premier Daladier and another to be given to Prime Minister MacDonald), he spiritedly waved Davis off on his way to the European capitals and Geneva: "Bon voyage, and all the good luck in the world. If you pull off disarmament they will bury you in Arlington when you die, if that is any comfort to you now!" In the instructions contained in the letter to Davis, Roosevelt reiterated his deep interest in the success of the conference and his concern for the future of European peace in the event of failure. He had the feeling, the President wrote, that if MacDonald, Daladier, Mussolini and Hitler could get together, the perplexing problems could be solved; so if preliminary talks in Europe led Davis to conclude that a meeting of these four heads of state was feasible, he should feel authorized to use his good offices to bring this about. But one paragraph seemed to me to indicate that whatever purpose might be served by such a meeting it would not result in an arms agreement. It read: "One further matter seems at this distance to be fairly clear — the crux of the problem seems to lie mainly between France and Germany. Obviously neither the United States nor Great Britain would want France to disarm if this would mean that Germany would later take advantage of this and seek revenge. Neither do we want to have Germany assert the right to re-arm as a result of failure on the part of the heavily armed nations to take immediate, substantial and constructive steps towards general disarmament." [6]

I recall two messages which, at the time, confirmed my sense that the conference was just staggering to a futile end. One was a report that Daladier had told Davis on September 19 that in order to get the French people to accept the idea of a disarmament treaty it would be necessary to have — he would not call it a guarantee — at least some form of assurance from England and the United States in regard to the position they would take if it should be shown patently that Germany was violating the terms of the treaty through rearming.[7] The American government was unwilling to give assurances that would satisfy French authorities.

The other was a message which our American ambassador in Italy, Breckinridge Long, sent to the Secretary of State on October 12. He repeated what the British and French ambassadors had told him about their separate talks with Mussolini. To the British ambassador, Sir Ronald William Graham, Mussolini remarked "that he considered most serious the situation developed as the result of the German attitude vis-à-vis disarmament proposals. He said it was the more serious because it was necessary to deal with those whom he characterized as a dreamer in the person of Hitler and a former inmate of a lunatic asylum in the person of Goering; that they were quite irresponsible; that they could not be scared or bluffed into acquiescence because of their abnormal mentality nor could they be importuned into acceptance of the specific conditions because they lacked any fear of consequences." [8]

The German government stood fast in the position that it could not compromise on the right to have armaments equivalent to those of France, without having first to prove its peaceful intentions during a probationary period. Thus having summoned the senile President von Hindenburg from his isolated estate in East Prussia, Hitler informed the world that the German government was not going to participate any longer in the Disarmament Conference.

Secretary Hull, on so learning and after thinking it over for half an hour, merely indulged in one of his futile laments — expressing regret at the occurrence and revealing his disappointment at this check to the disarmament movement. "Germany's action," he told reporters, was a "break-up of our team play." [9]

The representatives of the other chief powers decided to adjourn the conference for some ten days since they felt it necessary to consult their governments. These consultations and Davis's previous talks with senior officials of the English, French and Italian governments aroused suspicions in the United States that the American government was getting deeply implicated in the political problems of Europe. The President telephoned Norman Davis on October 16 to let him know that this rumor was abroad and to tell him, "I think you should make it very clear that we are in Geneva solely for disarmament purposes; that we will continue there as long as there is a possibility of carrying on disarmament negotiations, but we are not interested in the political element or in the purely European aspect of peace." [10]

Concordantly, the Secretary of State sent Davis the text of the President's comments to guide him in a public statement which he made at once. This statement was almost word for word the same as that suggested by the State Department and bluntly dismissed all possibility that the United States might associate itself with European powers in order to check aggression.[11] It repeated the affirmation that "We are not . . . interested in the politial element or purely European aspect of the picture." I thought at the time, and still think, that the effect of this statement of our policy was momentous.

In France, elements mistrustful of the United States regarded this statement as a reprimand to the French government. Even elements trustful of the United States concluded that there would be no common front against German aggression and that the task of the temperate Foreign Minister, Joseph Paul-Boncour, would become more dangerous and difficult.

In Germany the statement was hailed. The press printed it under headlines which read, AMERICA STAYS OUT OF PURELY EUROPEAN QUESTIONS, and AMERICAN POLICY OF COMPLETE EXCLUSION OF EUROPEAN POLITICS.[12]

But Hitler's dual strike — or stroke — against the League of Nations and the Disarmament Conference caused an adjustment of American policy, the consequences of which Hitler would live to regret. The American government, which had up to then continued to express the ardent wish that the conference would take a decisive step toward reducing armaments, now began to draw back. Hull informed Davis on October 28 that he agreed that special care must be exercised not to put pressure on the principal European powers to reduce their armaments against their better judgment, lest it be charged that the United States was assuming a moral commitment toward them.

The Germans hastened on with their rearmament. The French became still more firmly convinced that they had to maintain their military power and seek new alliances. The British were discouraged and bewildered, as yet unready and unwilling to face the prospect of entering into a more costly arms race which was likely to be the prelude to another agonizing war. The United States was about to enter a period during which it would try to exorcise the danger to its own security and remain at peace by remaining aloof from the quarrels in Europe and the Far East. Most Americans believed any attempt we might make to settle them was doomed to futility.

The further ebbing of international relations left Hull more dejected than ever. But in an effort to circumscribe and possibly arrest the fall, the American government took two initiatives which would leave it uninvolved. Hull took off for Montevideo, there to try to draw the American republics more closely together; and

Roosevelt proceeded to resume diplomatic relations with the Soviet government — broken since the Bolsheviks came into power. Of that more consequential act I shall tell next.

CHAPTER 24

We Recognize the Soviet Union

ON being urged to accord recognition to the Soviet government, Secretary Stimson had maintained — for example in his letter to Senator Borah of September 8, 1932 — that he thought if it did so the United States would lose its moral stature, particularly among the Japanese. In answer to appeals to act for the sake of American trade, he had expressed doubt whether recognition would bring about a substantial increase of Russian purchases in the United States.

Roosevelt's judgment had a different trend. He was inclined to believe it foolish and futile for the United States to remain distant toward so important a power as the Soviet Union. In his first weeks in office he had told his colleagues that he intended to try to arrange for a resumption of diplomatic relations if a satisfactory agreement could be reached, and when it might be done without arousing strong domestic opposition. He waited and watched.

Close at his side were two intimates who led him toward recognition by nourishing his sense of drama.

One was Bullitt. As a young man he had been Woodrow Wilson's emissary to the Bolsheviks early in the Revolution. His recommendations that the Western allies should enter into converse with the leaders of the Bolsheviks had been disregarded by both Woodrow Wilson and Lloyd George. His testimony before the Senate Committee on Foreign Relations had been influential in causing that body to reject the proffered treaty with Germany. He had married the widow of John Reed, the American journalist and friend of the Bolshevik leaders, whose body still lies in the Kremlin. These experiences, which won him favor in Russian official circles, had remained alive in his memory.

The other intimate of the President who had a marked interest in dealing with the Soviet government was Henry Morgenthau, Jr., director of the Farm Credit Administration. In that position he favored any and all moves that would increase the exports of American farm products and improve their prices — and incidentally show the President how useful he could be.

Other American officials who contributed much to the definition of the desired conditions of recognition and worked closely with Secretary Hull in the ensuing discussions were Robert F. Kelley and R. Walton Moore. Kelley was a career foreign service officer, at that time chief of the Division of Eastern European Affairs. He was reliable and industrious in his study of, and reports on, Soviet affairs. Memos prepared under his direction provided the factual basis for the negotiation. Since he considered the world revolutionary aims and practices of the Soviet Union precluded the maintenance of friendly association with it, he would have been content had the American government refrained from any attempt to enter into closer relations with its government. But as a career official he did his best to assure that the United States got whatever advantage could be had by doing so.

R. Walton Moore was appointed Assistant Secretary of State in midsummer. A Virginian, with the amiable spirit and courteous manners of his region, he had served several terms in Congress and was a well-liked crony of the Secretary of State. He had friends and friendly associations on the Hill, mainly with conservative Democratic Southerners whose support Roosevelt and the State Department were to need. Another reason why he was favored by Hull and Phillips, many felt, was that they hoped to foreclose the possibility that the President might implant Bullitt permanently in the State Department. (They may not have known that Moore's and Bullitt's fathers had been roommates at the University of Virginia Law School and were lifelong friends. Bullitt had the affectionate regard of the Moore household, of Moore — a bachelor — and his two spinster sisters. This regard Bullitt sprightly returned.)

Economic calculations brought the question of recognition to the fore. Despite the many measures under way, prevailing conditions in the United States made the lure of any new foreign market attractive; and the Russian market was thought to be potentially a great one. The German, Italian and British governments were underwriting credits by their nationals to Soviet purchasing agents in their countries; and the officials of the Soviet purchasing agency in the United States (Amtorg) were intimating to American farm organizations, grain and cotton brokers, commercial bankers and industrial concerns that it would buy much more in this country if the American government emulated these others.

Not long after the new administration took office the Farm Credit Board, the Reconstruction Finance Corporation and the Treasury had all begun to discuss with various American groups then in touch with Amtorg the possibility of financing sales to Russia of farm products and manufactured goods.

For several reasons these talks had not come to a conclusion. The Russian bargainers tried to play off the different branches of the American government against each other in their search for the best terms. None of the Russian representatives in the United States seemed to have sufficient authority to dare to make a commitment. Impatient over the faltering course of the discussions, Roosevelt remarked to Morgenthau on May 9: "Gosh, if I could only, myself, talk to some one man representing the Russians, I could straighten out the whole question. If you get the opportunity, Henry, you could say that you believe, but have no authority to say so, that the President would like to send some person to Moscow as Trade Commissioner in order to break the ice between the two countries and in that way gradually get people of the United States used to doing business with the Russians." [1] Morgenthau said that he doubted whether he would have a good chance to get this across since he was dealing with Amtorg only through intermediaries.

But still, in June, when Jones informed the President that the RFC had nearly completed arrangements for financing the sale of about seventy thousand bales of cotton to Russia (payment to be made 30 per cent in cash and 70 per cent in a one-year credit), Roosevelt took his time about giving his clearance to the bargain; and while it was still being considered, Amtorg backed away. Perhaps the Soviet government was teasing American trade interests in order to influence them to urge the government to accord recognition. This conjecture is suggested not only by the tactics of the Russian negotiators to conclude any trade deals but also by the drift of remarks made by Maxim Litvinov, the People's Commissar for Foreign Affairs, to Bullitt in London while they were together at the Monetary and Economic Conference. Litvinov then said that the British officials were arguing with him that it was not fair for Russia to trade with the United States since we had not recognized the Russian government. He asked Bullitt whether the American government was contemplating recognition. Bullitt felt well enough versed with the situation to inform him that he thought the President's general attitude was friendly, as indicated by the fact that the American representatives to the conference were conversing with him in the same way as with officials of other governments, and that trade negotiations were "in progress" in Washington. But, Bullitt added, he hadn't the slightest idea when the President might consider it desirable to grant recognition; it might be soon or it might be quite a long way off. Then he had gone on to say that of course the President would require an absolute pledge from the Soviet government to refrain from all propaganda directed against American institutions. Litvinov's response was that the Soviet government would be glad to give such an understanding provided the American government gave a similar one. [2]

Less frequently on Roosevelt's tongue, but more decisive in his thoughts, were the political purposes that might be served by entering into relations with the Soviet government. Reports were reaching Washington that it was worried lest clashes resulting from Japanese interference with the Chinese Eastern Railway (which ran from Siberia through Northern Manchuria to Vladivostok) might precipitate a war. The Japanese military leaders were thought to be willing to have that happen. The Soviet authorities were thought to be intent on avoiding it. On the Western front, as just recounted, Hitler was casting off the restraints of the Treaty of Versailles, giving orders for armaments to industrial firms which had come to terms with National Socialism, and shrieking his blessings on the processions of uniformed youths who were goosestepping through the cities and villages of Germany. The idea was forming in both Roosevelt's and Hull's minds that Japan and Germany might be sobered if the breach between the United States and the Soviet Union were healed.

Officials in the State Department had begun to worry lest the American government rush into trade deals with the Soviet government and/or an agreement for recognition before the many vexing problems in Russian-American relations were settled. Kelley and his assistants made a comprehensive examination of them. Of the various informative and advisory memos he produced, one dated July 27 is the most thorough. In its prefatory paragraph the opinion was stressed that the experiences of other nations which had recognized the Soviet Union showed conclusively that, unless obstacles to friendly cooperation were eliminated before recognition, "official relations, established as a result of recognition, tend to become . . . the source of friction and ill-will, rather than the mainspring of cooperation and good-will. It would be essential, therefore, that every endeavor should be made to remove these obstacles prior to the extension of recognition." [3] Phillips gave the President a copy of this memorandum and there was reason to believe that it was carefully read.

The President continued to bide his time. In August, Peter Bogdonov, the head of Amtorg, was proposing to buy seventy-five million dollars worth of raw materials and fifty million dollars worth of machinery. The President, upon being consulted by Morgenthau about this and another bid by Bogdonov, said that he thought the American government ought to limit its sales to Russia during the next few months to one hundred million dollars and ask 15 to 20 per cent down payment.[4] Possibly due to this last requirement no deal was consummated.

Roosevelt may have been mindful of the pleas of the State Department not to approve loans to the Soviet government except in connection with an agreement to accord diplomatic recognition; and not to agree to recognition until and unless the main questions which troubled the relations between the two countries were straightened out — as for example in a long and vigorously phrased letter which Bullitt and Kelley composed, and which they besought the Secretary of State to send to the President. In this they set forth the reasons for their belief that the Soviet authorities valued American recognition highly. Then they advocated that all available means should be used to obtain a satisfactory settlement of the causes of dissension between the two countries. The two concluding sentences read, "It is evident that if loans of any considerable amount should be extended to the Soviet government, except as a part of an agreement involving a satisfactory settlement of such problems, one of our most effective weapons would be taken from our hands — possibly the most effective — since the Soviets, it is believed, prefer at the moment credits to recognition. It would seem, therefore, highly undesirable that any loan should be extended to facilitate purchases by the Soviet government in the United States, except as part and parcel of a general settlement of our relations with Russia." [5]

The Secretary fingered this letter hesitantly. He signed it and took it over to the White House but brought it back again. Being still of two minds, he had not given it to the President. But within the next day or two he succumbed to persuasion and did so. Soon afterwards he told the President that he was in favor of recognizing the Soviet government provided satisfactory assurances were obtained. Roosevelt remarked dryly "I agree entirely." The President was by then actively giving thought to the tenor of a message which he might dispatch to the President of the Soviet Union, Mikhail Kalinin, asking him to send over a representative to discuss the possibility of resumption of diplomatic relations.

The next day, September 26, when Morgenthau, in whose hands the handling of all financing of exports to Russia had just been concentrated, asked the President whether, in view of all the publicity, he wanted him to go ahead and make loans to Russia, the President fended him off. He let Morgenthau know that he had a definite plan of action in mind. The President said, "What would you think of bringing this whole Russian question into our front parlor instead of back in the kitchen?" Morgenthau said, "That is fine if you want to do it, but it is up to you." Whereupon the President said, "I have a plan in mind." He did not at that time explain it. But he suggested that Morgenthau send for Boris Skvirsky — whom, with boyish humor, he called Schmirsky — then acting as a secret diplomatic agent for the Russian government. He might be led to understand that the American government had the whole Russian question under consideration and that the delay in arranging a credit was in no way prejudicial.[6]

Under-Secretary of State Phillips, Bullitt and Kelley were all still alarmed lest the President might approve credits in order to grease the way to a resumption of the diplomatic relations. So at this juncture they again pelted him with advice not to do so pending discussions in which we could ascertain whether the Soviet government would grant our wishes.* All were overestimating the importance which the Soviet authorities attached to obtaining credits. Thus, for example, while lunching with Morgenthau on September 27, Bullitt said that the Russians were "absolutely broke," and that there was a 50 per cent chance that Japan would attack the Russian maritime provinces in the near future. But if Russia secured a loan from us, Japan would draw the inference that the American government would also finance its purchases of planes and other war materials.

* As, for example, in a succinct and firm memo which Kelley sent to Phillips on September 25, 1933. *Foreign Relations of the United States* — 1933-1934, p. 14.

Another reason, Bullitt thought, why the Soviet government valued American credit highly enough to meet its wishes was that it would lessen or end its dependence on Germany for financial help.

Bullitt then went on to repeat to Morgenthau, who had not yet seen Skvirsky, that the State Department was opposed to the extension of any loans except in connection with a firm settlement which would convey assurances greatly wanted by the American government — among them guarantees that the Third International (Comintern) would not engage in propaganda in this country and that American ships would be given protection in Russian ports.[7]

Bullitt began to probe the prospects with Skvirsky. The President gave him an easy rein in his efforts to find out what the chances were of obtaining the assurances we wanted — at the same time warning him to be careful to maintain the appearance of serving merely as assistant to Hull and charging him not to go over Hull's head, as Moley had.[8]

Skvirsky was unable to give Bullitt any conclusive answer. Suspecting that Roosevelt might plunge ahead without delaying longer, Bullitt and Moore once again emphatically argued that it was essential not to accord recognition except as the final act of an agreement on matters that were causing trouble between the two countries. They restated tersely the most important conditions and understandings which they considered significant in the development of plans for the recognition of the Soviet government. Hull transmitted their respective memos to the President with the cautious remark that he was doing so "for whatever the information may be worth." [9]

The President decided to put the matter to the test. He requested Bullitt to compose a letter to Kalinin. He asked Hull to look it over: "Here is my effort at a suggested letter to Kalinin to be submitted confidentially in draft to see what kind of reply he would make if we sent it. What do you think?" [10] Hull found no fault with the draft.

Bullitt told Morgenthau that the President had finally authorized him to proceed. Morgenthau thereupon located Skvirsky in New

York and asked him to be at his office the next morning, Wednesday, October 11, at 10 A.M. Skvirsky was on time. Morgenthau and Bullitt acted out the script which the President had drawn up. As described by Morgenthau in his diary: "I said to Mr. Skvirsky, 'Several weeks ago I told you that for the time being our negotiations were off, pending consideration by the White House. You asked me if this was a friendly move and I said yes. I will now give it to you. In about five minutes Bullitt, from the State Department, will come here with a piece of paper unsigned, and show it to you.' His face lit up with a big smile. Bullitt made his entry on the stage as arranged by the President, sat down, and said to Skvirsky, 'I have a piece of paper in my hand, unsigned. This document can be made into an invitation for your country to send representatives over to discuss relations between our two countries. We wish you to telegraph the contents of this piece of paper in your most confidential code, and learn if it is acceptable to your people . . . have your people send a draft of an answer to us and we will let you know if this proposed draft is acceptable to the President. If both drafts are accepted, the President will sign this piece of paper, and both letters can be released simultaneously from Moscow and Washington. If they are not acceptable, will you give me your word of honor that there will never be any publicity in regard to this proposed exchange of letters and that the whole matter will be kept a secret?' Mr. Skvirsky assured Bullitt that would be the case. He then said, 'Does this mean recognition?' and Bullitt parried with an answer by saying, 'What more can you expect than to have your representative sit down with the President of the United States? ' " [11]

The message to Kalinin was brief and friendly. Roosevelt said that since he had become President he had contemplated the resumption of normal relations between the Russian and American peoples. "The difficulties," he went on, ". . . are not insoluble, but could be removed only by frank, friendly conversations. Hence . . . If you are of similar mind, I should be glad to receive any representatives you may designate to explore with me personally all questions outstanding between our two countries." [12]

Kalinin answered within a week. After agreeing with Roosevelt that the situation between their two countries was abnormal and regrettable, he said he would sent Litvinov to Washington to represent the Soviet government in discussions of questions of common interest.

On releasing these letters to the press, Roosevelt explained that this step did not constitute recognition of the Soviet government. The Japanese authorities put the best face upon that eventuality that they could. The Foreign Minister first informed inquiring reporters that he doubted whether the talks would result in American recognition of the Soviet Union. And he added, "If those two countries continue in favorable relations for years to come they will teach a lesson to the world that capitalism and communism can agree . . . If anyone observes that the possible American-Soviet agreement means pressure on Japan's position in the Far East, he knows nothing of the Far Eastern situation." [13]

But Ambassador Grew reported that Saburo Kurusu, chief of the commercial bureau of the foreign office (whose name was later on to become unhappily familiar to Americans), had said that the Japanse foreign office was worried because it was afraid Japanese military elements might stir up trouble if they came to believe that our recognition of the Soviet government was in any way directed against Japan.

Litvinov, a devoted Communist, was an astute negotiator. It was said of him (as now is being said of Anastas Mikoyan) that he was "able to come out dry from the water." But he was more familiar with, and trustful of, Western ways and ideas than most Soviet diplomats, was married to an Englishwoman, and spoke English. For these very reasons, which led to his selection as negotiator for recognition in 1933, his weatherproofing was to fail when years later relations between the Soviet Union and the West again became stormy.

Litvinov landed in New York on November 7 and hurried on to Washington without pause. This disappointed the manager of the elegant Waldorf-Astoria Hotel, who had wired James Dunn, head of the Division of International Conferences and Protocol of the

State Department: "would like to have Litvinov stay at Waldorf
. . . appreciate if you can assist us."

Waiting on the platform at Union Station in Washington when
Litvinov arrived were the Secretary of State, several other officials
of the State Department and Marvin McIntyre, secretary to the
President. The visitor wore an ordinary business suit, not formal
diplomatic garb. After a brief exchange of greetings he was driven
by the President's military aide directly to the White House. In the
Blue Room, Roosevelt, standing, welcomed him cordially.

To leave critics groping at the time, and frustrate students in the
future, Roosevelt and Litvinov agreed that no records should be
made of their talks.* Nor has any official record of the conversations held within the State Department been found. But several of
Roosevelt's and Hull's advisers who sat in on some of their talks,
or to whom the President recounted what was said, kept journals.†

The discussions went on for a week without remission — a week
during which the curious world had to conjure up what was happening from terse communiqués. Both Litvinov and Roosevelt
guarded themselves well against leaks that might interfere with
their effort to reach an accord.

Litvinov at first balked at discussing other issues before the

---

* Assistant Secretary Moore prefaced the account which he gave on the
radio on November 25 of the agreements with the Soviet Union by stating,
"There were no stenographers present and no reports made and thus, as far
as the conferences at the White House are concerned, this will be a bare
outline and not a full picture exposed to the eye of the future historian."
Counting myself among these, I find that my frustration in not being able
adequately to tell of the talks between Roosevelt and Litvinov is not dispelled by Moore's next remark that, "But after all, to repeat the legend of
the coat of arms of the Washington family, 'It is the result that proves the
work.'"

† Of those known to me, the journal of William Phillips, Under-Secretary
of State, and one entry made on November 14 in Morgenthau's diary are the
most informative. I made some brief notes of information passed on to me
at the time by the Secretary and Under-Secretary of State, Bullitt and Kelley
on how the talks were going.

William Bullitt gave me to believe that somewhere in the "tank" (he said
"tank" not "bank") of his personal papers there are notes he made about
these discussions in the White House and State Department. But he dismissed
the thought of looking for them as "impossibly troublesome."

American government agreed to accord recognition. The President and the Secretary stood fast. They explained that the decision about recognition must await agreement on the several other questions which had to be settled amicably if recognition was to be a prelude to genuine friendliness, and if the needed support in the United States was to be won. Litvinov grudgingly gave in, saying that he feared that many of his colleagues and fellow countrymen would feel that Russia was being unfairly put in the wrong.

The endeavors of the American negotiators centered on achieving five purposes: (1) a pledge that the Soviet government and all organizations under its control would refrain from activities aimed at injuring the United States or subverting its government; (2) a settlement of the loans which the American government had made to the provisional government of Alexander Kerensky in 1917; (3) a promise to compensate private American holders of Russian government bonds and Americans whose property had been confiscated; (4) a pledge that American nationals in Russia would be accorded religious freedom, and (5) assurances that any American nationals who might be placed under arrest by the Russian authorities would have good treatment and legal protection.

Litvinov gave reasons for denying, or qualifying, or countering each of these stipulations. During the morning and afternoon sessions in Hull's office on the next day, November 8, the talk swirled around our request for assurances regarding freedom of religion. Litvinov interpreted some remarks made by Moore to mean that we were asking the Russian government for a formal statement according freedom of religious worship to all Russians. He said emphatically that he could not agree to make any statement to this effect, formal or informal. Hull quickly explained that all we had in mind was freedom of religion for American nationals in Russia.[14]

Litvinov in subsequent discussions contended that actually American nationals were being permitted to exercise this freedom, and that none of them had ever complained against religious restrictions while they were in Russia. "We cannot," he said, "set up a privileged class." Hull persisted and gave Litvinov a memorandum on the subject. On doing so he said he would be willing to make the exchange of pledges reciprocal.* Whereupon Litvinov answered that the Russian government would not make any similar request of the American government as it was not interested in the religion of its nationals in the United States. Incidentally, he remarked, Soviet authorities took special precautions against emissaries from the Vatican.

The talks about payment on American loans and claims similarly went around and around without arriving anywhere. Litvinov suggested that American and Soviet counterclaims be dealt with through diplomatic channels after recognition was accorded. Hull said that would subject the American government to criticism. Litvinov's rejoinder was, "We have not discussed debts in sixteen years with the United States of America. Now if we have recognition at least we will be making some progress." He also indicated that he believed some of the private claims for compensation which the American government was espousing were unjustified and excessive.

The records available to me of the talks about Soviet abstention from subversive activities is so slight and murky that I can do no more than note a few markers along the trail. I believe the discussions on this subject were more prolonged and acrimonious than on any other. The text of the agreement to which the American negotiators asked Litvinov to subscribe did not name the Comintern specifically, because of the chance that the Russians might merely change its name and later contend that the accord did not apply to it. But in the light of what happened afterwards it is of interest that in the talks with Hull on November 8 and 9, Litvinov disclaimed all responsibility for the activities of the Third Communist International in the United States. He said at one point that this organization did not have any government standing and added, "We are not asking for anything. We have no request to make of any of the organizations of the United States, so why ask us about some of our organizations?" The Secretary pointed out that Stalin

* In the entry for November 14 in the Morgenthau Diary from which this information is derived the word "unilateral" is used, but I am sure that this is a mistake and that Hull meant "reciprocal."

was a director of the Third International and thus the Soviet government was involved in its activities. "Litvinov denied this allegation completely and refused to discuss it," noted Phillips. Litvinov was in this discussion, of this subject, "absolutely intransigent," noted Morgenthau.[15] When the talks ended on November 9, it almost seemed as though an impasse had been reached.

However, on November 10, when the President spoke for the second time with Litvinov, some progress was made. Under-Secretary Phillips left this conference with a heightened admiration for the President which is reflected in the entry he made in his journal: "Mr. Litvinov came at twelve o'clock, when the President reviewed the whole situation with him. It was one of the most remarkable performances I have ever seen. Somehow the President succeeded in changing the whole atmosphere. He did it by a combination of humor, sincerity, clearness and friendliness — a combination of all four which brought the first response that Mr. Litvinov has given out since his arrival in Washington." [16] Litvinov agreed to consider the proposition on propaganda which had been presented to him and which he had previously refused to consider.

The President then urged him to assent to our proposal that the Soviet government sign a written pledge to allow Americans in Russia to practice their religion. Up to then Litvinov had contended that this would be both an intrusion into Soviet affairs and offensive to Soviet authorities. He, Bullitt thought, was fearful of what would happen to him upon returning to Moscow if he agreed to this precedent. But the President, with incisive bluntness, said that such a promise was essential — if the Soviet government refused to give in, Litvinov could return to Moscow, his mission a failure.

James Farley, the Postmaster General, relates in his memoirs that while the talks about this subject were going on, the President told Litvinov that he was "willing to wager that five minutes before his [Litvinov's] time came to die, and he was conscious of it, that he would be thinking of his parents and wanting to make his peace with God." [17] Perhaps it was this intimation of the desolation of dying in a godless world that brought Litvinov around. But more probably it was an instruction from Moscow which led him to defer to Roosevelt's earnest insistence. In any case, the next day, November 11, Litvinov said he was authorized to try to draw up a statement which would satisfy the wishes which the President had expressed.

However, Litvinov turned down the request to accord Americans placed under arrest in Russia protective procedures similar to, or equivalent to, those in the United States. He maintained that they would be fairly treated in accordance with Soviet laws and he could promise nothing else or more. The President recognized that Litvinov could not be brought to reconsider after talking with him again that evening from nine o'clock till midnight.

During the following five days — from November 12 to 16 — Litvinov became a little more yielding on almost all points discussed. The American negotiators on their part whittled down their stipulations. During these days neither the White House nor the State Department issued any bulletins about the progress of the talks. And I cannot illuminate their silence.

On the evening of November 16, the President gave his annual dinner to the cabinet, followed by a musicale. After the guests left, the President invited Phillips, Morgenthau (who had just been made Acting Secretary of the Treasury) and Bullitt to join Litvinov and him in his study. On the desk were the several sets of letters in which the understandings reached were set forth. The President read them aloud. Litvinov objected to the use in several of the documents of the phrase "The Government of the United States expects" as being in the nature of an ultimatum. The Americans insisted it be kept in, and Litvinov gave way when the President agreed to change the phrasing to "will expect." The President and Litvinov took up their pens and scratched their signatures at the same time. Then they exchanged the letters. Roosevelt seemed to be in high good humor at the outcome of this venturesome negotiation. Litvinov was more repressed but also clearly pleased. The group quaffed only beer in celebration. No ceremonial champagne was served.

By the foremost pair of letters the resumption of diplomatic relations was effectuated.[18]

In his letter Roosevelt said that he was happy to inform Litvinov that the American government had decided to establish normal diplomatic relations with the government of the Union of Soviet Socialist Republics, trusting that the future relations between the two countries would "forever remain normal and friendly." Litvinov in his acknowledgment stated that the Soviet government was glad to establish normal diplomatic relations with the United States and affirmed that he shared the President's hopes.

This pair of letters was supplemented by four other sets. In one set the Soviet government averred that it would be its fixed policy not to interfere in any manner in the internal affairs of the United States, and "to refrain, and to restrain all persons in government service and all organizations of the Government or under its direct or indirect control, including the organizations in receipt of any financial assistance from it, from any act overt or covert liable in any way whatsoever to injure the tranquillity, prosperity, order, or security of the whole or any part of the United States. . . ." and also "not to permit the formation or residence on its territory of any organization or group . . . or of representatives or officials of any organization or group which has as an aim the overthrow or the preparation for the overthrow of, or the bringing about by force of a change in the political or social order of the whole or any part of the United States . . ."

Could the phraseology of this promise have been made more comprehensive or explicit? It may safely be assumed, I think, though the fragmentary records of the discussion available are not definitive in this regard, that the American negotiators made it clear that they understood that this pledge applied to the activities of the Third Communist International — the Comintern. But it is obvious that this was wishful thinking. Litvinov was prompt if not candid in his denials — as when on November 17, the morrow of the day the agreements were signed, in talking to the National Press Club in Washington, he said: "The Third International is not mentioned in the documents. You should not read more in the documents than was intended." *

Needless to say, this promise and the reciprocal one given by the American government have not survived wear and tear. The first slash, in fact, occurred only a month after the agreements were signed. Then the executive committee of the Comintern, meeting in Moscow, adopted a resolution stating that "there is no way out of the general crisis of capitalism other than the one shown by the October revolution, via the overthrow of the exploiting classes by the proletariat, the confiscation of the banks, of the factories, the mines, transport, houses, the stocks of goods of the capitalists, the lands of the landlords, the church and the crown." The several national Communist parties who were members of the International were instructed to continue to do what they could to make this resolution effective. In 1933, when the suffering caused by the prolonged depression was still deep and widespread, this was inciting doctrine. But when the American government reproached the Soviet government for what it regarded as a violation of the pledged word, Litvinov again disclaimed responsibility for the utterances and actions of the Comintern. Having done so, the Soviet authorities appended to this rejection various statements made by individual Americans in both private and public life which in effect called for the repudiation of the Communist system and form of government.

In another set of letters Roosevelt expressed the deep wish that American nationals in Russia would be able to exercise liberty of conscience in religious worship without suffering in any way therefrom. He enumerated those religious activities which American nationals were to be allowed to carry on without annoyance or molestation of any kind. Litvinov answered by citing various provisions of Soviet law which could be deemed to guarantee the requested rights and privileges.

In a third set of letters the Soviet government promised to con-

* The subject is discussed interestingly in Donald G. Bishop, *The Roosevelt-Litvinov Agreements*, Chapter II.

clude at once a consular convention which would grant American nationals in the Soviet Union the right to the same legal protection enjoyed by nationals of any other foreign country. Litvinov also, in a separate statement dealing with the particular question of prosecution for "economic espionage," gave assurances that the Soviet government would not interfere with efforts to obtain such economic information as was procured by legitimate means, and which was not regarded as secret, or the dissemination of which was not forbidden by regulations. Hedged as the statement was, it probably did subsequently in some measure safeguard inquirers against arrest and punishment. Roosevelt in his acknowledgment stated that American diplomatic and consular officers in the Soviet Union would be zealous in guarding the rights of Americans — especially the right to have a fair, public and speedy trial, and to be represented by counsel of their own choice; and that the American government would also expect that its representatives would be notified at once of the arrest or detention of any American national and promptly afforded the opportunity to communicate and converse with him. This too probably did make the existence of Americans in Russia more secure.

In still another set of the communications exchanged, the Soviet government waived its claim for damages because of the participation of American military forces in the expedition to Siberia during the years 1918 to 1921. Litvinov agreed to relinquish any such claim after being shown documentary evidence that the American purpose had been to counteract Japanese activities in Russian territory. Roosevelt and Litvinov issued a joint statement in which they said that they had exchanged views in regard to methods of settling outstanding financial questions and that their talks permitted hope that these could be solved quickly and fairly. What they had in mind, probably, was that on November 15 the President and Litvinov entered into a "gentlemen's agreement." This stipulated that over and above all claims of the Soviet nationals against us, the Soviet government would pay, on account of the loans made to the Kerensky regime, not less than seventy-five million dollars — in the form of a percentage above the usual rate of interest on a loan to be granted it either by the government of the United States or by its nationals. The President had on this occasion told Litvinov that he believed he could persuade Congress to accept one hundred and fifty million dollars but he was afraid it would not accept any smaller amount. Litvinov answered that he could not on his own authority agree to any such sum, as his government considered it excessive. He added that he personally would be inclined to advise his government to agree to pay one hundred million dollars.[19]

It was arranged that Litvinov should remain in Washington for a few days after the end of the formal negotiations to review more thoroughly this complicated field of claims and counterclaims. But the ensuing talks did not disentangle them. He left this country with the understanding that negotiations would commence once more after the American ambassador took up his post in Moscow. No agreement, it may be noted, was ever reached and no payment was ever made on these obligations. The American government ignored them when it included the Soviet Union among the recipients of lend-lease after Germany had hauled it into the Second World War.

Similarly, the subsequent effort to formulate a favorable basis for Soviet-American trade — now that the two countries were again in diplomatic relations with each other — got nowhere for a long time. The President was hesitant to ask Congress for authority to extend large credits to the Soviet government. The sums provided by the Export-Import Bank were relatively scanty due to the refusal of the Soviet government to settle American claims satisfactorily. The Soviet government continued to buy where it could buy cheapest and on the best credit terms. Moreover, at this time it had only small quantities of desirable raw materials to offer American purchasers who would pay dollars wherewith the Soviet government could purchase American products; and such foreign funds as accrued to it were used to buy machinery and industrial plants, not goods for consumption such as wheat, cotton, tobacco and automobiles.

For the next several years the businesses and banks which had looked forward to a large and profitable trade with Russia (made safe by government credits) continued to try to make their wishes come true. Their agents hurried from one government department to another in an effort to find out what was happening. When, discouraged, they took the train back from Washington, they were almost as perplexed as they had been when they arrived. All the while the Soviet government was pressing the American government to consent to the appointment of a trade commissioner who would reside in New York but be attached to the Russian embassy in Washington. The State Department delayed until it could decide how to limit the diplomatic immunity of any such official.

Ultimately — in 1935 — the two governments entered into a simple arrangement which provided that Soviet exports to the United States should be as well treated under American laws as those of any other country; and the Soviet government in return promised to purchase at least thirty million dollars worth of American products during the following twelve months. Thus the hope of economic benefit, which was among those that impelled the American government toward recognition of the Soviet government, was scantily fulfilled.

But my appraisal of the results of the agreements has run ahead of my story. The texts of the accords were published at once. The President told the cabinet that he thought that generally speaking he had driven a good bargain not only for the United States but for the world and that these agreements would go a long way toward preserving future peace. Hull, aboard the S.S. *American Legion* on his way to Montevideo, told press correspondents on the ship that he thought "the badly confused world situation will be improved by this natural and timely step which is proof of the marked progress possible in all international dealings where there exists such splendid initiative as that displayed by the President and the mutual disposition and will to approach serious world problems in a friendly and fearless spirit." [20]

Few of the articulate commentators in the American press and radio challenged the pleased and optimistic estimates of the accords, although many took the position that time and experience alone could reveal their actual value. An analysis of the opinions expressed by three hundred American newspapers that the State Department made and sent to the President on October 19 stated, "The Northeastern and North Atlantic states do not appear to be enthusiastically in favor of recognition; the majority of Southern and Midwestern states are in favor of recognition, and the Pacific Coast states are somewhat indifferent." Corn, wheat, cotton and tobacco were having their say.

The comment in the controlled Soviet press dismissed the idea that the American government was granting a boon to the Soviet Union by recognizing it. The prevailing theme there was exemplified by the boast of the editor of *Izvestia* that the American capitalists had agreed to recognize the Soviet government because they realized that they could not solve their economic problems in isolation.*

In a circular instruction which the State Department sent to all diplomatic missions on November 17, our representatives abroad were told that they should "enter into cordial and official and social relations with your Soviet colleagues . . ." [21]

Skvirsky was named Soviet chargé d'affaires. He entered into occupation of an embassy in Washington which had been in the custody of those almost forgotten diplomats whom the provisional government of Russia sent to Washington in July 1917. Shortly after recognition Alexander Troyanovsky was named ambassador. As soon as the old embassy on 16th Street was renovated, the limousines were bringing to its doors American officials and businessmen eager to get to know their newly recognized colleagues, and enjoy the food and drink lavishly laid out on the long buffet tables. For the first time I had my fill of caviar and concluded that the resumption of relations was in better taste than I had realized. Later, during the period of the Nazi-Communist friendship, and after an aggravating session with one truculent Soviet ambassador,

* A long and interesting account of the contemporary Soviet comment can be found in a dispatch sent by the American chargé in Riga (Cole) on November 23, 1933. *Foreign Relations of the United States* — The Soviet Union 1933-1939, pp. 821-823.

I found myself musing that sturgeon was the only Soviet diplomatic agent I liked.

The President at once asked the Soviet Union to agree to the appointment of Bullitt as ambassador to the Soviet Union. Bullitt's opinion of his fitness for the post had changed since talking with Litvinov in June. The Soviet Commissar for Foreign Affairs had then said that he hoped if Russia were recognized, Bullitt would be sent as the first American ambassador. Bullitt had answered that he couldn't think of a worse person for the post and that he would say so to the President. This he did, telling Roosevelt that he had no idea whether such an action would be contemplated, but if it were he would like to argue against it.

But subsequently he had come to want this responsible and formidable assignment. Like the President, he regarded the resumption of diplomatic relations as the first step in cooperation between the two countries that might preserve future international peace.

As soon as the Russian government stated that it would be pleased to have him as ambassador, Bullitt left for Moscow. His hurry was due not only to a wish to present his credentials but to an urgent need to arrange residential and working facilities for the American diplomatic mission.

In presenting his letters of credence on December 13 to President Kalinin, he said in part that he conceived his task to be to create not merely normal but genuine friendly relations between the two nations. These, he avowed, being "bound by the tie of their mutual desire for peace . . . will find many other fields for fruitful cooperation."

While in Paris, on his way back to Washington, he informed the President exultantly, "It is difficult to exaggerate the hospitality with which I was received by all members of the Government including Kalinin, Molotov, Voroshilov and Stalin. Especially noteworthy is the fact that Stalin, who until my arrival had never received any Ambassador, said to me: 'At any moment, day or night, if you wish to see me you have only to ask and I will see you at once.' " [22]

It was hard to remain inert when caught in the current of Bullitt's exuberance. How far off course that exuberance could carry his judgment is indicated by his impression of Vyacheslav Molotov, then President of the Soviet Council of People's Commissars. In the longer report of his visit to the Soviet Union of December 10 to 22, which he wrote while sailing home on the S.S. *Washington,* he said he had found that he had underrated not only Kalinin but Molotov, who "has a magnificent forehead and the general aspect of a first-rate French scientist, great poise, kindliness and intelligence." [23]

For a brief period after the resumption of diplomatic relations — to cast a glance beyond the bounds of this narrative — the diplomacy of the two countries did conjoin.

Before leaving Washington, Litvinov had suggested to Acting Secretary Phillips that an attempt be made to negotiate two non-agression pacts: one between the United States, the Soviet Union and Japan; the other between the United States, the Soviet Union and China. Phillips had discouraged the idea on the grounds that Japan would certainly reject the overture as it had two previous Soviet proposals. But behind his answer was the President's determination not to have the United States involved in direct responsibility for events in the Far East, and his wish to avoid arousing the suspicions of the Japanese military.

The anxieties of the American government in this regard were evidenced in a reprimand sent by Phillips on December 11 to Ambassador Dodd in Germany. This began: "The President and I are somewhat concerned over your reference to the Far East," and went on to emphasize that "we are particularly anxious to avoid any step which might give the appearance of endeavoring to isolate Japan. During the recent visit of Litvinov . . . great care was exercised not to give the impression that recognition carried with it any thought of cooperation with Russia against Japan." The message ended by reminding Dodd of the dual aspects of our policy: "We do not feel any move should be made by us toward either condoning the breaking of treaties or bringing to bear upon Japan pressure

suggestive of coercion in regard to the Manchurian situation."
During Bullitt's first hasty visit to Moscow, Litvinov informed
him that the Soviet government was under great pressure from
France to join the League of Nations. The Commissar went on to
explain that the government was disposed to accede to the French
request because its entry into the League was connected with a
complementary agreement with France for joint defense against attack by Germany. Litvinov, Bullitt thought, genuinely believed that
both Germany and Japan were likely to attack the Soviet Union
before long. Since the American government was not a member of
the League, would it have, Litvinov asked, any objection if Russia
became a member? The American government had none. The Soviet Union joined the League in 1934 and also signed a mutual
assistance pact with France.

Events subsequent to those related in this narrative revealed that
mutual mistrust between the Soviet Union and the United States
had not been permanently allayed by the establishment of diplomatic relations. Before long they again regarded each other as
scheming enemies rather than friends. This led Japan as it did Germany each to feel confident that it would not encounter the combined resistance of Russia and the United States to its aspirations
and plots. That inference turned out to be correct, until in 1940
and 1941 the United States — dismayed by the defeat of France,
worried lest China be compelled to submit to Japan and the Soviet
Union forced to accept Germany as master of all Western Europe
— threw its weight into the struggle.

CHAPTER 25

Prohibition Passes

WHAT made December 1933 memorable to many Americans was not any great turn in foreign affairs but the end of the stealthy era of prohibition.

The potential demand for wine and liquors was keen and tremendous, the clamor for large importations loud. The legal provisions governing the taxation, imports, sale and trade in these beverages were obsolete.

In October an interdepartmental Wines and Spirits Committee was formed to advise on these problems. I was named the State Department member — an honor not sought and soon regretted. Haste was in our assignment, urgency in our decisions. For the President himself had been surprised at the rapidity with which some states had voted for repeal of the Eighteenth Amendment. He had reckoned that prohibition would not end until about March 1934.

It was apparent that there would have to be two stages in the restoration of the trade and formulation of governmental policy. The first would be the interval between repeal and the enactment of permanent legislation by Congress — an interval of three or four months. The second would be the permanent government system of control and taxation.

At about the same time that the committee started work, officials of the American government began discussions with members of the distilled spirits and alcoholic beverages industries about a code to regulate their actions. The committee took it for granted that private trade was to be restored, subject to later determination by Congress and/or the several states of the union of the methods to be employed, including possible state monopolies.*

The idea occurred to some of us that the reopening of the American market for foreign wines and spirits might provide a chance to sell to the producers more of our surplus agricultural products. Why not require governments of those countries who wished to export wines and spirits to us to agree in return to lower their tariffs against imports of our farm products, or to allow entry of increased quotas? Why should not Britain be asked to buy more of our cotton or lard or corn or wheat if we bought a large part of its stock of Scotch whiskey; and Canada, if we purchased its supplies of bourbon; and France, Italy and Germany, if we permitted the purchase of their table wines; and Spain and Portugal, if sherry and port were allowed freely to appear on our buffet tables and in our barrooms; and Holland, if we were to down its gin; and Norway, if we were to sip aquavit after our meals; and even Greece, since the Greeks in this country liked to drink its resinous wines. Then there were South Africa and Chile and other new wine-producing countries that were eager to have their products make a name for themselves. In short, why not, as we imbibed, help the hard-working farmer and revive the American economy?

* The plank in the Democratic platform of 1932 had left that implication. It read: "We advocate the repeal of the Eighteenth Amendment. To effect such a repeal we demand that the Congress immediately propose a Constitutional Amendment to truly representative conventions of the State called solely for that purpose. We urge the enactment of such measures by the separate states as will actually promote temperance, effectively prevent the saloon, bring the liquor traffic into the open under supervision and control by the State."

The notion appealed to the officials of the Agricultural Adjustment Administration and the Treasury and no less to myself. Here was the opportunity for the Office of the Economic Adviser to prove that it was not only a fount of advice but a fount of prosperity! The other members of the committee yielded to our importunities. But how, and by what branches of the government, were these exchanges of products to be negotiated and supervised? The system envisaged by the committee and suggested to the President in its reports was seemingly a simple one. Licenses to import from each country of origin minimum amounts of wine and spirits would be issued unconditionally. But licenses to import more than the minimum would be granted only if the government of the country of origin agreed to make it easier for us to sell their peoples more American farm products. Thus we would play their game of tit-for-tat, or favor-for-favor.

The licenses were to be issued to importers in the United States by the AAA in cooperation with the Alcohol Control Division of the Treasury, subject to the approval of the State Department. We were to consult the AAA as we sought to swap American farm products for extra batches of licenses. After importing houses had procured licenses and placed their orders abroad, the State Department was to inform the American consuls in the country where the imports were purchased, and the consuls were to certify that the shipping invoice was in accordance with the license.

What system could be simpler and surer than that? The only trouble with it was that it rested on an all-around misjudgment of the situation; it did not reckon with the excited competition among the concerns that wanted to share in what was certain to be a most profitable trade — not only those that had been in the liquor business before prohibition but also the even more numerous ones that were eager to enter the business now. Each and every one of them rushed an executive abroad to sign up one or more producers of a well-known brand of spirits, or an esteemed vineyard or dealer in wines. Reports from foreign service officers who were traveling at the time on ships to Europe said that in the smoking rooms, usually haunts of good cheer, rivals watched each other with uneasy suspicion. The plan also failed to take account of the fact that governments of the countries that had good-quality wines and spirits to sell would not feel compelled to bargain for the chance to sell them in the United States during this period; the demand was obviously irresistible. Moreover, at will their governments could first increase the obstacles they imposed against the import of American farm products and then promise to decrease them in return for larger quotas. But all this was wisdom learned only after a month or two of staggering confusion.

The interdepartmental Wines and Spirits Committee, after about forty days of work, presented a preliminary report to the President on November 7. Two days later the committee met with the President for the first time, his cabinet officers also attending. The discussion that evening veered from the report to a basic question of policy to which the committee had given only incidental attention, having taken its disposition for granted.

True, while the committee had toiled Tugwell had been going about town with a superior air saying that no matter what the committee recommended the Department of Agriculture, under the AAA act, had the power to control what would be done. At this meeting Secretary of Agriculture Wallace tried to exert that power.

The committee proposed that the domestic trade in liquors be regulated in some respects by marketing codes and agreements (under the NRA), and in other respects by legislation on the statute books (or by new enactments in Congress). But Wallace, with the support of Daniel Roper, Secretary of Commerce, recommended instead that the government establish a federal monopoly for the wholesale distribution of liquor. It, and it alone, was to buy wines and spirits from domestic and foreign producers and resell them to the retailers under regulations that the federal government would impose.

The reasons for not adopting this plan were diverse and conclusive, and I was not backward in expressing them. I was sure the American government, struggling as it was to revive and reshape the American economy, should not take on this immense and troublesome task. If it did, a new and great realm of corruption might be created. For this and other reasons, all members of the committee itself (except the representatives of the AAA) joined me in opposing this proposal.

A week or so later the same group met again with the President, along with the chairmen of the committees of the Senate and the House of Representatives in which legislation in the field would originate. Our group explained at length why it thought the monopoly idea unsound. The President scanned the committee's revised report impatiently and critically. He seemed receptive to the suggestion that the whole business be entrusted to a federal monopoly.*

But the committee had added a supplementary recommendation to its report. This contemplated the creation of a Federal Alcohol Authority with vaguely defined powers and responsibilities, and it was this provision that saved the report from the trash basket. When the President reached the sentence suggesting the creation of a Federal Alcohol Authority, he remarked that although the report bestowed the name on the new agency it projected, it did not specify what authority the agency was to have. For all he could tell, its only function was to make reports. The members of the committee hastily endowed it with more genuine powers.

After a pause, during which the President seemed to be weighing the possibility, he asked how the agency was to be brought into existence and given these powers. Eager to prevent a resurgence of the prosposal for a federal liquor monopoly, I remarked that it would be possible to establish such an authority under the codes for the industry that would be drawn up under the NRA. The idea struck the President favorably. He asked whether any comparable arrangement had been made under any of the other codes or industry agreements. Sections of the code for the oil industry were cited as a precedent. At this juncture the President had to turn his atten-

* My impression is confirmed by a note in *The Secret Diary of Harold L. Ickes* (the Secretary of the Interior), Vol. I, p. 228. Entry for November 10, 1933. "We the Cabinet had some discussion of liquor control. The President seems to be leaning toward a Government monopoly plan. I favor government monopoly myself."

tion to other matters, so he asked the group to continue their talk in the Cabinet Room.

In the ensuing discussions, support for the monopoly plan waned. Wallace seemed to renounce the idea of a federal monopoly in favor of an authority — provided it be given powers of initiation and not merely of negative control. He remarked further that he did not want the responsibility for regulating the industry or bargaining with foreign governments to be located in his office; if it were, he foresaw that the selection of the Secretary of Agriculture would be subject to extraneous influences. The suggestion that a liquor authority be created was supplemented by a proposal that under the liquor industry codes those engaged in the business should be required to promise not to engage in the various types of objectionable activity that were so common before prohibition — such as lobbying and political contributions. Both suggestions were approved and both, I believe, were among the considerations that influenced the President eventually to entrust the task of regulation to an authority and shelve the idea of a federal monopoly.

At this meeting and in subsequent ones, consideration was given to methods of trying to secure compensatory commercial favors in return for the new and inviting market for foreign wines and spirits in this country. Decision was put off, leaving the State Department on the anxious seat. It was compelled to prolong the doubts which were already disturbing the foreign governments and the American importers. I fretted over the probability that since time would be so short and the pressure for imports so strong, the chance of winning sales for American farm products would be small.

It was finally decided that temporary four-month basic minimum import quotas should be fixed for each country, based on one-third of its average annual sales of wine and spirits to the United States in the years 1910 to 1914. The task of allocating licenses for this volume of imports among the many clamorous liquor importers and dealers was imposed upon Raymond Miller of the Agriculture Adjustment Administration and Daniel Doran of the Alcohol Control Division of the Treasury. As soon as the doors of their offices were opened they were overwhelmed. After twenty-four hours they were compelled to suspend the issuances of licenses until they could cull out the requests and secure information about the applicants. When they started again — and this was only about a week before the end of prohibition — the number of their eager clients had tripled.

Amazingly, no attempt had been made to recruit a special staff. Needed printed forms were lacking because of the many changes of judgment about the nature and contents. Confusion reigned. The resultant tasks that fell upon the State Department almost drowned out all other duties of officers in the geographical divisions; the clerks and stenographers in the code room were soon worn out with the chore of writing and sending off to our consulates the notices of licenses issued enabling them to certify invoices. The consuls were beaten by the number of requests for certification; their offices were as crowded as barrooms the night prohibition ended. The paper work was parching.

At the same time members of half the foreign embassies in Washington — from commercial attachés up to ambassadors — began to visit the State Department. Some merely sought information about the arrangements for the importation of liquors. Others came to complain about the size of the basic quota granted their country. Still others wanted to begin talks about the possibility of getting enlarged quotas in return for increased purchases of American farm products. As they waited in the hall for their appointments, more and more American businessmen who were seeking licenses to import mingled with them. Some came to appeal rulings which either denied them licenses to import or set the amount that they were authorized to import too low. Others came to ask the foreign diplomats to use their influence to get the State Department to increase either the national quota or their own quota.

Having helped to bring this system into existence, I turned over the task of talking with this assembly of aspirants and claimants to my assistant, Frederick Livesey, a tireless, genial and able man. During the next fortnight, as the numbers of visitors outside his room grew not only in numbers but in noisiness, and as members of the liquor trade fell to quarreling with one another, I found it prudent to take refuge in other caves. The two officials responsible for issuing the licenses were even more harrassed. Ray Miller of the AAA sent me a note saying that he did not intend to send me any more reports on the liquor situation, but rather instead to issue bulletins as from a sickbed in a hospital.

On the eve of the repeal of the Eighteenth Amendment the uproar was as loud as ever. Yielding to the demand on this day, it was decided to license without bargaining the importation from Canada of ten million gallons more of rye and bourbon whiskey for blending purposes. The State Department also recommended that the allowable purchases of Scotch whiskey from Great Britain — where ten million gallons were waiting to be sold and shipped — and wine and brandy from France be similarly enlarged. But the AAA was opposing such additional authorizations unless Great Britain promised to buy more American bacon and ham, and France, more American apples and pears.

These working difficulties were properly ignored when Acting Secretary of State Phillips, at six o'clock on the evening of December 5, read the proclamation of repeal over the radio. On the next night, when the repeal became effective, the President gave his annual reception for the diplomatic corps. As they were walking along the reception line, Sir Ronald Lindsay whispered to Moffat, who in turn whispered it to me, "You are now looking at a parade of the best-dressed men in town and have you stopped to think that the one thought each and every one has in mind is, 'How much whiskey can I sell in this country? ' "

Two days later Moffat was writing in his diary, "The liquor situation is more and more confused. . . . The problem had been transferred from State to Treasury to the Agricultural Adjustment Administration, back to State, all within a week, and in the State Department it has been variously assigned to Feis, Wiley, Culbertson [of Western European Division] and Livesey."

During this fortnight the first and only real success of the bargaining system was achieved — but after much squabbling. The French government offered to accept a substantially larger supply of American apples, pears, meats and hams in return for a larger quota of French wines — particularly champagne. But within a few days we learned that the French government was going to impose import license taxes on these American products. *Marchandage!*

At this stage the question reached a lofty level. The State Department thereupon held up the deal, and the French ambassador, André de Laboulaye, a suave and highly educated diplomat who had rarely in his career bothered with questions of trade, took the trouble of telephoning to Paris. He brought to the Acting Secretary of State a written guarantee that the new French taxes would not be allowed to interfere with the importation into France of the increased amounts of fruits produced in the American Northwest. So seriously was the question taken in American circles that Phillips thought it well to submit this guarantee to the cabinet that afternoon and obtain not only the approval of Secretary of Agriculture Wallace but of the President. Then a public statement was issued explaining the arrangement. In his diary for December 21 Phillips wrote, "Although it [the arrangement] is not wholly satisfactory, of course we could not delay any further because the demand for French champagne was growing hourly and could not have been restricted any longer."

In a talk with Moffat this same day I told him that I was becoming more and more upset over the quota system since I thought it was causing trouble everywhere; moreover, foreign countries were learning how to penalize us one day and then remove the penalty the next day in return for increased quotas. The American dealers were appealing to members of Congress to compel the government to relax its restrictions on imports.

The administrative riot of our own creation was quieted during January when stocks of almost all liquors in the United States were running out and fears arose that bootlegging was about to start on a vast scale all over the United States. Therefore it was decided to end the quota system for rye and bourbon and subsequently for all other kinds of liquor. Congress was starting to give consideration to the future regime for regulating and taxing both domestic products and imports. Gladly the committee and the negotiators relinquished their ill-managed duties.

Livesey wrapped up our records of this hectic episode in brown paper and made a present of the bundle to the chairman of the Federal Alcohol Administration. Joseph H. Choate, Jr., had been persuaded to accept that post. He had an envious rival. In the course of a long letter which Felix Frankfurter, then at Oxford, sent to the President he wrote, "When last I saw you, you told me that you almost got me a very good job, that of Administrator of the Booze Industry. I never quite understood why you did not land it for me. If it was for lack of experience, I'm somewhat making up for my deficiencies. Recently I attended two perfectly swell dinners, at one of which, Grand Day at Inner Temple, they had nine courses of wine, and at the Founders Day Feast at Kings College, Cambridge, there were seven."

Americans had no need any longer to envy these self-indulgent scholars or take trips to Europe to emulate them. In 1933 to 1934, prices of wine were still so low even college professors and government officials could afford a bottle of vintage wine now and again for themselves and their guests! This led them to regard the plight of the world with greater equanimity.

CHAPTER 26

Epilogue

FRANKLIN D. ROOSEVELT had entered the presidency with lively spirits and grand aspirations. As the year 1933 ended — the year when nations and men were awash — his desire for improvement in our relations with foreign countries had not waned. But this had been so tried and tattered by events and experiences that he transmitted it through a fractured prism.

Of the state of his spirit and energies I will let William Phillips, his old friend, tell: "He [Roosevelt] shows a remarkable insight into every point brought up for discussion and I have never seen a sign of ignorance on his part on a single subject brought into Cabinet. His capacity for overcoming the difficulties that arise, for putting the different departments together, and breaking into the atmosphere cheer and confidence is utterly remarkable and there is no sign of irritation coming from him." [1]

Whether his cheery confidence was a sheath against doubt or dejection no one except perhaps his wife and Louis Howe knew. Probably not usually, because of his way of putting mistakes behind him and quickly trying again, and of finding release for frustrations in laughter or ridicule.

But that there was a great gap in thoughts about foreign affairs between his aspirations and his command of the means of attaining them was evidenced in an address he made on December 28 at the annual dinner of the band of Woodrow Wilson devotees — of which he had once been a leader. The crystal and silver on the white tablecloths as well as the up-looking faces all gleamed the more warmly as he spoke. But his utterance, I reflected as I listened, was really a speech in defense of having to turn at least half way from Wilsonian ideas, and of the American people for requiring him to do so. In this he seemed to me to be trying to cover over or cover up the gap, but he failed.

"In the wider field . . . a change of events has led of late, we fear, away from, rather than toward, the ultimate objectives of Woodrow Wilson.

"The superficial observer charges the failure to the growth of nationalism. He suggests a nationalism in the wrong sense, a nationalism in the narrower restrictive sense; he suggests a nationalism of that kind supported by the overwhelming masses of the people themselves in each nation.

"I challenge that description of the world population today. The blame for the danger to world peace lies not in the world population but in the political leaders of that population."

And a little further on in the address:

"The League of Nations, encouraging as it does the extension of non-aggression pacts, of reduction of armament agreements, is a prop in the world peace structure, and it must remain.

"We are not members and do not contemplate membership. We are giving co-operation to the League in every matter which is not primarily political and in every matter which obviously represents the views and the good of the peoples of the world as distinguished from the views of political leaders, of privileged classes and of imperialistic aims."

Ah, but the quarrels were "primarily political" — struggles for security, power, trade and territory! From these, he was repeating, the United States would and should continue to remain aloof. As had his Republican predecessors, he would rely on pacts which would ban aggression without obligating governments to combine to resist or stop aggression — while continuing to hope that the popular will would in time bring about disarmament and lead to "practical peace, permanent real peace, throughout the world."

He and the American people were gradually and grimly to learn that challenging nations could not be dissuaded from their course; that their peoples followed aggressive leaders enthusiastically or were intimidated; and that their willingness to resort to force became readier and more gruesome.

The war came and Roosevelt felt compelled to lead the United States into it. And after victory the United States entered into vital obligations of the sort that were eschewed in 1933 — involving itself, probably, in too many troubled and unmanageable situations. It was impelled to do so because of the menace of new antagonists, especially the Soviet Union and China. National armaments are vastly more powerful than ever before, and more brutally vaunted — one is tempted to write "almost worshiped," as they sustain the mutual terror on which peace at present so largely depends.

Yet the student of the events of the year 1933 may be almost sure that the younger Roosevelt, the unfatigued Roosevelt, would have faced this prospect — our present prospect — undismayed and with unremitting will to try to dispel the worldwide danger. It is not only the achievements of the dead that keep their memories alive, but their efforts, and the work they leave behind for the living to carry on.

Notes

3. THE NEED FOR LIAISON

1 It was published by the British government as a White Paper — Cmd. 4129.

4. LIAISON: ACT ONE

1 Stimson Diary, November 13, 1932.
2 Raymond Moley, *After Seven Years,* p. 70.
3 *Ibid.,* pp. 71-72. The long list of questions is printed in Appendix B. To listen to the answers, Roosevelt and Moley would have had to stay in Washington at least a week.
4 Stimson Diary, December 22, 1932.
5 *Ibid.,* November 23, 1932.
6 *Ibid.*
7 Moley, *After Seven Years,* p. 78. This book was written in the year 1939.
8 Stimson Diary, November 23, 1932.
9 *New York Herald Tribune,* December 12, 1932.

5. LIAISON: ACT TWO

1 Stimson Diary, December 22, 1932.
2 *Ibid.,* December 23, 1932.
3 *Ibid.*
4 *Ibid.,* December 24, 1932.
5 Letter, Frankfurter to Roosevelt, January 4, 1933.

6. LIAISON: ACT THREE

1 Stimson Diary, January 9, 1933.
2 Memorandum by Secretary of State Stimson. *Foreign Relations of the*

United States — Japan 1931-1941, Vol. I, pp. 107-108.

3 Stimson Diary, January 6, 1933.
4 *Ibid.,* January 9, 1933.
5 *Ibid.,* January 12, and 16, 1933.
6 Moffat Diary, January 17, 1933.
7 Stimson Diary, January 17, 1933.
8 Moley, *After Seven Years,* p. 95.
9 In Tugwell's *Notes from a New Deal Diary,* quoted by William E. Leuchtenburg in his book *Franklin D. Roosevelt and the New Deal, 1932-1940,* p. 214.
10 Stimson Diary, February 24, 1933.
11 *Ibid.,* February 24 and 25, 1933.

7. LIAISON: ACT FOUR

1 Stimson Diary, January 9, 1933.
2 This memorandum is included in Stimson's diary entry for January 15, 1933.
3 *Ibid.*
4 *Ibid.*

8. LIAISON: ACT FIVE

1 Stimson Diary, January 19, 1933.
2 *Ibid.,* January 20, 1933.
3 Moley, *After Seven Years,* p. 98.
4 Stimson Diary, January 20, 1933.
5 Hoover memorandum in Stimson Diary, *ibid.*
6 *Ibid.*
7 Moley, *After Seven Years,* p. 98.
8 *Ibid.,* p. 102, quoting from an entry Moley made in his journal on January 21, 1933.
9 Stimson Diary, January 21 and 22, 1933.
10 Moley, *After Seven Years,* pp. 113-114.
11 Stimson Diary, January 27, 1933.
12 *New York Times,* January 25, 1933.

9. LIAISON: THE RANCOROUS END

1 Stimson Diary, February 25, 26 and 28, 1933.
2 *Ibid.,* February 17, 1933.
3 Letter from John S. West, operative, to W. H. Moran, Secret Service Division of the Treasury, February 27, 1933. Ogden Mills Papers.
4 William S. Myers and Walter H. Newton, *The Hoover Administration. A Documental Narrative,* pp. 338-340.
5 *Ibid.,* p. 541.
6 Stimson Diary, February 22, 1933.
7 Moley, *After Seven Years,* pp. 139-141.
8 Letter, Roosevelt to Hoover, March 1, 1933.
9 This account of the discussions between New York and Washington is

based on the record of a special meeting of the Board of Directors of the Federal Reserve Bank of New York, March 3, 1933. George Harrison Papers.

11. THE NEW GROUP

1   Moley, *After Seven Years,* p. 116.
2   Moffat Diary, March 1, 1933.

12. THE DOLLAR GOES OFF GOLD

1   Marriner S. Eccles, *Beckoning Frontiers,* p. 117.
2   *New York Times,* January 29, 1933.
3   Meeting of the Board of Governors of the Federal Reserve Bank of New York, February 23, 1933. Harrison Papers.
4   A request to the Congress for authority to effect drastic economies in government, March 10, 1933.
5   Letter, Thomas to Roosevelt, April 17, 1933.
6   Warburg Journal, April 18, 1933, 8:30 A.M. and 10:30 A.M.
7   Moley, *After Seven Years,* p. 159.
8   Record of Session of the Executive Committee of the Federal Reserve Bank of New York, April 24, 1933. Harrison Papers.

13. THE FLURRY OF FOREIGN MISSIONS

1   Davis to Hull, April 4, 1933. *Foreign Relations of the United States—* 1933, Vol. I — General, p. 484.
2   The texts of all the joint press releases issued by the President and heads of the visiting foreign missions are printed in pp. 490 *et. seq.*
3   Dodd Diary, June 16, 1933, pp. 4-5.

14. WE AGREE TO DISCUSS STABILIZATION

1   Warburg Journal, April 30, 1933.
2   May 6, 1933. *Foreign Relations of the United States* — 1933, Vol. I — General, p. 504.
3   This memorandum, by Landreth M. Harrison of the Division of Eastern European Affairs, is in *ibid.,* pp. 553-561.
4   *Ibid.,* p. 144.
5   *Ibid.,* pp. 608-609.
6   Morgenthau Diary, May 29, 1933.
7   Memorandum by J. C. Crane of telephone conversation, Harrison with Robert Lacour-Gayet of the Bank of France, May 26, 1933. Harrison Papers.
8   Moley, *After Seven Years,* p. 216.

15. MEANWHILE, FISSION IN EUROPE

1   Telegram, Klieforth to Hull, February 2, 1933. *Foreign Relations of the United States* — 1933, Vol. II, p. 186.
2   *Ibid.,* p. 226.
3   Messersmith to Hull, *ibid.,* Vol. I — General, pp. 120-121.
4   Dodd Diary, June 16, 1933, the opening day of the Monetary and Economic Conference.

5 Moffat Diary, March 31, 1933.
6 *Ibid.,* April 20, 1933.
7 Gibson to Hull, March 12, 1933. *Foreign Relations of the United States* — 1933, Vol. I — General, p. 31.
8 Hull to Davis, *ibid.,* p. 107.
9 The text of this appeal is printed in *ibid.,* pp. 143-145.
10 Marriner to State Department, May 17, 1933. *Ibid.,* pp. 147-148.
11 Text in *Documents on International Affairs* — 1933, pp. 196-208. Published by Royal Institute of International Affairs, London.
12 Walter Lippmann, *New York Herald Tribune,* May 19, 1933.
13 Wilson to Hull, May 18, 1933. Hull Papers.
14 *Foreign Relations of the United States* — 1933, Vol. I — General, p. 416.

16. OFF TO THE CONFERENCE

1 This interesting message of May 9 is in *Foreign Relations of the United States* — 1933, Vol. I — General, pp. 597-600.
2 Quoted in William E. Leuchtenburg's *Franglin D. Roosevelt and the New Deal, 1932-1940,* pp. 199-200.
3 Moley, *After Seven Years,* p. 217.
4 Resolution No. 5 read:

Whereas, various nations have been constrained, on the one hand, to impose restrictions upon imports in the nature of tariffs, quotas, embargoes, etc. and, on the other hand, to subsidize exports, and

Whereas, this tendency has resulted in nationalistic action in all nations, which, if carried to its logical conclusion, will result in the almost complete elimination of international trade and a return to a medieval isolationism, and

Whereas, it is agreed that this tendency must be arrested if a world recovery is to be achieved and a decent standard of living widely maintained,

Now therefore, be it *Resolved,* that all the nations participating in this Conference agree

(a) That it is against the common interest for any nation to adopt or continue a policy of extreme economic nationalism and to raise additional trade barriers and discrimination;

(b) That embargoes, import quotas and various other arbitrary restrictions should be removed completely as quickly as possible; and

(c) That tariff barriers should be reduced as quickly as possible by reciprocal bilateral agreements or by multilateral agreements to a point where trade can once more move in a free and normal manner; and

(d) That care should be taken in making bilateral or multilateral agreements not to introduce discriminatory features which, while providing an advantage to the contracting parties, would react disadvantageously upon world trade as a whole.

* * *

The instructions to the American delegation as well as the memorandum on policy for the American delegation, which contains the text of the six

resolutions, is in *Foreign Relations of the United States* — 1933, Vol. I —
General, pp. 620 *et seq.*

Resolution 1, concerned with the tariff truce, and Resolution 5 as printed
above were interpreted in a supplementary memorandum. This retains
enough historical interest to quote:

"The instructions to the American Delegation to propose Resolutions 1
and 5 as contained in the memorandum of instruction, implies that the
American government will not raise any additional barriers, excepting possibly compensating duties as provided by the Farm Bill or protective measures
against discrimination adopted by other countries, unless and until it becomes
reluctantly convinced that a method to effect world recovery cannot be developed through international cooperation. The Delegation is at liberty to
state that if the American government does not find a spirit of cooperation
on the part of other nations, the American government will then be forced
into a policy of nationalistic protection, but the American government would
consider such a development a sign of the failure of present-day civilization.
The American Delegation is instructed to point out and emphasize that all
nations collectively and individually are now faced with the decision of a
choice between a broad policy of practical international co-operation for
purposes of business recovery with the resulting increase of profits and wages
and living standards in every country, or of embracing in still more extreme
and impracticable forms the present policy of world economic warfare."

5 Cordell Hull, *Memoirs,* Vol. I, p. 251.
6 *Ibid.*

17. THE CONFERENCE STARTS AND STALLS

1 This message, sent on June 11, is in *Foreign Relations of the United
   States* — 1933, Vol. I — General, p. 633.
2 *Ibid.,* p. 634.
3 *Ibid.,* pp. 636-640.
4 *Ibid.,* p. 641.
5 These are printed in *ibid.,* pp. 642-644.
6 *Ibid.,* p. 646.
7 The messages from Sprague and Warburg and the President's answer are
   in *ibid.,* pp. 642-646.
8 *Ibid.,* pp. 647-648.
9 Memorandum of meeting of Executive Committee of the Federal Reserve Bank of New York, June 19, 1933. Harrison Papers.
10 *Foreign Relations of the United States* — 1933, Vol. I — General, p.
   650.
11 *Ibid.,* p. 648. The paper which I submitted was called "Suggested Agenda
   of the Economic Commission in the Fields of Tariffs and Commercial
   Policy." (CNF NE/CE 4)
12 *Foreign Relations of the United States* — 1933, Vol. I — General,
   p. 651.
13 This and the foregoing information are derived from Warburg's Journal
   and his statement in the Oral History Project at Columbia University.

14   *Foreign Relations of the United States* — 1933, Vol. I — General, p. 652.
15   *Ibid.*, pp. 653-654.
16   This message of June 24 is in *ibid.*, p. 655. Its substance was relayed to Moley on board the S.S. *Manhattan* on June 26. The suggestion contained in it may well have misled Moley.

18. THE CONFERENCE CHAMPS

1   Moley, *After Seven Years*, pp. 230-231.
2   Farley, James M., *Jim Farley's Story*, pp. 40-41.
3   Moley, *After Seven Years*, p. 235.
4   *Ibid.*, pp. 235-236.
5   *Ibid.*
6   These are excerpts from letters in the collection of Baruch's correspondence in Princeton University Library.
7   *Foreign Relations of the United States* — 1933, Vol. I — General, pp. 656-657.
8   Hull to Moley, June 26, 1933. Hull Papers.
9   *Foreign Relations of the United States* — 1933, Vol. I — General, p. 658.
10 Memorandum of telephone conversation with Sprague, June 27, 1933, 2:10 P.M. Harrison Papers.
11 *Foreign Relations of the United States* — 1933, Vol. I — General, pp. 660-661. Sent from U.S.S. *Ellis*, June 28, 1933, 7 P.M., and received in Washington June 29, 3 A.M.
12 *Ibid.*, pp. 661-663. Sent from Washington to Roosevelt 9 P.M. (Washington time), June 28. It was prepared by Baruch after consultation with Woodin and concurred in by Harrison, Douglas and Acheson.
13 *Ibid.* Sent 6 P.M. (Washington time), June 29.

19. THE CONFERENCE GASPS

1   This statement and various others scattered throughout this and the next chapter are derived from a memo written up for Moley from notes made by himself, Swope, Mullen and his secretary Celeste Jedel on the steamer during their return trip to the United States.
2   Memo from Bullitt to Hull, July 2, 1933. Hull Papers.
3   Moley, *After Seven Years*, p. 246.
4   *Ibid.*, p. 248.
5   *Ibid.*, p. 249. Italics in the original.
6   *Ibid.*
7   *Ibid.*, p. 250.
8   *Foreign Relations of the United States* — 1933, Vol. I — General, pp. 668-669.
9   The article, entitled "The Theory of Trade," appeared in the July 1, 1933, issue.
10 Morgenthau Diary, June 29, 1933.
11 Moley, *After Seven Years*, p. 250.

12 Cordell Hull, *Memoirs,* Vol. I, p. 261. Hull reported substantially the same version in a letter he wrote to the President on July 11.
13 Moley, *After Seven Years,* p. 253.
14 It was sent over from Campobello to the U.S.S. *Indianapolis;* sent off the ship by naval radio at 2 A.M. to Phillips in Washington; transmitted by Phillips to Hull at 8 A.M. (Washington time); and received in London in the early afternoon of July 1 (London time).
15 *Foreign Relations of the United States —* 1933, Vol. I — General, pp. 669-670.
16 *Ibid.,* p. 671.
17 James M. Cox, *Journey Through My Years,* p. 378.
18 Moley, *After Seven Years,* p. 255.
19 Cordell Hull, *Memoirs,* Vol. I, p. 261.
20 Memo written by Hugh Cumming on July 16, 1933, at Secretary Hull's request. Hull Papers.
21 Warburg Journal, July 1, 1933.
22 Moley, *After Seven Years,* p. 257.
23 Alfred B. Rollins, Jr., *Roosevelt and Howe,* pp. 297-298.
24 Moley, *After Seven Years,* p. 258.
25 *Ibid.*
26 *Foreign Relations of the United States —* 1933, Vol. I — General, pp. 674-675.
27 Morgenthau Diary, July 1, 1933.
28 *Foreign Relations of the United States —* 1933, Vol. I — General, pp. 673-674.

20. THE CONFERENCE EXPIRES

1 Warburg Journal, July 3, 1933.
2 *Foreign Relations of the United States —* 1933, Vol. I — General, p. 679.
3 *Ibid.,* p. 680. An appended footnote states, "Original not found in the Department files."
4 This appeared in the *London Daily Mail,* July 4, 1933.
5 House of Commons Debate, 5th Series, Vol. 280, p. 786, July 10, 1933.
6 Moley, *After Seven Years,* p. 263.
7 *Foreign Relations of the United States —* 1933, Vol. I — General, pp. 681-683.
8 *Ibid.,* pp. 680-681. Sent July 4, 1 P.M., from the U.S.S. *Indianapolis.*
9 Stimson Diary, July 15, 1933, recounting a talk with MacDonald.
10 July 3, 1933, midnight. *Foreign Relations of the United States —* 1933, Vol. I — General, pp. 688-692.
11 Moley, *After Seven Years,* p. 265. No such passage appears in the memorandum of the first telephone conversation on July 5 between Roosevelt, Hull and Moley which is in *Foreign Relations of the United States —* 1933, Vol. I — General, pp. 688-692. Nor did I come across it in the record of the second conversation not printed in *Foreign Relations.*

12 Letter, MacDonald to Hull, which Hull transmitted to the President on July 12, 1933, along with the answer to MacDonald that he had made on July 11, 1933. Roosevelt Papers.

13 Memo of telephone conversation, Roosevelt with Hull and Moley, July 5, 1933. Hull Papers. No record of it was found in the State Department. See footnote on page 692 of *Foreign Relations of the United States —* 1933, Vol. I — General.

14 Moley, *After Seven Years*, p. 266. The entry in the unpublished Moley memo read, "My dear Moley, why wasn't this issued on Friday? It would have saved the Conference."

15 *Ibid.*, pp. 266-267.

16 The text of this cable is in *Foreign Relations of the United States —* 1933, Vol. I — General, p. 680. In a footnote the editors state that the original of the cable was not to be found in the State Department files.

17 Hull to Howe, July 8, 1933. Hull Papers.

18 Telegram, Hull to Roosevelt, July 11, 1933. Roosevelt Papers.

19 Their talk was on July 13, 1933, but is recorded in the memo which Stimson dictated on October 18, from his pencil notes made at the time of the occurrence.

20 Letter, Bingham to Howe, August 3, 1933. House Papers.

21 Letter, Bingham to House, July 31, 1933. House Papers.

22 Morgenthau Diary, July 30, 1933.

23 *Foreign Relations of the United States —* 1933, Vol. I — General, pp. 703-704.

24 Stimson Diary, July 15, 1933.

25 Memo of telephone conversation, Harrison and Norman, July 14, 1933. Harrison Papers.

26 This episode is described in the entry of July 18, 1933, in the Stimson Diary.

21. AFTER THE CONFERENCE

1 This report, addressed to Secretary Hull, is in *Foreign Relations of the United States —* 1933, Vol. I — General, pp. 934-936.

2 Morgenthau Diary, May 15, 1933.

3 Letter, Child to Roosevelt, May 25, 1933. Roosevelt Papers.

4 Stimson Diary, October 26, 1933.

5 Its report, in which the directors of the corporation are named, is in *Foreign Relations of the United States —* 1933, Vol. I — General, pp. 937-939.

22. THE DOLLAR IS THRUST DOWN

1 A summary of Warren's recommendations is given in Acheson's *Morning and Noon*, p. 175.

2 Morgenthau Diary, August 16, 1933.

3 Warburg Journal, August 15, 1933.

4 Minutes of meetings of the executive committee of the Federal Reserve Bank of New York, August 21, 1933, and September 14, 1933. Harrison Papers.

5 Quoted in John M. Blum, *From the Morgenthau Diaries,* pp. 66-67.
6 Morgenthau Diary, October 18, 1933.
7 *Ibid.,* October 19, 1933.
8 *From the Morgenthau Diaries,* p. 71.
9 *Ibid.,* p. 69.
10 Morgenthau Diary, November 13, 1933.
11 *Ibid.*
12 Letters, Colonel Edward M. House to Secretary of Commerce Daniel Roper, November 12, 1933; and Franklin D. Roosevelt to Colonel House, November 21, 1933. House Papers.
13 Meeting in White House, 3 P.M., October 29, 1933. Harrison Papers.
14 Memo by J. C. Crane of discussion with the President at the White House, November 13, 1933. The others present were Woodin, Jones, Harrison, Rogers, Warren, Morgenthau, Black and Henry Bruere. Harrison Papers.
    Information about other discussions in the preceding intervals is in a memo of telephone conversations between Harrison and Norman on November 2 and 6, 1933.
15 Roosevelt to House, November 21, 1933. House Papers.
16 Memorandum of Roosevelt written by him for the historical record to which a memorandum by Harrison of his talk with Norman is attached. Roosevelt Papers.

23. THE FURTHER EBB OF THE INTERNATIONAL SITUATION

1 John W. Wheeler-Bennett, *Munich: Prologue to Tragedy.*
2 Dodd to Hull, October 19, 1933. Hull Papers.
3 Dodd to Roosevelt, November 27, 1933. Roosevelt Papers.
4 *Foreign Relations of the United States* — 1933, Vol. — General, pp. 505-506.
5 Dorothy Borg, *The United States and the Far Eastern Crisis of 1933- 1938,* pp. 37-38.
6 Letter from President Roosevelt to the chairman of the American delegation, Norman Davis, August 30, 1933. *Foreign Relations of the United States* — 1933, Vol. 1 — General, pp. 209-210.
7 *Ibid.,* p. 223.
8 *Ibid.,* p. 253.
9 Moffat Journal, October 14 and 15, 1933.
10 Excerpt from memorandum of transatlantic telephone conversation between President Roosevelt and Secretary of State Hull in Washington and Norman Davis in Geneva, October 16, 1933. *Foreign Relations of the United States* — 1933, Vol. I — General, pp. 273-274.
11 Hull message is in *ibid.,* p. 277.
12 Dodd to Hull, October 17, 1933. *Ibid.,* p. 285.

24. WE RECOGNIZE THE SOVIET UNION

1 Morgenthau Diary, May 9, 1933.
2 Letter, Bullitt to the President, from London, July 8, 1933. Roosevelt Papers.

3   *Foreign Relations of the United States* — The Soviet Union 1933-1939, pp. 6 *et seq.*
4   Morgenthau Diary, August 16, 1933.
5   *Foreign Relations of the United States* — The Soviet Union 1933, pp. 12-13.
6   Morgenthau Diary, September 26, 1933.
7   These are excerpts from a long and somewhat disorderly account of Bullitt's remarks contained in the entry of September 27, 1933, in the Morgenthau Diary.
8   *Ibid.*, October 11, 1933.
9   The two memoranda and Hull's covering note are in *Foreign Relations of the United States* — The Soviet Union 1933-1939, pp. 16 and 17.
10 Letter, Roosevelt to Hull, no date. Roosevelt Papers.
11 Morgenthau Diary, October 18, 1933.
12 The message to Kalinin and Kalinin's reply are in *Foreign Relations of the United States* — 1933-1939, Vol. II, pp. 794-795.
13 *Foreign Relations of the United States* — The Soviet Union 1933-1939, p. 20
14 Phillips Journal, November 8, 1933. Phillips ended this entry about these discussions, "None of us were enthusiastic about this day's work."
15 Phillips Journal, November 9, 1933, and Morgenthau Diary, November 14, 1933.
16 Phillips Journal, November 10, 1933.
17 *Jim Farley's Story*, pp. 113-114.
18 The text of these letters in *Foreign Relations of the United States,* Vol. II, pp. 805-814.
19 This is recorded in a joint memo signed by Roosevelt and Litvinov on November 15, 1933. *Foreign Relations of the United States* — The Soviet Union 1933, p. 804.
20 *Ibid.*, p. 817.
21 *Ibid.*, p. 816.
22 Messages sent by Bullitt to Roosevelt from Paris, December 24, 1933. *Ibid.*, pp. 831-832.
23 *Ibid.*, pp. 833-840. This whole long message is a lively and fascinating account of the short gush of mutual goodwill that followed recognition.

26. EPILOGUE

1   Phillips Journal, December 21, 1933.

Index